# THE PRICE
# OF A CONSTITUTION

# THE PRICE
# OF A CONSTITUTION
## The Origin of Japan's Postwar Politics

**Tetsuya Kataoka**

Hoover Institute, Stanford University

**CRANE RUSSAK**
A member of the Taylor & Francis Group

New York • Philadelphia • Washington • London

| USA | Publishing Office: | Taylor & Francis New York, Inc. |
| | | 79 Madison Ave., New York, NY 10016-7892 |
| | Sales Office: | Taylor & Francis Inc. |
| | | 1900 Frost Road, Bristol, PA 19007-1598 |
| UK | | Taylor & Francis Ltd. |
| | | 4 John St., London WC1N 2ET |

**THE PRICE OF A CONSTITUTION: The Origin of Japan's Postwar Politics**

Note: In this book, Japanese names are written with surnames first, except in footnotes, where the convention of first names first is observed.

2 3 4 5 6 7 8 9 0   B R B R   9 8 7 6 5 4 3 2 1

Cover design by Berg Design, Inc.
Printing and binding by Braun-Brumfield, Inc.

A CIP catalog record for this book is available from the British Library.

**Library of Congress Cataloging-in-Publication Data**

Kataoka, Tetsuya.
   The price of a constitution: the origin of Japan's postwar
politics / Tetsuya Kataoka.
      p.    cm.
   Includes bibliographical references.

   1. Japan—Politics and government—1945-   2. Japan—Foreign
relations—1945-   I. Title.
JQ1611.K28   1991
952.04—dc20
                                                            90-47714
                                                                 CIP

ISBN 0-8448-1700-7 (case)
ISBN 0-8448-1714-7 (paper)

# Contents

# Preface

This book can trace its conception to the turmoil and tension in the Cold War alliances I witnessed in the wake of the Soviet invasion of Afghanistan in 1980. Afghanistan heralded the beginning of a particularly stressful decade for the alliance between the United States and Japan. So-called friction, mostly in the guise of trade dispute, became endemic between them. But it was obviously rooted in more generic causes. I felt then, as I do now, that a revision of the U.S.–Japanese strategic relationship toward greater equality was necessary and inevitable. I made the point in my *Waiting for a Pearl Harbor: Japan Debates Defense* (Stanford: Hoover Institution Press, 1980). Toward the end of the decade, the tension produced revisionist thinkers in America as well. David P. Calleo, *Beyond American Hegemony: The Future of the Western Alliance* (New York: Basic Books, 1987) heartened me by basically agreeing with my position. Others—such as van Wolferen, Prestowitz, and Fallows—dismayed me with their irrationality.

In the wake of Afghanistan, a Japanese prime minister recognized for the first time that there was an alliance with America, but Japan's change was at best opaque and obscure. The United States was torn between two opposed impulses: "Japan will be criticized if it does not substantially increase its spending upon arms, and it will be denounced if it does," as Yela historian Paul Kennedy put it later (in *The Rise and Fall of the Great Powers: Economic Change and Military Conflict from 1500 to 2000* [New York: Random House, 1987], p. 470.). I knew that the problem will not go away. But I decided that the best contribution I could make toward its solution was to conduct a rigorous inquiry into the origin of the strangely lopsided relationship between the two nations, as seen from Japan. As I conclude the inquiry with this preface, another war seems only a week away. Once again, the United States is bearing most of the burden, and Japan is standing on the sideline. But this time I have the personal satisfaction of knowing how we have come to this.

There are several people and institutions whose generous assistance made this book possible and to whom I am deeply in debt. I was blessed at the outset, in 1985, with a fellowship at the Woodrow Wilson International Center for Scholars at the Smithsonian Institution in Washington, D.C. I thoroughly enjoyed the company of Dr. James Billington, its director, and the staff members. Chalmers A. Johnson, my long-time friend since the days of our Chinese studies, encouraged me to undertake this study and read the manuscript. Kenneth Pyle and Donald Hellmann of Henry M. Jackson School, University of Washington in Seattle, also gave me a fellowship, encouragement, and advice. Professors Ito Takashi and Igarashi Takeshi, both of Tokyo University, have been my valuable companions in writing this book. I have benefited much from the works of those who took part in the Hoover Workshop on the 1955 System of Japan in 1988: Masumi Junnosuke, Nagao Ryuichi, Iokibe Makoto, Tsutsui Kiyotada, Otake Hideo, Tani Satomi, Kent E. Calder, Peter Duus, and Haruhiro Fukui.

I must single out the Hoover Institution for special thanks. Few research centers in the world can equal Hoover for the freedom it offers, the caliber of its resident fellows, and the quality of its libraries and archives. I am grateful to Glenn Campbell, former director, John Raisian, current director, and Ramon H. Myers, Senior Fellow and Curator of East Asian Collection, for bringing me to this marvellous environment and for their encouragement. My thanks also go to the following publishers for permission to make lengthy citations from their publications: Time Warner Inc., The University of Chicago Press, The University of California Press, and W. W. Norton. As always my wife Barbara and daughter Drue have been generous and loyal to me and tolerated my total absorption in my work.

*Tetsuya Kataoka*

# Chapter 1

# Introduction

In 1952, while negotiating the Administrative Agreement to the security treaty with the Japanese, Dean Rusk, assistant secretary of state in the Truman administration, thought that Japan was "schizophrenic" on strategic questions. Japan, he said, was like "the man who wanted to sleep with a woman one night without having to say hello to her in public the next day."[1] This is a very apt metaphor for Japan's conduct in the world, and I use it as the leading question for this book: How is it that Japan has come to behave in this way?

Our task is to ask what the essence of the postwar regime is. Today that regime is exposed to intense pressure for change from sources both external and internal, and the process of change has already begun. It is clearly part of the denouement of the Cold War and the realignment of world powers. Something about the Japan that thrived in the Cold War environment is becoming brittle and obsolete. But the critics of Japan ought to know that, in railing at its ruling party, the FSX (fighter support experimental) project, trade surplus, or its alleged niggardliness in dispensing foreign aid, they are chipping away at the tip of a huge iceberg whose submerged portion they scarcely know or comprehend. Now that the iceberg seems to have begun slowly drifting away from the mooring, it behooves them to know precisely what it is—and what they are doing.

The Japan that Rusk spoke of in 1952 was nurtured by the conservatives who have been calling themselves the Liberal Democrats and who have been running the country for some 35 years without interruption. To be precise, it was not all of them but a group that today innocuously calls itself the "conservative mainstream" that should take both the praise and blame for Japan. The group used to consist of a distinct faction with partisan fire in its belly and carried the somewhat pejorative label of the "Yoshida School." Prime Minister Yoshida Shigeru is universally recognized today as the man who has had a strongly held view about Japan's place in the world and who prevailed with that view in the Sturm und Drang of early postwar days.

Kosaka Masataka, Kyoto University political scientist who has been for some

time the unofficial spokesman both for Yoshida and Japan, likens Japan to medie-
val Venice, an unarmed merchant state that lived by sheer wits in the world of
armed and dangerous neighbors.[2] Perhaps the oldest and most persistent jibe at
Yoshida's Japan is that it indulges American goodwill to get a military free ride.
Rusk's metaphor is clearly a diplomatic way of putting the same point. Held in
abeyance for a long time, this criticism was revived in the decade of the 1980s
when the Reagan administration went into a huge military expansion. In the
minds of congressional critics of Japan, who repeat and repeat the charge, Japan's
economic success stems from the savings derived from a free ride.

As if to conceal an inner torment, Japan responds to the charge not by daring
to rearm once and for all but by referring the interlocutors to its own earlier
resolve to be born again as a peace-loving nation following a disastrous defeat
in war. In the first instance, it points to the no-war constitution, which it fastidi-
ously upholds, or to the constitutionally derived principle of "passive defense,"
by which Japan swore never to send its armed forces beyond its territorial
space. But a formal answer such as this is really no answer, so the American
interlocutor presses for a prior reason. Then the Japanese disclose somberly
that the new Venice harbors an impulse deep in its heart to return to the old
mistaken ways, as revealed in occasional indiscretions of rightwing cabinet
ministers and that America is well advised to leave Japan alone or face unpleasant consequences. There is a strange combination of willfulness and self-
abnegation here. In any case the Japanese mind remains impenetrable to American legislators or media whose memory span is short and who are in any case
indifferent to the weight of history that propels other nations.

There are other charges against the foreign policy of Japan, charges that
seem to stem from its alleged schizophrenia. For instance, Japan is said to be
opaque, inscrutable, and lacking in principle. Japan has scrupulously eschewed
conflict, avoided a potentially divisive situation, seldom acted without consult-
ing Washington, and refrained from asserting its will. On most important matters, it has been the established custom for Washington to lead and Tokyo to
follow. Hence it is said that Japan is "docile," that it has a "foreign policy of a
trading company," that its conduct is reactive, not proactive, and even that
Japan is not a state.[3] Not a few Japanese agree with such views. Miyazawa
Kiichi, the last of Yoshida's disciples and a leader of an important LDP faction,
has vowed that Japan is a "special state" because the constitution pledges in the
preamble that it trusts in "the justice and faith of the peace-loving peoples of
the world" and that Japanese diplomacy must necessarily "preclude all value
judgments."[4]

The fact is, however, that Japan's diplomacy is not value-free. Japan pursues
success according to is own definition: in commerce, manufacturing, finance,

and high tech. Far from being reactive or destitute of ambition, Japan flexes a muscle in these endeavors, inspiring awe in America and compelling Europe to integrate itself as a way of competing. By the 1990s, Japan's industrial machine had trounced Pittsburgh, Detroit, Silicon Valley, and is still on the march. By middecade, its whopping trade surplus compelled Washington to devalue the dollar, which in turn hastened the fall of the United States to debtor status and transformed Japan into the world's biggest creditor. Japan is now the supplier of America's capital needs both in Washington and Wall Street. Juggernaut is the metaphor often applied to Japan, and in 1987 a work of serious scholarship, by Paul Kennedy, drew a parallel between the "rise and fall" of Great Britain, the United States, and Japan. Kennedy touched the raw nerves in America because he seems to reinforce the perception that Japan is gaining at the expense of America or that it is continuing to fight World War II by peaceful means.[5]

The paradox posed by Japan is put recently as "power without purpose."[6] Van Wolferen, who has accused Japan of not being a state, concedes that it is nonetheless the "System." By general consent there is in Japan a strange combination of strength and weakness, resilience and fragility, expansiveness and subservience, aggressiveness and self-effacement, keen competitiveness and placid stupor, cohesion (or "consensus") and apparent headlessness, and cynicism and innocence. Those who mind only one side of the coin and ignore the other may do so at peril to themselves.

Japan's relationship with the United States may be the embodiment of this paradox. A former conqueror, the United States enjoys preponderant influence over Japan. But this is not to be equated with suzerainty pure and simple—far from it. Until recently America has been generous to Japan in providing physical and material well-being, so long as Japan paid generous tribute in the coin of political honor. Obviously this tribute stems from Japan's military self-abnegation and, hence, dependence, constitutionally mandated. But far from placing Japan at the mercy of the United States, this self-abnegation enabled it to do as it pleases while binding the United States to the role of tutor-protector, short-tempered at times but always paternalistic. Today, Japan has become the "hand that finances" the hegemon, and America seems to be controlled as much by Japan's constitution as Japan is. How has it come to such a pass?[7]

As in the case of all nations, Japan's external conduct is closely related to its domestic politics and above all to its regime. It is the inherent nature of the regime that has produced the following characteristics of its domestic politics:

1. *The LDP's one-party dominance.* This party has ruled Japan for some 35 years without interruption since its founding in 1955. For better or worse, it is a synonym of postwar Japan. Obviously the LDP rule ex-

cluded the chances for a fuller democracy based on an alternating party
system. The LDP's monopoly of power was made possible by the fact
that it has been a catch-all party, so-called, catering to the needs of di-
verse constituencies: big business, small business, farmers, the white
collar workers, and, increasingly, urban independent voters. The diver-
sity of its constituencies went hand-in-glove with the fact that the LDP
shunned articulating itself in ideological or programmatic terms and con-
centrated instead on the politics of patronage. Its instinctive anticommunism aside, the LDP is a parochial party with greater aptitude for
promoting purely self-regarding policies such as industrialization. The
LDP can without question take credit for Japan's economic "miracle,"
but it is also justly blamed for having fostered "money politics," the
materialist social ethos, and a good deal of political corruption.
2. *The LDP's factionalism.* This follows logically from the fact of the LDP's
monopoly of power, for it is only among the factions that power can be
passed around. The LDP's factions behave as though they are virtually
independent political parties, preventing the articulation of the will of the
ruling party and, hence, of the nation. No one has ever asked why a
nation that set so much store by consensus has such a fractured political
party.
3. *Decision-making by log rolling until unanimity is obtained.* Van Wolferen
accuses Japan of having no political "center," i.e., the ultimate decision-
maker who stops the buck from circulating. But he is barking up the
wrong tree. The buck stops somewhere. It just takes time circulating
because the Japanese political system demands unanimity (consensus)
rather than the majority rule. Why the Japanese prefer such a system
cannot be answered until we see the nature of substantive issues, to which
consensus decisions are applied.
4. *The power of central ministry bureaucracies.* Much is made of this
power. There has been a running debate on its nature and scope, but the
result is at best inconclusive. The reason, I suggest, is that we know so
little of the genealogy of this power. I uphold Chalmers A. Johnson's
thesis that it is a heritage of the imperial bureaucracies, but he does not
explain how such a power could have survived intact the wholesale occupation reforms, nor how the principle of Diet supremacy, written at Mac-
Arthur's insistence into the constitution, has been subverted. The missing
piece of the puzzle is the nature of the occupation regime, on the one
hand, and the struggle between the bureaucratic politicians and the professional politicians during and following the occupation, on the other.
The contention between Yoshida and Hatoyama is the clue to the answer.[8]

To explain the origin of the postwar Japanese politics with fairness and objectivity necessarily calls for a revisionist stance. Deliberately ignored until today for the sake of "consensus," a titanic political contest took place in the early postwar years over the issues of Japan's purpose and its relationship with the United States. The struggle began early in the occupation and kept Japan in turmoil until 1960. The engine of that struggle was the rearmament issue that was thrust upon Japan as it signed the peace and security treaties in 1951. In a successful appeal to anti-American sentiment, the Socialists and the Communists called for disarmed neutrality, resting their case on the constitution. Arrayed against them along the Cold War fault line were all the conservatives, who endorsed the security treaty.

But the conservatives were split on the issue of rearmament, with Yoshida pitting himself against those whom I label the Japanese revisionists. Yoshida advised Japan to avoid the traditional avenue to autonomy—through rearmament—and to concentrate on economic development. To shield Japan from American pressure to rearm, Yoshida opted to retain the constitution, and became the Socialists' bedfellow. That is to say, he was for straddling the security treaty and the constitution. In time he consented to partial rearmament but never to constitutional revision.

With American support, the revisionists—led by Hatoyama Ichiro, Kishi Nobusuke, Miki Bukichi, and Kono Ichiro—collided with Yoshida and his double-pronged policy. The revisionists were concerned less with rearmament itself than with diplomatic equality and mutuality that went with rearmament, not with military hardware but with possible corruption of the body politic that may result from avoiding all international entanglements. Gaullists at heart, they found Yoshida's policy of reaming through the backdoor sly and illegitimate and called for his ouster, rearmament, and constitutional revision.

Although the conservatives outnumbered the JSP in the Diet and at the polls two to one, their internal division had in effect created a three-way split in politics. Major decisions became a matter of putting together shifting alliances of two groups against a third. It was not until the upheaval of 1960, nearly 10 years after the conclusion of the peace and security treaties in San Francisco, that Japan gave a grudging consent to them. The constitution was retained so as to prevent Japan's participation in regional collective security, and the Japanese simply learned to ignore the American military bases in their midst. They decided that their self-respect was best served by the pursuit of economic excellence.

The history of postwar Japan as we have it today—the orthodox, received, standard version—was written by Yoshida's followers in the Yoshida School and his apologists, calling themselves the realists. It is partisan and less than complete, because it deliberately obscures what Bertram Wolfe calls the history of the defeated, that is, the revisionists and the Socialists.[9] The task of disentangling and revising the postwar history and of restoring the revisionists to their rightful place faces more than an ordinary share of difficulty, because it runs into the stonewall of Yoshida's friends in America as well. Until recently, the United States government (the State and Defense departments in particular) and the Eastern establishment have been united in their support of Yoshida's line and the history that puts him in favorable light. This attitude goes back to the day when America was trying to enlist Japan as an anti-communist ally in the early Cold War.

Marxism burst on the defeated Japan with a vengeance. Convergence of several factors account for it. The total defeat in the total war unleashed in a delayed reaction the resentment of the oppressed part of the Meiji regime against the government. America's war against Japan was conceived in a radical scheme to remake the world through a crusade, a "punishment" against "crimes," and the occupation of Japan rested originally on that scheme. New Deal liberalism, which shaped that scheme, defined the defects of the old Japan as emanating from "feudalism" embodied in the domestic institutions, to be completely replaced. The war as a violent form of power struggle invoked corresponding instincts in America and Japan, and those instincts dominated their relations in the early postwar years. It is not surprising therefore that extremist ideologues and nationalists should have keynoted American pubic opinion and provided policy frameworks. Andrew Roth, Owen Lattimore, and E. Herbert Norman are among the writers who advocated the view that Japan was lacking in any saving grace and was ripe for revolutionary remedies.[10] But it was in 1948—the year in which the U.S. occupation policy was reversed because of the Cold War—that the decisive drift toward the Left began.

John Foster Dulles, who visited Japan during the Korean War as President Truman's chief negotiator for the peace and security treaties, was struck by the strength of neutralism there. From Prime Minister Yoshida on down, the Japanese were rather lukewarm toward national defense. Correctly Dulles diagnosed Japan's problem as the absence of public support for the conservative rule after it was discredited in defeat. Presumably he knew that nationalism was the most natural counter to communism. At the minimum Japan had to reaffirm itself and the Japanese be disabused of their self-flagellation. In 1952 Dulles persuaded the state department to set in motion a "psychological program" for creating a new ideology to combat Marxism. Edwin O. Reischauer, distinguished Harvard historian of Japan, and his fellow Japanologists were entrusted with the task. In the hands of the academics, however, the efforts went beyond "psychological program" to a search for a new paradigm of Japan's modern history.[11] The concept of modernization, a slightly milder affirmation than nationalism, was the answer. In the new history based on that paradigm, Japan was no longer the semifeudal oppressor and aggressor as the Marxists said it was. Instead, it was the leading modernizer and the first to introduce constitutional democracy in Asia; far from deriving from some innate native traits, Japanese militarism was now viewed as an aberration in an otherwise uninterrupted flow of "continuity"; the concept of feudalism was replaced by "tradition" or "early modernity"; and the "secrets of Japan's success" were sought in its tradition.

But Reischauer did not slay the ghosts of Japanese "militarism." He had to reintroduce it. As he put it in 1950,

> No matter how feasible it would be to make Japan our military ally, it probably could not be done without seriously endangering Japanese democracy. In view of *Japan's strong militaristic tradition* and the record of recent history . . . , it would be too much to hope that Japan could be both a military and an ideological ally.[12]

Japan was "modern," not "feudal." But a race of samurai warriors, Japan nevertheless nursed "militarism" in its "tradition."

This is a politically loaded point, conjuring up the bogey of "militarism" behind the attempt to rearm the postwar Japan. Traceable to the joint decision of MacArthur and Yoshida to preserve the no-war constitution of Japan, the "militarist" bogey has been the primary justification for that constitution and the lopsided U.S.-Japanese defense relations, as this book will show. Whether the bogey was intended to be a part of the modernization paradigm constructed by the distinguished historians is not known. It is my judgement, however, that through custom, usage, and sheer repetition it did become an integral part of the paradigm. In this roundabout way, John Foster Dulles's call for an anti-Marxist ideology has produced a paradigm and a history—which I choose to call standard history—based on it.

Standard history reflects the interests of the parties who constructed the new Venice. Douglas MacArthur was interested in maintaining the myth that the Japanese people had freely willed the constitution. He has had to conceal the fact that he wrote it, that he saved Emperor Hirohito in exchange for the emperor's acceptance of it, and that the emperor was not quite so free of responsibility for World War II, as he had to insist at the time in order to consummate the exchange.[13]

Standard history did succeed in eradicating Marxist influence but at a cost: the baby called power was thrown out with the bathwater of Marxism.[14] Evaporation of power as an analytical tool might have been ordained in any case by pacifism practiced by the new Venice. As a result, standard history has a certain quality that makes it seem unreal, inauthentic, and Alice in wonderland-like. In standard history, postwar Japan became a seamless web of good feeling, "consensus," and the "new middle mass" harnessed to the end of industrialization, best described in terms of the inanimate process of macroeconomics. In Japanese universities, Marxists gave way through attrition to the younger generation of scholars trained in the Anglo-Saxon tradition of empiricism, and, through the unique process of conversion, not a few firebrands of Zengakuren became academic apologists of the establishment. They began to pay lip service to the alleged advantages of one-party rule or conservative factionalism. A precious few Japanese continued to decry the inauthenticity of a Japan free riding in the cocoon of Pax Americana, but their voices were drowned out.[15]

Standard history reflects the concern of the U.S. Department of State for amour propre of Japan as an ally and a sovereign nation. The State Department leans over backward to concede equality to Japan by calling it a "partner," even though "mutuality" goes only one way and is not real. But this is not simple altruism but enlightened self-interest for America, for, as Reischauer noted above, any attempt to make an ally out of Japan would arouse its militarist tradition. Japan can remain a democracy only so long as it is chained to the constitution and only so long as it is successful in peaceful pursuits. Hence America must not only protect Japan but keep on absorbing interminable Japanese exports at the expense of its own industries.[16]

And yet Japan is an equal partner only as a matter of diplomatic protocol. In reality it is a military protectorate (partly by its own choice). Big powers do act ruthlessly toward their small neighbors, and the United States has not been an exception. How should American interventions in Japan's politics be treated? Standard history's answer has been to ignore them and to treat Japan as if it were autonomous and/or living in total isolation from the rest of the world. This tradition, too, has its origin in MacArthur: he wrote the constitution but assiduously maintained the fiction that the Japanese chose it of their own free will. In the name of U.S.-Japanese friendship, other milestone events that have shaped the bilateral relationship have also become taboos, untouchable, and off limit. They are skipped over entirely, covered up with elliptical allusions, or with fictions. Those who defy the taboo find it difficult to publish their works.[17]

Finally, standard history reflects the interests of the new Venice itself. Indeed the modernization paradigm was unsurpassed as an ideological sanction for the merchant state's pursuit of "income doubling" and technological and commercial success. At the Hakone conference and as a U.S. ambassador to Japan, Reischauer tirelessly kept up his proselytizing, and Japan's establishment welcomed him with open arms. Together the Japanese and American establishments extolled the virtues of the new Venice and warned against the "militarist" vice. The textbook controversy, so-called, of 1982 was just another instance in which the old bogey was paraded so as to forestall the Reagan administration's pressure on Japan to undertake the defense of its sealanes.

While stressing consensus, standard history does not neglect to show how Yoshida compares favorably to the Japanese revisionists.[18] Today it is widely assumed, incorrectly, that Yoshida founded the LDP. In contrast, Hatoyama, who should have been enshrined as the LDP's founding father, is a non-entity, best ignored.[19] Prime Minister Kishi who had sacrificed his political career to give birth to the existing security treaty is dismissed simply as a reaction to Yoshida's "democracy."[20]

But standard history is an ideology of the new Venice, not the truth. The policy it sanctioned was bound to be challenged once Japan emerged as a major economic power and America began to entertain doubts about the cost of hegemony. The American revisionists who emerged in 1988–89 are angry men who argue that Japan's economic power and edge threaten America's security.[21] Without knowing exactly why, they perceived Japan's differences from all the other states. Hence, they call for its containment, for managed trade, for the "structural impediment initiative," or for a revolution (to eliminate its differences from the normal states).

Their radical zeal brings us full circle back to 1945 and to Andrew Roth, Owen Lattimore, and E. H. Norman. Once again Japan's virtues—as defined by standard history this time—are turned on their heads: its stability is viewed as resistance to change, its economic "miracle" as resulting from selfishness, and its consensus as lack of political will (or "political center"). The apologists of the new Venice—who used to boast, "The Yoshida doctrine is forever"— have fallen silent.[22] Standard history that once successfully fended off Marxism seems powerless against the new enemy.

Karel van Wolferen, the author of *The Enigma of Japanese Power: People and Politics of A Stateless Nation,* gave me the immediate motive for writing this book. His thesis that Japan is a "Stateless" nation is not new. The Japanese themselves have been saying so for decades.[23] But van Wolferen is in error in assuming that Japan chose this condition of its own accord. The truth is that what he assails as The Japan Problem is a joint creation of U.S. and Japanese foreign policies, a fact that standard history has concealed from us. It is pointless to denounce The Japan Problem while leaving the constitution, its premise, untouched. At least van Wolferen ought to know that that sort of revisionism has already been tried and failed.

But this book is not an adjunct to a polemical purpose. It stands on its own as the first, uninhibited, truthful, scholarly account of the origin of Japan's postwar politics. Japan built by MacArthur and Yoshida nearly half a century ago stands in the twilight today. I want to see the Owl of Minerva take a flight in freedom, transcending both the ignorance of Japan's critics and misinformation peddled by its self-appointed defenders.

# NOTES

1. Michael Yoshitsu, *Japan and the San Francisco Peace Settlement* (New York: Columbia Univ. Press, 1983), p. 89.

2. *Kaiyo kokka Nihon no koso* [Japan as a seafaring nation: a proposal] (Tokyo: Chuo Koronsha, 1974). His biography of Yoshida is a revealing, important book: Masataka Kosaka, *Saiso Yoshida Shigeru* [Prime Minister Yoshida Shigeru] (Tokyo: Chuo Koronsha, 1968), p. 86.

3. Ronald Steel, "With Japan Rearmed," *New York Times,* December 7, 1982, op-ed page; Donald Hellmann, *Japanese American Relations* (Washington, DC: American Enterprise Institute, 1975); Kent E. Calder, "Japanese Foreign Economic Policy Formation: Explaining the Reactive State," *World Politics* (July 1988), pp. 517–41; Karel van Wolferen, *The Enigma of Japanese Power: People and Politics in A Stateless Nation* (New York: Alfred A. Knopf, 1989).

4. Cited in Soichiro Tawara, "Soren wa kowai desuka" [Is the Soviet Union threatening?], *Bungei Shunju* (March 1980).

5. van Wolferen, p. 425; James Fallows, "Containing Japan," *Atlantic,* May 1989, pp. 40–54; Theodore H. White, "The Danger from Japan," *New York Times Magazine,* July 28, 1985, pp. 15–83.

6. R. Taggart Murphy, "Power without Purpose: The Crisis of Japan's Global Financial Dominance," *Harvard Business Review* (March/April), 1989, pp. 71–83.

7. Raymond C. Togtman, *Atlantic,* September 1989, p. 8.

8. Chalmers A. Johnson, *MITI and the Japanese Miracle: The Growth of Industrial Policy, 1925–1975* (Stanford, CA: Stanford Univ. Press, 1982, Chapter I. Van Wolferen's attempt to explain that survival by saying that the "tail" of Japanese bureaucracies "wagged the dog," the occupation army, is not an explanation but a restatement of the problem. Van Wolferen, p. 352. He is more confusing than enlightening: on the one hand the bureaucracies are all powerful, but on the other they have no "core."

9. Bertram D. Wolfe, *Three Who Made A Revolution* (New York: Beacon Press, 1957).

10. Marxism and power were two elements that dominated American views of Japan during the war and the early occupation. Marxism was represented by E. H. Norman, *Japan's Emergence as a Modern State* (Westport, CT: Greenwood Press, 1940). Power struggle was stressed in, Andrew Roth, *Dilemma in Japan* (Boston: Little, Brown, 1945); Owen Lattimore, *Solutions in Asia* (Boston: Little, Brown, 1945); Willis Church Lamott, *Nippon: The Crime and Punishment of Japan* (New York: Doubleday, 1944). See Dower's analyses in John W. Dower, ed., *Origins of the Modern Japanese State: Selected Writings of E. H. Norman* (New York: Random House, 1975). Dower's *War without Mercy: Race and Power in the Pacific War* (New York: Pantheon Books, 1986) shows that America's wartime view of Japan was largely a result of wartime hysteria and propaganda.

11. Dower, *Origins,* p. 41.

12. *The United States and Japan* (Cambridge: Harvard Univ. Press, 1957), xx. Emphasis added.

13. Professor Reischauer defended the myth of Emperor Hirohito's innocence on U.S. television networks on the occasion of the emperor's death.

14. Note that this is one of Dower's reasons for returning to E. H. Norman. Dower, *Origins,* pp. 65–90.

15. Tsuneari Fukuda was one. See *Nichi-bei ryo kokumin ni uttaeru* [An appeal to the peoples of Japan and the United States] (Tokyo: Takagi Shobo, 1974); *Heiwaron ni taisuru gimon* [Skepticism toward pacifism] (Tokyo: Bungei Shunjusha, 1955); *Yukoku no ronri* [The rationale for patriotism] (Tokyo: Nihon Kyobunsha, 1970).

16. Mike Mochizuki and Richard Samuels, "Japanese Security Requires No Choice Between Evils," *New York Times,* December 19, 1982, op–ed page.

17. Theodore Cohen's very important book, *Remaking Japan: The U.S. Occupation as New Deal* (New York: Basic Books, 1987), could find a publisher only in Japan for several years. *Nihon senryo kakumei: GHQ kara no shogen* [Japan's occupation revolution: a testimony from GHQ] (Tokyo: TBS Britanica, 1983).

18. Masamichi Inoki, previously the president of the Defense College, and Kosaka Masataka, professor at Kyoto University, are the chief protagonists of the school. See Inoki, *Hyoden Yoshida Shigeru* [Yoshida Shigeru: A Biography] (Tokyo: Yomiuri Shimbunsha, 1978); Kosaka, *Saiso Yoshida Shigeru.*

19. U.S. Ambassador John M. Allison's posting to Tokyo, 1953–57, almost overlapped the Hatoyama administration's tenure, 1953–56. But in his memoir Allison mentions Hatoyama in only four places. *Ambassador from the Prairie: Or Allison Wonderland* (New York: Houghton Mifflin, 1973).

20. Mike Mochizuki, *Managing and Influencing the Japanese Legislative Process: The Role of Parties and the National Diet* (dissertation submitted to the department of political science, Harvard University, 1982), p. 465. In Martin E. Weinstein's book, the security treaty of 1960, concluded at enormous personal cost to Kishi, is credited to Yoshida's foresight. *Japan's Postwar Defense Policy, 1947–1968* (New York: Columbia University Press, 1969), p. 87. He also argues that the constitution was altogether irrelevant as a factor in Japan's foreign policy.

21. "Unfortunately, the major external threat to America's ability to pay the costs of leadership is Japan's uncontrolled, unbalanced economic growth," says James Fallows, in "Containing Japan," *The Atlantic,* May 1989, p. 42.

22. Yonosuke Nagai, "Yoshida dokutorin wa eien nari" [The Yoshida doctrine is forever], *Bungei Shunju,* May 1984, pp. 382–405;

23. Among the Japanese revisionists was Ikutaro Shimizu and his *Nihon yo kokka tare!* [Japan, be a state!] (Tokyo: Bungei Shunjusha, 1980). Yoshida's own camp used to call Japan a "moratorium state."

# Chapter 2

# A Constitution to Save the Emperor

---

The most puzzling thing about Yoshida Shigeru and the key to the postwar history of Japan is this: why did this man—a staunch royalist, strong nationalist, imperialist, and sometimes called a Churchill for those reasons—fight so arduously to defend the war-renouncing constitution? Did Japan's defeat transform him into a pacifist, or did he defend the constitution because he remained a nationalist?[1]

For answers, we must go back to the beginning, to the negotiations that led to Japan's surrender in 1945, touching on the special character of World War II, unprecedented and perhaps unrepeatable. President Franklin D. Roosevelt, who shaped the outcome of the war, took as his point of departure Woodrow Wilson's failure to make a lasting peace out of World War I and its settlement. Roosevelt was Wilsonian, but he was determined to avoid Wilson's mistakes: Wilson's internationalism was too idealistic to carry the isolationist public opinion of America with him; with its fastidious deference toward the Allies' sovereign equality, the United States lost control over their bickering; "peace without victory," Wilson's goal, prevented the Allies from achieving a decisive military conclusion on the battlefield and led to their negotiating rather than dictating the peace terms. The Wilsonian vision of world government and free international trade was in need of political teeth to be made good.

Roosevelt's solution was to use the idea of unconditional surrender, which he enunciated in Casablanca in 1942, to turn World War II into an even more intense moral crusade than the first. He viewed the war as a punishment against crimes, a punishment to deter war and banish it forever from international relations. The mobilized public gave him an unshakable mandate at home, enabling him to project America's power abroad. In the conduct of the war, over its settlement, and in the postwar world order, America was the determining voice. Whether at the UN Security Council, in GATT (General Agreement on Tariff and Trade) meetings, or over international currency, the United States was to enjoy hegemonic power, without which the new world order could not function. Only FDR's blend of power and moral principles, of punishment and utopianism made that order possible. The splendor and decay of that order—including the U.S.-Japan tension today—can be traced back to this innovation in the means of implementing the Wilsonian principles.

But a trouble with that vision surfaced even before the Axis powers were subdued, as it became evident that the United States was exchanging one set of enemies for another as a direct consequence of the policy of unconditional surrender. Some second thoughts about the policy surfaced in the Allied war council in Yalta in 1945. At the Anglo-American combined chiefs of staff meeting, Winston Churchill voiced his doubts about it in regard to Japan, the doubts he had earlier suppressed at Casablanca out of deference to Roosevelt.[2] However, for Roosevelt, Soviet cooperation was the cornerstone of peace, and at this point it was already impossible to rehash Allied decisions about Germany: the only thing the powers could agree on was the blank check called unconditional surrender.

But Churchill's voice fell on the receptive ears of the American military leaders who were present, George Marshall, chairman of the Joint Chiefs of Staff (JCS), William D. Leahy, and Ernest J. King, none of whom was eager to exclude political negotiation with the enemy. Upon returning from Yalta in March, moreover, they learned of a shocking fact. In the one month of fierce fighting it took to invade Saipan, defended by 23,000 Japanese troops, U.S. casualties were 23,000 (6,000 killed). Only 200 defenders survived. A full-scale race war of a savagery scarcely matched in the fight with the Germans was raging in the Pacific. The military came to note the connection between the emperor and Japanese fighting morale. They also inferred that unconditional surrender, which threatened to liquidate the Japanese state, was driving the Japanese in fierce resistance. Hence they came to the support of a negotiated peace upon FDR's death on April 12, 1945.[3]

Five days before FDR's death, a new government under General Suzuki Kantaro was installed in Tokyo. He understood the emperor's command to search for peace. But the U.S. policy of unconditional surrender stood in the way. No one could advocate surrender with impunity without assurance for the safety of the emperor and the emperor system. The imperial army was still bent on fighting one decisive battle on the mainland. But the German capitulation and Soviet transfer of forces to the Far East induced the army to agree to a diplomatic probe of Moscow's intentions. Japan's aims were to prevent Soviet participation in the war and to seek Soviet good offices in concluding the war on terms other than unconditional surrender.[4] But in reality, Moscow was an alternative that had to be exhausted before the army agreed to a talk with Washington.

Of primary importance in changing the Truman administration's policy toward

Japan was the increasing suspicion of Moscow's intentions regarding Poland. Soviet unilateralism and exclusiveness were beginning to erode the Roosevelt-bequeathed American taboo against negotiating with the Japanese. Joseph C. Grew, former ambassador to Japan and acting secretary of state while Secretary Edward R. Stettinius, Jr. busied himself with the founding of the United Nations, was acutely afraid of repeating in Asia the mistake committed in Europe, yet the Yalta accord had to be honored. In Grew's mind, the only way to minimize the damage from that accord was to induce Japan to surrender speedily to the United States. Equally important, he wished to obviate the need to use atomic bombs, of which he had learned on V-E Day. He personally supervised the drafting of an Allied statement to be addressed to Tokyo from Potsdam.[5]

Already, beginning in May 1943 he launched a one-man campaign to spread his view on Japan, which amounted to dangerous heresy—he wanted to spare the emperor. The emperor was the "queen bee" in Grew's metaphor. Promise honorable treatment for the emperor and the nation would lay down its arms, he argued. Grew found in Henry Stimson, secretary of the army and increasingly the elder statesman in the Roosevelt cabinet, sympathy for a negotiated end to the war. The original draft of the Potsdam Declaration was completed by Eugene Dooman, Grew's assistant at state, on May 26 and was redrafted by the sympathetic hands of Stimson and McCloy, assistant secretary of the army. It adhered to the rubric of unconditional surrender in deference to Roosevelt and public opinion, but sought to remove the biggest obstacle to Japan's acceptance of it by allowing the retention of "constitutional monarchy." But it left ambiguous the subject of unconditional surrender as between the Japanese state and armed forces.

But a strong objection to the Stimson draft arose at the State Department about the time of James F. Byrnes's succession of Stettinius as secretary in early July. The officials at State were determined to liquidate the superstructure of the Japanese government. The reference to the retention of monarchy in the surrender condition was struck out. The term "unconditional surrender" was used only in connection with the armed forces, not the state, of Japan. The declaration was to be addressed not to "Japan" or "the Japanese government" but to "the Japanese people," implying a revolutionary design to reconstitute the government during occupation. When the new draft was referred to the British government for comment, the following revisions were recommended and accepted. The addressee was changed back to "Japan" and "the Japanese government"; the subject of democratic reforms was "the Japanese government"; and the area of occupation was reduced from "the Japanese territory" to "points" in Japan.[6]

But neither Truman nor Stimson seemed to be in a hurry to issue a warning to the Japanese about the atomic bomb before its practicality was demonstrated at Alamogordo on July 16. In fact, they held Grew—impatient to preempt its use by an early Japanese surrender—at bay through May and June. During this time Washington, which had broken PURPLE—the Japanese code—in September 1940, became deaf as Japanese diplomatic traffic with Berlin ceased upon Germany's fall. Traffic resumed in July as Tokyo began to negotiate with Moscow, and its interception had two consequences for the decision makers in Washington. It indicated beyond doubt that the Japanese were ready to surrender if the monarchy could be retained, as both Grew and Stimson had suspected. It also suggested that should the United States press on with military assault, the Soviet Union might reap a windfall.

But from late July on Byrnes—supported by Archibald MacLeish and Dean Acheson, assistant secretaries for public and cultural affairs and for congressional relations, respectively—prevailed with his hardline views and excluded Grew and Stimson from the final drafting process. Byrnes, MacLeish, and Acheson were sensitive to public opinion, which rapidly grew vengeful toward Japan as the end of war came into sight, more so than toward Germany.[7]

The Potsdam Declaration of July 26 gives the impression of being a treaty or contract by expressly stating the "terms" to which Japan was to agree. It included articles that bound the Allied powers: Article 12 promised to terminate occupation upon Japan's fulfillment of the terms of the declaration; it also promised the Japanese people the right to choose a government through their "freely expressed will." The declaration further stated that Japan was to retain sovereignty over its territory (Article 8); that the "Japanese government" was to preside over the revival of democratic tendencies (Article 10); that occupation would be confined to "points in Japanese territory" (Article 7); that the "Japanese government" was to declare and guarantee the "unconditional surrender" of its armed forces (Article 13).[8]

But the declaration was deliberately vague on the point on which Japan's surrender hinged: there was no guarantee for the throne. "Its formulation was a compromise . . . [and] a lowest common denominator that satisfied the concern of the U.S. Army that nothing be done to preclude the emperor's continuation in office during the postwar occupation."[9] The army wanted to use the imperial authority for peaceful disarmament. Thus the United States was legally fortified to take either of the two steps if Japan accepted the declaration: to eliminate or retain the monarchy and the emperor.

On August 6 the bomb named "Little Boy" was dropped over Hiroshima. Three days later Radio Moscow announced the Soviet declaration of war and the second bomb was dropped on Nagasaki. The Soviet entry was more of a psychological shock than the bombs to the imperial army, but its resolve was not affected. Prime Minister Suzuki called the war council on the same day. The double-edged nature of the Potsdam Declaration was understood by those present. Hence the army minister and the army and navy chiefs of staff argued for the last decisive battle on the mainland to bargain for an explicit guarantee for the throne. That weakened Foreign Minister Togo's case for immediate acceptance of the surrender terms. He argued that the Potsdam Declaration was better than nothing and that it was wiser to take a chance on that than on another battle, for if the battle failed, the Allies would be so embittered as to give no quarter. Implicitly Togo was asking only for the safety of the throne and the emperor.[10] The war council deadlocked. Under the Meiji constitution, all ministers of state had to affix their signatures to a decision before it became valid.

An imperial conference had to be called late that night to debate two draft plans of reply to the Allied powers. Both drafts included the condition that "prerogatives of His Majesty as a sovereign ruler" be preserved. Draft B demanded in addition that (1) foreign armies be withdrawn speedily, (2) war criminals be tried by the Japanese government, and (3) a regime of control (supervising the terms of peace) not be imposed. The army minister and army and navy chiefs of staff insisted on draft B, whereas the remainder of the council agreed on draft A. To save the deadlocked conference, the prime minister asked the emperor to intervene. He upheld draft A.

The imperial government replied to the Allies on August 10 that it accepted the Potsdam Declaration, with the understanding that the "declaration does not comprise any demand which prejudices the prerogatives of His Majesty as a Sovereign Ruler."[11] There was a last-minute dispute in the Truman cabinet as to whether this understanding gave the Japanese too wide a latitude, enabling them to subvert the intent of the declaration. A reply was drafted, stating, "From the moment of surrender the authority of the Emperor and the Japanese Government to rule the state shall be *subject to* the Supreme Commander of the Allied Powers who will take such steps as he deems proper to effectuate the surrender *terms.*"[12] On the question of monarchy, the reply evaded Japanese inquiry by simply repeating the phrase in the Potsdam Declaration that the ultimate form of the Japanese government would be decided by the "freely expressed will of the Japanese people."[13]

When the Allied reply reached Tokyo on the 12th, it touched off another dispute over the implication of the phrase "subject to." On the 14th the emperor convened another conference on his own initiative and decided to accept the Potsdam Declaration. His intervention alone stopped the war, and he alone could command the armed forces to lay down their arms. Therefore, it was unavoidable that the imperial rescript, calling on the armed forces to surrender, stated that *kokutai,* or the emperor system, had been preserved.[14] The rescript, personally read by the emperor, was broadcast nationwide on August 15. The war ended, and the occupation was about to begin. But there was a serious disagreement between the belligerents as to the meaning of the Potsdam Declaration.

On August 14 the Japanese government asked the government of Switzerland to transmit to Washington several requests. Among them were requests to avoid entering the Tokyo region for occupation and to let the imperial government carry out the disarming of its armed forces. The requests were clearly an echo of the Potsdam Declaration, though the declaration as such was not mentioned.[15] Having secured the national consent to submit to the Potsdam Declaration, the government of prime minister and General Suzuki Kantaro resigned on August 15, the day of surrender. The Privy Council was temporarily in disarray, and the emperor personally appointed Higashikuni Naruhiko—an imperial prince, the emperor's uncle, and army general—as successor. A unit of the Imperial Guard Division had attempted a coup against surrender the night before, and it was felt that the task of persuading the armed forces to lay down their arms would be best carried out by an imperial prince. Higashikuni's foreign minister was Shigemitsu Mamoru, a career diplomat and former foreign minister who was to figure in subsequent conservative politics.

On August 22 the Japanese government established the Conference for Concluding the War (Shusen Shori Kaigi) in the cabinet and the Central Liaison Office, staffed by Foreign Ministry officials. The head of the Yokohama branch of the Liaison Office had been under instruction from the outset to do two things: to keep the Americans in Yokohama and to prevent them from issuing military payment certificates (mpc's). In addition, on August 23 and 28 Tokyo sent further requests by wireless to MacArthur in Manila, asking that mpc's not be used lest the Japanese public finance be thrown into chaos.[16] But no reply was received.

The advance party of the occupation forces arrived at the Atsugi air base of the imperial navy on August 28, followed by MacArthur and his headquarters on August 30. SCAP GHQ was housed in the New Grand Hotel in Yokohama, where it remained for 19 days. While in Yokohama, MacArthur moved with dispatch and energy, issuing major directives, accepting surrender of the imperial forces in Korea, and ordering the arrest of General Tojo as a war crimes suspect.

It was on September 2, after the surrender ceremony aboard the battleship *Missouri,* that a major issue between the Americans and the Japanese arose for the first time. During a conversation with General Sutherland, MacArthur's chief of staff, Suzuki Kyuman, head of the Yokohama Liaison Office, discovered that SCAP was to issue on the following day three proclamations addressed to "the Japanese people" in both English and Japanese. The first proclamation announced that Japan was to be placed under direct military government of SCAP, which would supersede all administrative, legislative, and judicial powers of the Japanese government and that English would be the official language. The second announced that military courts martial would try and punish anyone defying the terms of surrender, and the third that mpc's would circulate as legal tender alongside the issues of the Bank of Japan.

The news reported by Suzuki took the Japanese government by surprise. An emergency cabinet session was held, and Okazaki Katsuo, head of the Central Liaison Office, was dispatched late that night to GHQ in Yokohama with a request to put off the proclamations until a meeting between Foreign Minister Shigemitsu and MacArthur could be arranged. That meeting took place on September 3. Shigemitsu held fast to the terms of the Potsdam Declaration in insisting on the continued existence of the Japanese government. As for the use of mpc's, he pointed out that fiscal chaos would work against the purpose of the occupation. Surprisingly, MacArthur relented.[17]

The incident had underscored an important issue. As noted earlier, the Potsdam Declaration could be taken to mean that the Japanese government would remain sovereign and the subject of democratic reforms, existing side by side with the occupation authority, stationed at "points in Japanese territory; Japan's freedom to choose the form of government could mean in essence freedom from occupation interference. The Japanese government had to insist on its interpretation of the declaration if only because ultimately the fate of the throne depended on it.

What was Douglas MacArthur up to? My answer has to be highly conjectural. He was obviously aware of the State-War dispute over the disposition of the monarchy since Potsdam. Byrnes' radical policy posed a threat to the security of the U.S. forces, not to speak of the success of the occupation. MacArthur was already in receipt of a major occupation directive, authorizing indirect government for occupation but giving the supreme commander the discretion to set up a direct military rule if necessary.[18] By invoking a direct military rule, he could ask for a vast reinforcement. As a matter of fact, he was at this time asking for one. This request amounted to a warning to Byrnes and Truman that an attempt on the emperor's life would be extremely costly. Then why did he give in to Shigemitsu's plea? The foreign minister, I surmise, had persuaded him that sticking to the letters of the Potsdam Declaration— including the indirect government—was a better way of insuring the safety of the throne.[19]

The first full indication to Japan that the United States was seeking as a matter of policy very radical reforms including the possibility of eliminating the throne, and that it was reverting to the principle of unconditional surrender in carrying out these reforms came in the "United States Initial Postsurrender Policy for Japan," drafted by the State-War-Navy Coordinating Committee (SWNCC) and dated September 6, 1945. Staffed by assistant secretaries of the three departments, SWNCC was established in December 1944, and it rapidly developed into an executive organ with the powers of ultimate decisions over the conclusion of war and postwar policies. Its decisions became authoritative when President Truman, new to the executive office, began to refer to SWNCC for advice. The "Initial Postsurrender Policy," designated SWNCC 150/1, was originally drafted in June, prior to the Potsdam conference, but was revised successively through SWNCC 150/4 to take note of the Potsdam Declaration and subsequent development in U.S. policy. A summary of SWNCC 150/4 was radioed to MacArthur in Manila on August 29, and it appeared in final form on September 6 with Truman's approval. The document was to be made public in both the United States and Japan.

SWNCC 150/4 did not use the words, "unconditional surrender," but it indicated that the official American thinking was substantially changing. The most striking difference between the Potsdam Declaration of July or SWNCC 150/2 of August 12, on the one hand, and SWNCC 150/4 of September 6, on the other, is the addition of the following paragraph:

> . . . This policy, moreover, does not commit the Supreme Commander to support the Emperor or any other Japanese governmental authority in opposition to evolutionary changes looking toward the attainment of United States objectives. The policy is to use the existing form of Government in Japan, not to support it. Changes in the form of Government initiated by the Japanese people or government in the direction of modifying its feudal and authoritarian tendencies are to be permitted and favored. In the event that the effectuation of such changes involves the use of force by the Japanese people or government against persons opposed thereto, the Supreme Commander should intervene only where necessary to ensure the security of his forces and the attainment of all other objectives of the occupation.[20]

A violent overthrow of "feudal and authoritarian" government—including regicide—was to be encouraged and supported by the occupation forces, according to the postsurrender revision. Unconditional surrender, the original goal of the war, seemed to combine with the New Deal reformist zeal to inform the new policy.[21]

The story behind this radical shift still awaits scholarly inquiry. Hitherto, there has been deep ambivalence in orthodox interpretation of Japan's surrender, with some insisting that it was unconditional and others maintaining that the monarchy and emperor were preserved by the Potsdam Declaration. A most recent Japanese work says that the declaration specified conditional unconditional surrender. It was not until 1988 that Leon V. Sigal firmly established the double-option nature of the declaration.[22] The ambivalence is a reflection of both the U.S. and Japanese governments. The Japanese Foreign Ministry maintained throughout the occupation that its surrender was conditional. According to it, when the Potsdam Declaration—by itself a unilateral declaration of the four Allied powers—was incorporated into the instrument of surrender, it came to constitute a kind of contract binding on both parties. But in June 1950, just before the arrival in Tokyo of John Foster Dulles, then consultant to Secretary of State Dean Acheson and in charge of the Japanese peace treaty, the Foreign Ministry began to maintain retroactively that Japan's surrender was unconditional.[23]

The War Department and the JCS appeared to have been consistent throughout in seeking economy of force. In addition Henry Stimson, army secretary, was convinced that the Japanese monarchy was worth saving in its own right rather than as a means of securing a bloodless occupation. So the decision of the State Department could swing the U.S. position, and that in turn depended on Joseph Grew's fortunes. His influence reached its peak in late 1944 when he was promoted to undersecretary and acting secretary in Roosevelt's reshuffle of State, occasioned by the resignation of Cordell Hull and his succession by Edward Stettinius. Dean Acheson, a hardnosed liberal, was sidetracked from assistant secretary for economic affairs to assistant secretary of congressional relations. Even so, Grew faced an uphill battle in mustering his department's support for conditional surrender. But as long as he was successful in stonewalling any change in the monarchical institution, he could also hold at arm's length all the proposals looking to radical redistribution of wealth or politico-social engineering in Japan.

And many of these proposals were being drawn up at the middle level of bureaucracies all across Washington. Within the State Department itself, the "old Japan hands" inadvertently conceded influence to New Dealers in bureaucratic jockeying. When Grew was upgraded to acting secretary, Will Clayton moved into Economic Affairs. Apparently without much forethought, Clayton appointed Edwin Martin, a dedicated New Dealer from the Office of Strategic Services, his staff to assert the equality of his Economic Affairs with the traditional Japan crowd ensconced in Political Affairs. In April 1945 Dooman and Martin made an agreement to split political and economic affairs of Japan between themselves as coequals. In so doing, Dooman's autonomy over political affairs was held hostage to Martin's over economic. Martin began to introduce radical redistributive programs into his bailiwick as the early versions of SWNCC 150 were being drafted.[24]

Back in May 1943, the Army had appointed Major General John L. Hildring director of the Civil Affairs Division to draw up directives for future occupying commander in Japan. Because the "Japan crowd" at the State Department, all career diplomats, showed no interest in anything but foreign policy, Hildring enlisted the help of non-Japan-specialists at the Treasury Department, the Foreign Economic Administration, the Office of Strategic Services, the Office of War Information, and above all the Board of Economic Warfare, sponsored by Vice President Henry Wallace. This had two consequences. On the one hand, the control over policy began to slip out of the hands of the Japan specialists at State. On the other, Japan came to be treated as an adjunct to Germany.

In the summer of 1944, Henry Morgenthau, treasury secretary, was scandalized by the State Department's lenience in dealing with German reparations and, with President Roosevelt's enthusiastic support, intruded into postwar planning with his scheme to de-industrialize Germany. In response, the Civil Affairs Division produced the first and most severe version of JCS 1067, the occupation directive to General Eisenhower, which was in turn a model for JCS 1380/15, later sent to MacArthur in Japan.[25] JCS 1380/15 was the Army's counterpart of SWNCC 150/4.[26] Working under Hilldring as assistant executive officer, in close liaison with Harry Dexter White, Morgenthau's subordinate at Treasury, was one Lieutenant Colonel Charles Kades, who was destined to become a chief administrator of the initial occupation policy. The Morgenthau Plan met such resistance in the cabinet that it was temporarily shelved. But apparently nothing was done to JCS 1067. "[A] number of . . . German provisions did get into the Japanese directive, some of them verbatim."[27] Still this was the Army's directive.

The "old Japan hands" at State—consisting of Joseph Grew, Eugene Dooman, Joseph Ballantine, George Blakeslee, Robert Fearey—were alarmed by Treasury's incursion and decided to enlist the help of Stimson and his under secretary, McCloy, at the Army Department to reassert their control over postwar planning. In December 1944 the State-War-Navy Coordinating Committee was formed, with a subcommittee on the Far East called SWNCCFE, which did all the substantive work on Japan. Papers and decisions were routed from it through SWNCC, and on to the President. But "Hilldring now had a regular channel [in SWNCC] through which to present the war agencies' ideas."[28]

Then on July 3, Stettinius was succeeded by James Byrnes, who replaced Grew with Acheson as undersecretary. The coalition of the "China crowd" and Dean Acheson became decisive. John Carter Vincent, son of China missionaries and an "old China hand," replaced both Dooman, on SWNCCFE, and

Ballantine, head of the Office of Far Eastern Affairs. Earle Dickover, another Japan specialist, was replaced by Hugh Borton, formerly of Columbia University, who had written on peasant uprisings in feudal Japan. Asked to name a political adviser to General MacArthur, Byrnes skipped Dooman and chose George Atcheson, another son of a China missionary. Grew retired on V-J day, and Stimson followed in September.

When Japan accepted the Potsdam Declaration, a heated debate took place in Washington as to whether the Japanese monarchy can be eliminated within the terms of the Potsdam Declaration. On August 21, six days after Japan's surrender, Edward G. Miller, Jr., special assistant to Dean Acheson, drafted a memorandum supporting Acheson's views. He conceded that the Potsdam Declaration called for only the Japanese armed forces to surrender unconditionally and that it was addressed to the Japanese government. "However," he went on, "it seems to me that this particular point of construction of the Potsdam Declaration is rendered immaterial by the subsequent exchange of notes between the governments." Miller pointed to "the reply of the four powers of August 11 which stated that 'from the moment of surrender the authority of the Emperor and the Japanese government to rule the state shall be subject to the Supreme Commander of the Allied Powers . . .' " And he maintained that "this means in effect that the Supreme Commander has at any time the *right to dissolve or take such other action as he may wish* with respect to the present Japanese government."[29] Miller seemed to suggest that Japan surrendered under the terms not of the Potsdam Declaration but of the allied reply of August 11.

But in a memorandum to Assistant Secretary of State MacLeish, Joseph W. Ballantine of SWNCCFE conceded that the emperor could be eliminated within the terms of the Potsdam Declaration itself.[30] Some American officials insisted otherwise. For instance, George H. Blakeslee argued that regardless of rationalization the destruction of the emperor system now would be taken in Japan as a breach of faith and a betrayal and that the Japanese would then take the Potsdam Declaration as a ruse to induce surrender first so that the Allies could do as they pleased.[31]

What tipped the scale in favor of radicalization, it seems, was the shift in balance of power between Potsdam and the V-J Day. Japan's surrender to the United States had eliminated the chances of Soviet intervention in Japan proper. But Japan's position was weaker because of that intervention. "I cannot understand," Byrnes said, "why we should go further than we were willing to go at Potsdam when we had no atomic bomb, and Russia was not in the war."[32] A politician once considered for vice-presidency under FDR, Byrnes was also sensitive to public opinion and Congress. So were Acheson and Assistant Secretary Archibold MacLeish. As the end of the war came into sight, the American public's impulse to wreak vengeance on the enemy was on the surge.[33] A joint congressional resolution in late September demanded a trial of the emperor.[34]

With respect to the monarchy, SWNCC 150/4 kept the double-option of the Potsdam Declaration. But when Japan accepted the declaration, the "republican" option became a possibility. And that seemed to have opened the floodgate to all the radical engineering proposals, which were written into the final draft of SWNCC 150. Even if the monarchy were to survive, it would be emasculated and placed in a completely altered environment. Both SWNCC 150/4 and JCS 1380/15 shared the New Deal assumption that social structure is the source of political decisions. "The present economic and social system in Japan which makes for a will to war," said Dean Acheson in September, "will be changed so that the will to war will not continue."[35] Politically and economically, the existing ruling class in Japan was to be reformed out of existence and a new one established on its left through the instrumentality of large-scale purge.[36] The purge in turn made large-scale engineering possible.

Therefore, the most important difference between the Potsdam Declaration and SWNCC 150/4 was that the latter clearly implied the policy of (1) defining the monarchy in the minimalist sense, and (2) holding it hostage to Japan's acceptance of disarmament and radical reforms. Japan's surrender turned out to be unconditional, as the Japanese military had maintained at the imperial conference.

The sword of Damocles hung over the Japanese leaders. The table was turned on the Foreign Military, now responsible for the safety of the throne and the Japanese state. Even before the arrival of the first contingent of U.S. military forces in Atsugi air base on August 28, Foreign Military officials began to fight a desperate rear-guard action to defend their interpretation of the Potsdam Declaration. One official in particular, Yoshida Shigeru, felt an acute sense of responsibility because he had actively advocated peace[37] and because he was a staunch royalist.

Undoubtedly because of the gravity of SWNCC 150/4's implications—after all the Japanese armed forces still remained fully armed—MacArthur did not publicly release it, as was done in Washington, but secretly handed it to the Japanese government on September 24.[38] On September 30 the Foreign Military circulated a lengthy memorandum analyzing its content and commented, "The United States has refused to offer any guarantee for the preservation of our imperial system."[39] The United States was at liberty to interpret the terms of the Potsdam Declaration unilaterally, and whatever restraint may be implied by those terms was removed when the "freely expressed will of the Japanese people" was radically reinterpreted. There was no freedom from occupation because occupation was, ipso facto, freedom and liberation. MacArthur represented something like the General Will; he was the "sovereign" of Japan, as he used to call himself, possessing radically potent power that placed him above any law.[40] In the legal sense, therefore, it is impossible to say that there was democracy in Japan under the U.S. occupation. However, "democratization" of social and political institutions was carried out on a massive scale.

But the problem at hand in Tokyo was not theoretical but practical and downright explosive—scarcely two weeks after the end of fighting, the two nations were about to collide over the terms of surrender and the fate of the emperor. Because SWNCC 150/4 gave MacArthur a measure of discretion over the emperor question, he was in the eye of a storm. On September 17 President Truman sent an invitation to MacArthur "to return to the States to receive the plaudits of a grateful nation." But MacArthur declined, saying it was "unwise" for him to leave Japan because of the "delicate and difficult situation which prevails here." Truman persisted and extended another invitation on September 19—the day on which Dean Acheson's nomination as under secretary went to the Senate—promising a chance to address a joint session of Congress. Truman must have thought this was an honor MacArthur could hardly refuse. But Mac-Arthur once again declined because of "*extraordinarily dangerous and inherently inflammable situation* which exists here."[41] Alone, MacArthur stood between SWNCC 150/4 and the emperor.

On September 17, shortly after Shigemitsu's visit with MacArthur in Yokohama, a change of guard took place in silence at Gaimusho. Shigemitsu was dismissed by MacArthur for having leaked to the press the content of his meeting with the general.[42] Then he was arrested on suspicion of war crimes, at the insistence of Moscow which had a grudge against him dating back to his posting there as ambassador. Yoshida Shigeru, the central subject of this book, undoubtedly learned something from the incident as he took over as successor.

Ignoring the Japanese request, MacArthur moved SCAP GHQ from Yokohama to the U.S. embassy in Tokyo on September 17 and then to the Daiichi Building across from the imperial palace on October 2. The symbolism of the act was well understood by the Japanese.

Still the Japanese were confused about their freedom, promised without reservation in both the Potsdam Declaration and SWNCC 150/4. Hatoyama Ichiro (the leader of the former Seiyukai Party, now reorganized as the Liberal Party) who had spent the war years in self-imposed exile, but who had returned to active public life with the expectation of heading the government in the near future, publicly denounced the atomic bombing of Hiroshima and Nagasaki as atrocities and a violation of international law. To forestall similar moves, censorship was imposed in stages, on September 10, 15, and 21, the press code and precensorship going into effect on the last date.[43]

Since receiving SWNCC 150/4, Japanese officials were in a state of extreme anxiety. They sought to pry from Americans any clue as to what they had in store for the emperor. The emperor lived a stone's throw away from MacArthur's GHQ, and a meeting between them could not be postponed any longer. Yoshida went to GHQ to arrange one and asked the general point blank if he wished to be visited by the emperor. Momentarily nonplussed, MacArthur mumbled something, according to Yoshida. Then he said, to Yoshida's relief, that he had no intention to "embarrass" or "humiliate" the emperor. On September 27, ten days after MacArthur moved his GHQ to Tokyo, the emperor went to the Daiichi Building.[44]

According to MacArthur, the emperor surprised him by offering to "bear sole responsibility for every political and military decision made and taken by my people in the conduct of war."[45] It is also said that the emperor offered to abdicate in due course.[46] This is the last occasion for such offers, because owning up to war responsibilities and abdicating would be an invitation to prosecution. Kido Koichi, lord keeper of the seal and a privy councilor, noted in his diary that day: "MacArthur understood well that the emperor always worked for peace."[47] A new myth was in the making, to be honored in standard history later, a myth that, in an attempt to save the emperor's life, went to the extreme of maintaining that he had no responsibility whatever for the war or its conduct.

The day after the emperor's visit, GHQ released a photo showing the emperor in his cutaway, with the general towering over him in open-collared informality. The Interior Ministry censored the picture but was immediately countermanded by GHQ. The photo appeared on the front pages of newspapers on September 29, and it shocked the Japanese. On October 3, moreover, the interior minister had a press conference with foreign correspondents at which he vowed to "arrest in accordance with the Peace Preservation Law all those who advocate a change in the form of government, in particular, the abolition of the emperor system. They will be regarded as Communists."[48] He, too, was holding fast to the Potsdam Declaration. But SCAP's retribution was swift. In an executive order having the force of law and called the "Potsdam executive decree" (*Potsudamu seirei* in Japanese, SCAPIN for SCAP Instruction in English), issued the next day, SCAP ordered the dismissal of the interior minister and the head of police, immediate release of all political prisoners, abolition of "thought police," and repeal of all oppressive laws and regulations. The Higashikuni cabinet resigned to protest the unwarranted intervention in cabinet appointments and to hold MacArthur to the Potsdam Declaration.

The interior minister mentioned the Peace Preservation Law of 1925, enacted in the aftermath of World War I to stem the sudden spread of Marxist influence by making it sedition to advocate abolition of the emperor system and private property. It was directed emphatically at the Japan Communist Party (JCP) leaders. They were among the Japanese socialists who had earlier enlisted in the Third Communist International, or Comintern, but they had begun to quarrel among themselves over revolutionary strategies.[49] The quarrel ended up in a schism in 1932, when Joseph Stalin called for revolutionary overthrow of the emperor system in one of his theses. Those who shied away from lese majeste left the Comintern and became the leftwing of a socialist party. The hard-bitten Japanese Stalinists came to constitute the JCP, defying the secret police at enormous personal sacrifice, when most of the socialists went through "conversions" (*tenko*).

When the interior minister averred that the Peace Preservation Law would be upheld, he was insisting that those Stalinists would remain in jail. He certainly understood that the regicidal option in SWNCC 150/4 called for the use of Japanese collaborators, who would speak for the "freely expressed will of the Japanese people." To release the Communist prisoners and give them the mandate of SWNCC 150/4 was tantamount to suicide for the Japanese government.[50] Hence, he defied SCAP head-on. MacArthur had to dismiss him and order the release of the Communist prisoners.

Prince Higashikuni's successor was Shidehara Kijuro, a career diplomat, former prime minister, and well-known prewar liberal, whom MacArthur found acceptable for now because, for one thing, he spoke good English.[51] The Japanese government and the Foreign Ministry still clung to the pretense that Japan was something more than a protectorate under military occupation. Earlier, on August 15, Tokyo was given Washington's demand via the Swiss government that it must hand over all embassy and consular properties abroad to the Allied powers. Back in 1941, when all the Allied nations had severed relations with Japan, six neutral powers, including the Vatican, kept their diplomatic ties with Japan. The United States was ordering these ties terminated. The Foreign Ministry protested to Washington on the ground that the demand was not founded in the Potsdam Declaration.[52] On October 25, 1945, SCAP GHQ issued a directive repeating Washington's previous demand. Yoshida Shigeru, who had been retained in the Shidehara cabinet as foreign minister, protested again, to no avail. Soon thereafter Japan lost control of its foreign relations altogether. POLAD, or the Office Political Adviser, under SCAP, acted as Japan's as well as SCAP's foreign ministry from then on.[53]

Thus during the first month of occupation, the Japanese leaders became aware that they could not hold the U.S. government to the Potsdam Declaration. MacArthur's personal friendship for the emperor gave them a glimmer of hope. But arrests of war crimes suspects had been proceeding apace since General Tojo's apprehension by military police in September, and some Japanese leaders were committing suicide. It seemed difficult to avoid implicating the emperor if his ministers were to be tried and found guilty. In a meeting with Prime Minister Higashikuni in September, moreover, MacArthur "instructed" the drafting of "a plan for revision of the constitution,"[54] That could only mean tampering with imperial prerogatives.

On October 16 Secretary Byrnes wrote to George Atcheson, POLAD, informing him of the "[a]ttitude of Departmental officers" toward political reforms in Japan. One group, according to Byrnes, opted to "retain" the emperor system and the other opted not to, but both favored popular sovereignty.[55] On January 4, 1946, George Atcheson advised President Truman that execution of the emperor was one option.[56]

The Japanese leaders saw a threat to the emperor system from two sources—the war crimes trial and a "democratic" revolution. In February 1945, with Japan's defeat already a foregone conclusion, Prince Konoye wrote a lengthy memorandum to the throne expressing his deep apprehension that defeat would provide propitious conditions for a communist revolution.[57] Still, it was one thing to see a grassroots revolutionary movement and something else for the Japanese government, acting as an arm of SCAP, to encourage it as a matter of policy. Even after the dismissal of the previous interior minister, the Shidehara government continued to ignore the SCAP order to liberate the Communists. It would be a matter of time before the other shoe would drop.

The Japanese officials' nightmare came true in October when John Emmerson, a State Department official under POLAD, and E. Herbert Norman, acting chief of the Research and Analysis Section of the Counterintelligence Division in GHQ, proceeded to Fuchu Prison in the suburbs of Tokyo and released 16 political prisoners, including several Communists.[58] Norman was a Canadian citizen and a rather accomplished historian of modern Japan. At a time when such specialization was very rare, his book, *Japan's Emergence as a Modern State,* become a Bible of the New Dealer reformers in Tokyo. Perhaps the most important reason for his instant fame was the fact that he provided a theoretical justification for the view that a "feudal" *social structure* was the source of Japanese aggressions. For this formulation, he relied on the kozaha school of Japanese Communist historians, who postulated, two-stage revolution—a "French" or bourgeois-democratic revolution, followed by a communist revolution.[59] Japan's "feudal" traits, these historians maintained, stemmed from the "arrested" nature of the bourgeois-democratic revolution. In order to complete it and fully modernize Japan, some radical unleashing of shackles was necessary. This was precisely the theory underlying SWNCC 150/4.

It transpired later that Norman was a lifelong member of the Communist party.[60] Contemporaneously, he associated himself with progressive intellectuals at the Institute of Pacific Relations, and his works lent themselves to justifying the execution of the emperor. Owen Lattimore rested his case for execution on Norman's work.[61] Norman served briefly in Tokyo investigating Japanese war crimes, including those of former prime minister Konoye, who was driven to suicide soon thereafter.[62]

For the Japanese Communist leaders in jail, all seasoned Stalinists, the American welcoming party, made up of Norman and Emmerson, was quite an unexpected feat. Whether they were given a copy of SWNCC 150/4 is unknown. Promptly they declared that the "Allied powers are a liberation army," unfurled the old Comintern-inspired slogan, "overthrow the emperor system," made conspicuous visits to the Government Section of SCAP—the most powerful agency and spearhead of radical reform—and let it be known that SCAP stood behind them. SCAP pointedly issued no denials.[63] The first known assignment of the JCP members at GHQ was to draw up a list of class A war crimes suspects and help prepare the charges against them.

On January 7, 1946, the State-War-Navy-Coordinating Committee issued to SCAP a top secret directive, designated SWNCC 228, which conformed to the substance of Byrnes's letter of October 16, noted above. SCAP was ordered to carry out a thoroughgoing constitutional change to create a government of popular sovereignty.[64] In an atmosphere crackling with tension, the process of constitutional revision got underway between MacArthur and the government of Shidehara Kijuro. The Japanese leaders were duty-bound to defend the emperor. And it was Douglas MacArthur who came to the rescue.

There are three major themes in MacArthur's life that came to have a direct bearing on his administration of the occupation of Japan. They are (1) his sense of honor, which was part and parcel of his ambition to leave his name etched in history; (2) his sense of America's Manifest Destiny in Asia, the sense born of his father's and his own experience with the colonial administration of the Philippines; and (3) the tension between him and Franklin Roosevelt and the New Deal Democrats.

For all his foibles and the enigma surrounding him, Douglas MacArthur was beyond doubt a great man. This he owed to the fact that he tried to emulate the greatest—Caesar, Alexander, Lincoln, etc.—about whom he read voraciously. At a moment when the temptation for revenge was so strong, he rose above it and showed magnanimity toward the vanquished foe. His speech on the occasion of the surrender ceremony aboard the battleship *Missouri* in Tokyo Bay drove home that point, and it did not go unnoticed by the Japanese government. One infers in retrospect that his peroration, having the ring of Lincoln's Gettysburg Address and the second inaugural address ("With malice toward none . . ."), was a signal to Washington that he intended not to harm the emperor, though the Democratic president upstaged the *Missouri* speech in Washington.

MacArthur felt that the occupation of Japan was his greatest achievement. Asia was MacArthur's destiny, and the path of his career in Asia—from the Philippines, to Japan, and on to Korea—followed the sequence of America's involvement there. The sequence was not arbitrary but accorded with geopolitical logic. He who took the Philippines would have to come to terms with Japan. The Philippine archipelago lies athwart Japan's front line of defense in the western Pacific. As soon as the archipelago was taken—almost in a "fit of absent-mindedness"—the U.S. military had to draw up War Plan Orange, directed at Japan. And he who took Japan would have come to terms with Korea, the dagger pointed at the soft underbelly of Japan.

Genealogy fitted MacArthur for the role of military viceroy and benevolent dictator for a far-off land of Asian heathens. His father, Arthur MacArthur, a major general in the U.S. Army, took part in the Spanish-American war in the Philippines in 1898 and ruled the colony as a successful military governor. In year one of American colonialism, Douglas MacArthur entered West Point. Those were the times of Teddy Roosevelt and imperialism, Elihu Root and sea power; undoubtedly young MacArthur imbibed the sense of civilizing mission with which his father wielded the sword. But it was President McKinley who articulated that sense his father embodied. In his memoir, Douglas MacArthur cited at length a speech by McKinley, a benediction for American colonial rule:

> No imperial designs lurk in the American mind. They are alien to American sentiment, thought and purpose. Our priceless principles undergo no change under a tropical sun. They go with a fiat: "Why read ye not the changeless truth, the free can conquer but to save?"
>
> If we can benefit these peoples, who will object? If in the years of the future they are established in government under law and liberty, who will regret our perils and sacrifices? . . .
>
> . . . that group of islands . . . shall have become the gems and glories of those tropical seas, a land of plenty and of increasing possibilities, a people devoted to the arts of peace, in touch with the commerce and trade of all nations, enjoying the blessings of freedom, of civil and religious liberty, of education and of homes, and whose children and children's children for ages hence bless the American Republic, because it emancipated and redeemed their fatherland and set them in the pathway of the world's best civilization.[65]

The last paragraph above might as well have been uttered by MacArthur of Japan. Indeed it would become his dearest wish to Philippinize Japan. Both were Asian nations. Like McKinley, MacArthur assumed that Asians were in a "tuitionary" state, as MacArthur put it:

> If the Anglo-Saxon was say forty-five years of age in development in the sciences, the arts, divinity, culture, the Germans were quite as mature. The Japanese, however, in spite of their antiquity measured by time were in a very tuitionary condition. Measured by the standards of modern civilization, they would be like a boy of twelve as compared with our development of forty-five years. The German was quite as mature as we were. Whatever the German did in dereliction of the standards of modern morality, the international standards, he did deliberately. . . . But the Japanese were entirely different. There is no similarity.[66]

One event in Arthur MacArthur's administration of the Philippines left an indelible imprint on his son. After the Spaniards were put down, the U.S. Expeditionary Forces under Arthur MacArthur's command were unsuccessful in suppressing the guerrillas led by Emilio Aguinaldo, the leader of the Philippine independence movement, until the elder MacArthur hit upon a new, political solution: Capture Aguinaldo, the "queen bee" in Ambassador Grew's later metaphor for the emperor of Japan, and give him generous treatment. When this was done, Douglas later recalled with pride, the rest of the guerrillas surrendered their weapons and joined Aguinaldo, to the amazement of the Americans.[67]

Douglas MacArthur was appointed army chief of staff in 1930 by President Hoover. Following his suppression of the Bonus March by veterans, he had a falling-out with President Roosevelt, who maneuvered him out of his post in Washington. Roosevelt thought MacArthur was a "rare demagogue" and along with Huey Long "one of the two most dangerous men in the country," because they could be "Caesars."[68] FDR was more prescient than he knew. At the height of the occupation, in a conversation with George F. Kennan in 1948, MacArthur compared his rule of Japan to Caesar's occupation of Britain and France.[69]

MacArthur was a conservative Republican, and in the 1944 presidential election he showed an interest in running against Franklin Roosevelt. The soldier and the anti-Roosevelt Republican in MacArthur revealed themselves in his dislike of his role in the trial of Japan's political leaders for their "crimes against peace," the sine qua non of unconditional surrender.[70] On August 30, 1945, MacArthur embarked on the last leg of his journey from Manila aboard his C-54, *Bataan*. Unknown to the Japanese, he was already quietly resolved that the emperor must be saved if he were to compete with his father's success as a colonial viceroy.[71] Through historical revisionism, the initial phase of the U.S. occupation of Japan has come to be viewed as a benefaction or liberation simply, rather than as a punishment through unconditional surrender. It was MacArthur who originated this conception and acted on it, but at the time he was all alone in his fight against SWNCC 150/4 and its "vicious efforts to destroy the person of the Emperor."[72]

To return to constitutional revision, the idea was broached by MacArthur to Prime Minister Higashikuni when they met on September 15, 1945. But the first government under occupation resigned on October 5. The day before, the former prime minister, Konoye, met MacArthur, and four days later George Atcheson, POLAD. Both Americans impressed on him the need for constitutional revision. Konoye took these discussions as informal encouragement by SCAP to start drafting a revised constitution. With the Privy Council's sanction, he appointed himself to the task. Why a man from the cream of the Japanese establishment should have interested himself in constitutional revision at the behest of the Americans is a question of some importance. It appeared that the Japanese leaders were divided on the question of what was most conducive to the safety of the throne. Konoye represented those who argued for preempting the American decision with a mild reform retaining the emperor system. The Foreign Ministry bureaucracy, too, was inclined in this direction.[73] It is my inference that Shidehara and Yoshida argued the opposite. That is, any concession on the constitution would open the floodgates—the point was to hold the Americans to the Potsdam Declaration, the only protection left in Japanese hands.[74]

In any event, MacArthur dismissed Konoye's unsolicited help on constitutional revision with a formal announcement on November 1.[75] Konoye committed suicide on December 15, before he could be arrested on suspicion of war crimes. So his draft was stillborn. But it is interesting to speculate what he might have proposed, because following his stint as wartime prime minister between 1937 and 1941, he became highly critical of the Meiji constitution. At that time, the Japanese government was like a carriage pulled by two horses—the civilian political leaders and the military hierarchy—but without a driver. There were double ambiguities involved. The first had to do with the civil-military division of the power of the driver. The military was directly subordinated to the emperor as the commander-in-chief because there was unrest in the land at the time the Meiji constitution was drafted, and it was feared that the military might be politicized unless it was segregated from the political branch of the government. But there was no trouble with the two-horse carriage in the early Meiji era because the elder statesmen, the founders of the Meiji government, wielded real power behind the throne—they were the driver.

The second ambiguity had to do the emperor's power vis-a-vis his ministers, civilian or military. Whereas it is true that there was no presonal rule by an emperor, he was not a mere figurehead either. The imperial power was deliberately designed to be ambiguous in the Meiji constitution. On the one hand, the infant nation needed a charismatic figure to unite itself. Without a potential power—like that of a sword never drawn—the emperor could not have been sacred or charismatic. On the other hand, were he to exercise his power as ruler, he would have entered the cockpit of politics. He would have been held to account for the consequences of his decisions, the surest way of losing charisma. Therefore, the nature of imperial power gave rise to constitutional disputes. The prevailing usage seemed to affect theory. After Taisho democracy, Emperor Hirohito's civilian advisers always counseled him to emulate the British monarchy—reigning but not ruling. The constitutional theory of the time, propounded by Professor Minobe Tatsukichi of Tokyo University, held that the emperor was an "organ of the state" rather than the state itself. The Japanese militarists' abuse of imperial power, too, rested implicitly on something like Minobe's theory. They needed a figurehead, though they denounced Minobe.

The deterioration of the Japanese government in the 1930s took place because the Meiji statesmen had passed away, creating a power vacuum, which in turn created a hydra. It was pluralism that hobbled Japan. After struggling in vain to bring the military under cabinet control, Konoye and other imperial advisers handed power over to General Tojo in desperation. Being the most hawkish of the military, Tojo alone was capable of checking the military. The government did regain unity under him. But by then things were too far gone between Japan and the United States.[76]

George Atcheson understood why Konoye was forthcoming on the constitutional change. He feared that MacArthur might be placed in a position of having to override the "freely expressed will" of the Japanese people.[77] It is possible that Atcheson calumnied Konoye to the U.S. media to undermine him, thereby sabotaging MacArthur's scheme.

Prime Minister Shidehara, prince Higashikuni's successor, had a talk with MacArthur on October 11, at which he was handed a five-point proposal calling for a liberal constitution, women's suffrage, educational reform, abolition of the secret police, and the like. With this, Shidehara reluctantly ordered the establishment in the cabinet of the Constitution Problem Investigation Committee, headed by Dr. Matsumoto Joji, a distinguished constitutional lawyer and minister without portfolio.

But Shidehara was strongly opposed to formal revision of the Meiji constitution: he felt that a change in usage and ordinary statutes complementing the constitution would suffice for the time being. He felt it was highly improper to carry out a revision under foreign occupation and was angry that MacArthur demanded it.[78] Matsumoto recalled later, "According to the documents that resulted from the acceptance of the Potsdam Declaration, we certainly were supposed to be able to decide on the basis of the free will of the Japanese people. So I thought it best [to deal with the constitutional issue] after the peace conference. . . . I did not see any reason for hurry," he went on, "the reason being that it was none of their [SCAP's] business."[79]

Among the members of the Shidehara cabinet, Foreign Minister Yoshida Shigeru strongly endorsed Minister Matsumoto.[80] Unfortunately that is all we know of Yoshida's stand. Neither he nor Shidehara was sure that the Meiji constitution could be defended to the end, but they were duty-bound to try it.[81] And the government was hostile to Konoye as he was undermining its efforts at stonewalling.

After advising Higashikuni, Konoye, and Shidehara (October 9) on the necessity of liberalizing the Meiji constitution, MacArthur seemed to let the matter lapse, for reasons that cannot be ascertained. MacArthur was never the untrammelled autocrat he pretended to be but a high military commander executing orders coming from the JCS. Nonetheless, he enjoyed a larger measure of freedom during the first four months.[82] In October, MacArthur froze out POLAD, a State Department post—under the directorship of George Atcheson—from the issue of constitutional revision. Since Atcheson relied on the military channel of communication, MacArthur knew that he was toying with the idea of putting the emperor to trial.[83] The Government Section, established in the same month under General Courtney Whitney, one of the Bataan Gang, as director, began to handle all major political reforms thereafter. Colonel Charles Kades, the New Dealer who had a hand in drafting SWNCC 150/4 in Washington, was deputy director. The GS made no contact with the Matsumoto committee until early February 1946.

But major threats to MacArthur's scheme remained, and in the fall they began to gather force. One was the State Department, run by Byrnes and Acheson.[84] The other was the Soviet Union, which had been demanding an equal share in the occupation of Japan, similar to the arrangement in Germany. Soviet Foreign Minister Molotov made a strong demand to this effect at the London conference of the foreign ministers of the United States, the Soviet Union, Britain, France, and China in September. On the way back from the conference, Secretary Byrnes created the Far Eastern Advisory Commission, with a merely advisory role in occupation policymaking for Japan, with an American chairman. But neither the Soviet Union nor the other Allies were satisfied with it. This led in late November to a call by Byrnes for the three-power conference of foreign ministers in Moscow, slated for mid-December. One of Byrnes's reasons for his proposal was that he "had found it difficult to press for more authority for American representatives in Rumania and Bulgaria while denying Russian requests for a role in the occupation of Japan, and was now prepared to arrange a compromise even over the objections of General MacArthur."[85]

In a private session with Stalin during the Moscow conference, Byrnes agreed to the establishment of the Far Eastern Commission, a policymaking body in Washington, and the Allied Council for Japan, an advisory body in Tokyo. The Allied Council was rather innocuous. The FEC, composed of 11 belligerents, had no direct authority over SCAP either, MacArthur being accountable to the U.S. government through the JCS. But there was an exception—a U.S. directive dealing with constitutional matters had to be based on prior agreement and consultation with the FEC. It began to appear by December, therefore, that MacArthur might lose control over the fate of the emperor to Soviet intervention. MacArthur repeatedly floated rumors of resignation to protest the plans Byrnes was working out in Moscow.[86] The first session of the FEC, it was announced, was scheduled for February 26, 1946.[87]

As if to confirm MacArthur's fears, the most authoritative and final instruction from Washington to SCAP on constitutional questions arrived in Tokyo on January 11 in the form of SWNCC 228 (dated January 7). That was two weeks after the announcement of the Moscow agreement on the FEC.[88] SWNCC 228 demanded popular sovereignty. If the emperor system could not be adapted to this principle, it had to go. SWNCC 228 said, "the retention of the Emperor institution in its present form is not considered consistent" with the principle of popular sovereignty. Provided that popular sovereignty was safeguarded, however, the Japanese could be allowed to retain the emperor system.[89] Whether and at what point the Japanese government was told that a certain type of constitution could save the monarchy, and hence could be swapped for the monarchy, is unknown. With SWNCC 228, the Shidehara government's rearguard action was doomed. On Japan's means of military defense, SWNCC 228 said next to nothing. But it insisted on the principle of civilian supremacy, which implied that some sort of armed forces would be maintained. Nowhere did it ask for a permanent ban on war.

In the meantime, in December 1945, the Government Section of SCAP GHQ was preparing to launch a large-scale purge of Japanese leaders from public life. Some sort of purge was required by the Potsdam Declaration, but SWNCC 150/4 mandated a much more ambitious political engineering objective of decimating the existing political elites of conservative stripe and establishing on their left a new political center consisting of the socialists.[90] Since a new constitution was expected soon, the GS wanted to wipe the slate clean with the purge and hold a general election serving as a constitutional plebiscite.[91] Parallel with

political purge, there was to be a purge of business leaders with special emphasis on the liquidation of zaibatsu combines. There was a heated debate on the
scope of the purge at GHQ in mid-December, which practically split Mac-
Arthur's staff with Whitney on one side and General Charles A. Willoughby,
chief of G-2, another of the Bataan Gang and a strong anti-communist, on the
other. MacArthur supported the New Dealers.[92]

When the fist wave of the purge was announced on January 4, it stunned
Japan with its scope, but it kept expanding. Where the Japanese had expected at
most 200 or 300 people to be barred from public life, the purge eventually
removed 210,000 after screening nearly a million. Prime minister Shidehara,
who was in bed with flu on the day of announcement, felt personally betrayed
by MacArthur, since most of his cabinet members were wiped out. Outraged,
Shidehara resolved to resign.[93] But MacArthur would no permit such an affront;
he called in Yoshida and instructed him to have Shidehara change his mind.[94]

Throughout the fall of 1945, Washington and other Allied capitals kept float-
ing rumors about deigns on the emperor's life. In late December, Shidehara was
prompted to take a new tack to defuse the pressure. In consultation with SCAP
officials, he arranged for the emperor to issue a New Year's statement denying
divine attributes. But American editorial comments were sarcastic.

In early 1946, MacArthur and Whitney were most curious about the work
they had entrusted to Shidehara but about which they had scant information. In
addition to SWNCC 228 and the Far Eastern Commission, a general election
they scheduled for March was on their minds. Toward the end of January, a
sense of urgency suddenly seized the Government Section, and it ordered Shidehara to wind up his work.

On January 24, the prime minister visited MacArthur at the Daiichi Building
ostensibly to thank the general for penicillin given him for his flu. According to
MacArthur, Shidehara proposed in the course of a two-and-a-half hour talk that
"when the new constitution became final . . . it include the so-called no-war
clause. He also wanted it to prohibit any military establishment for Japan—any
military establishment whatsoever." Then the prime minister said, "The world
will laugh and mock us as impracticable visionaries, but a hundred years from
now we will be called prophets."[95] This was a fiction they had to maintain in
order to save the emperor and to keep the facade of democracy. But it was at
this meeting that they decided to (1) adopt a new constitution, (2) accept popular sovereignty, (3) turn the monarchy into a symbol of the unity of the nation,
and (4) add an article renouncing war forever. The constitution was exchanged
for the preservation of the emperor system.[96]

The next day, MacArthur sent a lengthy message, almost blackmailing Washington, as follows:

[The] investigation has been conducted here . . . with reference to possible criminal actions against the Emperor. No specific and tangible evidence has been uncovered. . . .

If he is to be tried great changes must be made in occupational plans and due preparations therefore should be accomplished in preparedness before actual action is initiated. His indictment will unquestionably cause a tremendous convulsion among the Japanese people, the repercussions of which cannot be overestimated. He is a symbol which unites all Japanese. Destroy him and the nation will disintegrate. Practically all Japanese venerate him as the social head of the state and *believe rightly or wrongly that the Potsdam Agreements were intended to maintain him as the Emperor of Japan.* They will regard allied action [to the contrary as a] . . . betrayal in their history. . . . It is quite possible that a minimum of a million troops would be required which would have to be maintained for an indefinite number of years. . . .[97]

But Shidehara evidently could not carry his cabinet with Yoshida and Matsumoto in the opposition. He was still operating under the old constitution, which required unanimous consent of all ministers for cabinet action. In the nature of the case, it had to be threatened—in due course. On February 1, the so-called Matsumoto Draft under consideration by the prime minister was inadvertently leaked and found its way onto the front page of *Mainichi.* The draft held fast to imperial sovereignty. "MacArthur decided that the Japanese shilly-shallying had gone on long enough."[98] On February 3 he ordered General Whitney and his staff in the Government Section to draw up a constitutional draft embodying three principles: retention of the emperor system as the symbol of the nation, renunciation of war, and abolition of the peerage.

It was most likely that the 1935 constitution of the Philippines was MacArthur's inspiration for the no-war article. Back in 1934, in order to ready the Philippine colony for independence, the U.S. Congress passed the Tydings-McDuffie Act, authorizing the Philippine legislature to convene a constitutional convention and to draft the constitution. The act required that the president of the United States "certify" that the constitutional draft conformed with the provisions of the act. Therefore, the 1935 constitution, promulgated with the approval of President Roosevelt, had a status similar to that of a state constitution. Article II, Section 2, of the 1935 constitution states: "The Philippines renounces war as an instrument of national policy, and adopts the generally accepted principles of international law as part of the law of the Nation."[99]

Responding to the general's instruction with great frenzy and exhilaration, the Government Section staff produced the draft in one week and reported it out to MacArthur on February 12. On February 13, General Whitney and two of his aides visited Foreign Minister Yoshida, Minister Matsumoto, and their staff.

The Japanese officials were told that their draft was completely unacceptable and that they must accept the draft that was handed to them. The Americans recorded the meeting as follows:

At this statement of General Whitney, the Japanese officials were obviously stunned—Mr. Yoshida's face particularly manifesting shock and concern. The whole atmosphere at this point was charged with dramatic tension.

[The Japanese officials were left alone to read the draft for a while before the Americans returned.] General Whitney then proceeded: ". . . As you may or may no know, the Supreme Commander has been unyielding in his defense of your Emperor against increasing pressure from the outside to render him subject to war criminal investigation. . . . But, gentlemen, the Supreme Commander is not omnipotent. He feels, however, that acceptance of the provisions of this new Constitution would render the Emperor practically unassailable. . . .

The Supreme Commander has directed me to offer this Constitution to your government and party for your adoption and your presentation to the people with his full backing if you care to do so, yet he does not require this of you. He is determined, however, that the principles therein stated shall be laid before the people—rather by you—but, if not, by himself. . . .

General MacArthur feels that this is the last opportunity for the conservative group, considered by many to be reactionary, to remain in power; that this can be done by a sharp swing to the left; and that if you accept this Constitution you can be sure that the Supreme Commander will support your position. I cannot emphasize too strongly that the acceptance of the draft Constitution is your only hope of survival, . . .[100]

The Japanese participants to the meeting were divided in their recollection on whether or not a harm to the "person of the emperor" was intimated here or not. Minister Matsumoto affirmed it, but Yoshida and the rest could not remember.[101]

Matsumoto and Yoshida still refused to capitulate. The deliberation centered on imperial prerogatives, almost to the exclusion of the war-renouncing article. In order to urge MacArthur to reconsider and relent, Shidehara went to see him on February 21, but to no avail.[102] The cabinet could not be persuaded either. The prime minister finally turned to the emperor, who ordered acceptance of the American draft. Once again and for the last time, the emperor saved the day—so he might never do so again. A little while later, Prime Minister Shidehara quipped to his confidant, "Let's say I asked for renunciation of war," and fell silent.[103]

The general election for the lower chamber was held on April 10, slightly behind schedule. The prewar Seiyukai party, now renamed Liberal party, under Hatoyama Ichiro, won 140 seats,[104] but just as Hatoyama was getting ready to organize his cabinet—on May 3—he was purged. With hardly anyone competent to run the government left, former Seiyukai leaders, in consultation with the establishment, settled on Yoshida as successor.

The 90th and last session of the Imperial Diet convened on June 20. MacArthur issued a statement, stressing the continuity between the old and new constitutions.[105] The debate in the House of Peers was particularly searching and intense, since several constitutional scholars sat there.

The debate was focused almost entirely on the question of whether or not *kokutai* (the emperor system) was preserved in the new constitution. The point of the interpellation was whether retaining the emperor as a "symbol" but no longer the sovereign was or was not a violation of the terms of the Potsdam Declaration. Professor Minobe Tatsukichi of Tokyo University, who was purged by the militarists for his emperor-as-the-organ-of-state theory, maintained that *kokutai* was lost. Yoshida, now prime minister, was forced to defend the document by pretending that it was "the freely expressed will of the Japanese people." It must have been painful, but it was his duty. To reassure the audience that nothing was amiss, he declared that Japan had accepted the Potsdam Declaration only on assurance that *kokutai* would be saved and that it was indeed saved in the government draft. Thereupon SCAP instructed him to retract his statement and to say that since Japan's surrender was unconditional, the Allied powers owed no obligation to it.[106] But Yoshida went ahead anyway with the argument that *kokutai* was indeed saved. On Article IX, he asserted that it proscribed even the right of self-defense. On October 6 the House of Peers and on October 7 the lower house voted the constitution into effect.

For the Japanese government the constitution was a contract to take the place of the Potsdam Declaration when the latter proved to be useless in safeguarding the throne and the emperor. It had little to do with Japan's choice of democracy, as so many people today assume. Leon V. Sigal's account of the drafting of the Potsdam Declaration does not suggest that the United States designed to have it both ways with the declaration—it was rather a bureaucratic compromise between those who sought to save the emperor and those opposed. But as a consequence, the emperor was held hostage while Japan swallowed most of the initial reforms. This was the major factor that explains the miraculous success of disarmament and democratization during the occupation. The Japanese had no legal case for complaining. But it is difficult to deduce SWNCC 150/4 or the open-ended use of the emperor from the Potsdam Declaration. Evidently, Yoshida Shigeru resented his experiences.

# NOTES

1. John W. Dower takes the first view, in *Empire and Aftermath: Yoshida Shigeru and the Japanese Experience, 1878-1954* (Cambridge: Harvard Univ. Press, 1979).

2. Makoto Iokibe, *Beikoku no Nihon senryo seisaku* [U.S. policy for occupation of Japan] (Tokyo: Chuo Koronsha, 1985), I, 131.

3. Ibid. 134.

4. Ibid., II, 148-51.

5. Ibid., II, 153-60.

6. Ibid., II, 196.

7. Leon V. Sigal, *Fighting to a Finish: The Politics Of War Termination In The United States And Japan, 1945* (Ithaca, NY: Cornell Univ. Press, 1988), pp. 94-95.

8. John M. Maki, *Conflict and Tension in the Far East: Key Documents, 1894-1960* (Seattle: Univ. of Washington Press, 1961), pp. 121-23.

9. Sigal, p. 154.

10. See an excellent article by Ryuichi Nagao, "Did Kokutai Change: Problems of Legitimacy in Postwar Japan," in Tetsuya Kataoka, ed., *The 1955 System of Japan's Politics: Its Origin and Consequences* (Stanford: Hoover Institution Press, forthcoming).

11. *Foreign Relations of the United States* (hereinafter cited as *FRUS*) (Washington, DC: GPO, 1969), 1945, VI, 627.

12. Ibid., pp. 631-32. Emphasis added.

13. Ibid.; Iokibe, II, 244.

14. Sigal, p. 274. The rescript was written by chief cabinet secretary Hisatsune Sakomizu. Yomiuri Shimbunsha, *Tenno no shusen* [The emperor's war termination] (Tokyo: Yomiuri Shimbunsha, 1988), pp. 313-16.

15. Kashima Heiwa Kenkyusho, *Nihon gaikoshi* [Diplomatic history of Japan], Vol. XXVI, Kyuman Suzuki, ed., *Shusen kara kowa made* [From the end of war to the peace treaty] (Tokyo, Kashima Heiwa Kenkyusho, 1973), pp. 12-13.

16. Suzuki, p. 25.

17. See the record of conversations, in Jun Eto, ed., *Senryo shiroku* [Historical record of the occupation], Vol. I, *Kofuku bunsho choin keii* [The process of signing the surrender document] (Tokyo: Kodansha, 1982), pp. 270-75; Suzuki, pp. 24-29.

18. An excerpt of SWNCC 150/4 was transmitted on August 22 and the whole text on August 29. Iokibe, II, 253-54.

19. It is reported that on September 3 MacArthur wired George Marshall, army chief of staff, protesting the "rigid and stringent" occupation policies as laid down in the summary of SWNCC 150/3. MacArthur is said to have argued that if SWNCC 150/3 was to be fully implemented, he would need a much larger occupation force than had been heretofore planned. Jun Eto, *Shusen shiroku*, Vol. IV, *Hondo shinchu* [The occupation of the mainland], p. 373. Eto cites National Archives, RG 165, Records of the War Department, General and Special Staffs, War Department Message Files. See also D. Clayton James, *The Years of MacArthur*, III, *Triumph and Disaster, 1945-1964* (Boston: Houghton Mifflin, 1985), 17-19.

20. Maki, p. 127. SWNCC 150/2, the only other version I have seen, is cited in *FRUS*, 1945, VI, 609-12. See also SWNCC 181/2 issued on the same day, in *FRUS*, 1945, VI, 712.

21. Yoshida said of SWNCC 150/4 that it "did not 'commit the Supreme Commander to support the Emperor or any other Japanese governmental authority' . . . The Japanese Government was not sure of protection by the Occupation forces even in the case of revolution should it happen that those concerned in it could convince the Occupation authorities that it was all in line with Occupation policy." *The Yoshida Memoirs* (Cambridge: Houghton Mifflin, 1962), pp. 127–28.

22. Herbert Feis, *Japan Subdued* (Princeton, N.J.: Princeton Univ. Press, 1961), insists on the unconditionality of surrender. Robert J.C. Butow, *Japan's Decision to Surrender* (Stanford: Stanford Univ. Press, 1954), stresses American magnanimity in sparing the emperor. Iokibe tries to straddle the two at the very end of his book, which is a fine piece of research up to then.

23. What lies behind this shift remains unknown. See Jun Eto, "Yoshida seiji no sai-kento" [Another look at Yoshida's politics], *Jiyu* (September 1983), pp. 19–27.

24. Theodore Cohen, *Remaking Japan: The American Occupation as New Deal* (New York: Free Press, 1987), p. 32.

25. Cohen, p. 28.

26. J.C.S. 1380/15, 3 November, 1945, "Basic Directive for Post-Surrender Military Government In Japan Proper," Government Section, SCAP, *Political Reorientation of Japan, September 1945–September 1948* (Washington, DC: GPO, 1949), II, 428–39.

27. Cohen, p. 28.

28. Cohen, p. 33.

29. *FRUS*, 1945, VI, 681–83. Emphasis added. Miller also said, "It is true that the Japanese note of August 14 does not expressly accept the terms of our reply of August 11, but this seems to me unimportant, particularly in view of the explicit reference to the August 11 note in the Japanese reply." See also Dean Acheson's letter of September 5 to Truman, in *FRUS*, 1945, VI, 711.

30. Referring to the portion of the declaration that said that "those who have deceived and misled the people of Japan" must be "eliminated," Ballantine said, "The wording in the ultimatum does not indicate to us that we should no longer imply or state that the Emperor has been deceived or misled." *FRUS*, 1945, VI, 591.

31. Iokibe, II, 256.

32. James Byrnes, *Speaking Frankly* (New York: Harper and Brothers, 1947), p. 209; see also Barton Bernstein, "The Perils and Politics of Surrender: Ending the War with Japan and Avoiding the Third Atomic Bomb," *Pacific Historical Review*, Spring 1967, p. 6.

33. See Lattimore in *Solution in Asia*, p. 184.

34. James, III, 105.

35. Dower, *Empire*, p. 277; for a full statement of this view in theoretical terms, see E. Herbert Norman, in John W. Dower, ed., *Origins of the Modern Japanese State*.

36. Cohen, p. 46.

37. For the activities of the so-called Yohansen group, see John W. Dower, *Empire*, pp. 227–52.

38. The political part of Hilldring's directive, designated JCS 1380/5, was dispatched on September 17, and the entire directive, JCS 1380/15, on November 3. Cohen, pp. 45–46.

39. Jun Eto, ed., *Senryo shiroku,* I, 312.

40. William J. Sebald, *With MacArthur in Japan: A Personal History of the Occu-

*pation* (New York: W. W. Norton, 1965), p. 119. Prior to drafting the constitution, MacArthur asked the government section whether it was within his competence as SCAP to do so. An affirmative reply was based on the argument that "the freely expressed will of the Japanese people" had been mandated by the Potsdam Declaration. MacArthur was that will. Kenzo Takayanagi, Ichiro Otomo, Hideo Tanaka, eds., *Nihonkoku kempo seitei no katei* [The making of Japan's constitution] (Tokyo: Yuhikaku, 1972), p. 92.

41. Harry S. Truman, *Memoirs* (New York: Doubleday, 1955–56), I, 520–21. Emphasis added. D. Clayton James cites these exchanges between the two men, and goes on to say that MacArthur was concerned about the "Reds"—not a very convincing explanation. James is too good a historian not to know what was at stake. James, III, 22.

42. Asahi Shimbunsha, *Yoshida Shigeru* (Tokyo: Asahi Shimbunsha, 1967), p. 129.

43. Toshio Nishi, *Unconditional Democracy: Education and Politics in Occupied Japan, 1945–1952* (Stanford: Hoover Institution Press, 1982), pp. 86–90.

44. Eto, *Shusen Shiroku*, I. 290–93, citing Yoshida's own report. See also Dower, *Empire*, p. 309, citing Shinobu Seizaburo; Rinjiro Sodei, *Makkasa no ni-sen-nichi* [The two thousand days of MacArthur] (Tokyo: Chuo Koronsha, 1976), p. 89.

45. *Reminiscences*, pp. 287–88; Faubion Bowers, "The Day the General Blinked," *New York Times*, September 30, 1988, op-ed page.

46. *FRUS*, VI, 826.

47. Koichi Kido, *Kido Koichi nikki* [Kido Koichi's diary] (Tokyo: Tokyo University Press, 1966), p. 1237. Note that Yoshida felt abdication would make the emperor vulnerable to prosecution and objected to it.

48. Junnosuke Masumi, *Sengo seiji, 1945–55* (Tokyo: Tokyo Univ. Press, 1983), II, 74.

49. This was the counterpart of the famous dispute between the *kozaha* school and *ronoha* school. The *kozaha* school followed the JCP line.

50. The Japanese government and MacArthur seemed to have shared an identical interest in keeping SWNCC 150/4 secret.

51. Sebald, pp. 98–99.

52. Eto, *Shusen shiroku*, Vol. II, *Teisen to gaikoken teishi* [Ceasefire and abrogation of diplomatic privileges] (Tokyo: Kodansha, 1981); Suzuki, pp. 59–68.

53. *FRUS*, 1945, IV, 786.

54. *FRUS*, 1946, VIII, 220.

55. *FRUS*, 1945, IV, 757. Archibald MacLeish noted that in strict legal interpretation, "there is nothing in the [Potsdam] Proclamation to exclude the taking by the *Allies themselves* of steps to revive and strengthen 'democratic tendencies among Japanese people.' " Ibid., p. 592. Emphasis added. On the following day, Byrnes transmitted the State Department's position that a constitutional revision—with or without the monarchy—was mandatory, to George Atcheson, *FRUS*, 1946, VIII, 221.

56. *FRUS*, 1946, VIII, 91.

57. Konoye's memorial to the throne, cited in Ryuichi Nagao et al., eds. *Nihon kempo-shi* [Constitutional history of Japan] (Tokyo: Tokyo Univ. Press, 1976), pp. 405–7.

58. Altogether, 3,000 Communists were released from jail. Yuzo Tamura, *Sengo Shakaito no ninaite tachi* [The leaders of postwar Socialist Party] (Tokyo: Nihon Hyoronsha, 1984), p. 57.

59. See John W. Dower, ed., *Origins of the Modern Japanese State*. Norman also sat as the Canadian delegate at the Far Eastern Advisory Commission, a predecessor to the Allied Council in Japan.

60. James Barros, *No Sense of Evil: The Espionage Case of E. Herbert Norman* (*Toronto: Ivy, 1988*).

61. See *Lattimore, Solution in Asia*. Norman's loyalty was called into question both in a U.S. Senate investigation and by the Canadian government. He committed suicide in 1957.

62. *FRUS*, 1945, VI, 971.

63. See George Atcheson, POLAD, in *FRUS*, 1946, VIII, 315.

64. *FRUS*, 1946, VIII, 99–101.

65. *Reminiscences*, pp. 19–20.

66. U.S. Senate, 82nd Congress, 1st Session, Committees on Armed Services and Foreign Relations, *Military Situation in the Far East* (Washington, DC: GPO, 1951), pp. 310–11.

67. *Reminiscences*, p. 24.

68. D. Clayton James, *The Years of MacArthur, 1880–1941* (Boston: Houghton Mifflin, 1970), I, 411.

69. *FRUS*, 1948, VI, 697. In his testimony before the Senate in 1951, MacArthur also stated that the success of his land reform in Japan was comparable to that of the Gracchi in Rome. Sodei, *Makkasa no nisen-nichi*, p. 194.

70. *Reminiscences*, p. 318.

71. Milo E. Rowell, a civilian official of the Government Section, SCAP, testified to this effect to Japanese investigators. Takayanagi, I, 22.

72. MacArthur, cited in James, III, 129.

73. See Eto, *Senryo shiroku*, I, 331, for Foreign Ministry commentary on SWNCC 150/4.

74. Toshio Sumimoto, *Senryo hiroku* [Secret history of the occupation] (Tokyo: Mainichi Shimbunsha, 1952), I, 85. Similarly, Yoshida opposed the emperor's abdication because off the throne he would be vulnerable to war crimes prosecution.

75. MacArthur was attacked in the American press for letting Konoye handle the revision. Jun Eto, *Senryo shiroku*, Vol. III, *Kempo seitei katei* [The process of constitutional revision], p. 116.

76. See George Atcheson's report on the outline of the Konoye draft as reported in the press, in *FRUS*, 1945, VI, 888–89. In this draft Konoye was clearly moving in the direction of Professor Minobe Tatsukichi's "emperor-as-the-organ-of-state theory." The cabinet was the locus of real power, though the emperor held some residual power. The military was strictly subordinated to the cabinet.

77. *FRUS*, 1945, VI, 884.

78. Sumimoto, I, 77.

79. Takayanagi, II, 71.

80. Shidehara Heiwa Zaidan [Shidehara peace foundation], *Shidehara Kijuro* (Tokyo: Diet Library, 1955), p. 656.

81. Shidehara said to the lord keeper of the seal in early October, "we cannot resist [constitutional revision] with force of arms. In that case, we will leave a record and submit." Kido, p. 1241.

82. Sebald, p. 103.

The Price of a Constitution

83. *FRUS,* 1946, VIII, 90.

84. James, III, 21–22.

85. John Lewis Gaddis, *The United States and the Origin of the Cold War* (New York: Columbia Univ. Press, 1972), pp. 273–76.

86. James, III, 29, 32.

87. However, D. Clayton James has studied the terms of reference for the FEC and ACJ and concluded that "it is difficult to view the majority of the FEC members in the sinister light in which MacArthur cast them at the time." James, III, 138.

88. SWNCC 228 restated the two points already made in the Initial Postsurrender Policy (SWNCC 150/4): The overriding goal of the occupation was U.S. national security, and Japan's "democratization" was a means to that end. This is from Annex B, which is not printed in *FRUS* but is available in Takayanagi, I, 418.

89. *FRUS,* VIII, 98–102.

90. Government Section, SCAP, *Political Reorientation of Japan, September 1945 to September 1948* (Washington, DC: GPO, 1949), Vol. I.

91. Masumi, I, 168.

92. Mark Gayne, *Tokyo Diary* (New York: William Sloane, 1948), pp. 162–64.

93. Masumi, I, 171.

94. Courtney Whitney, *MacArthur: His Rendezvous with History* (New York: Alfred A. Knopf, 1956), pp. 245–46. MacArthur never mentions the purge in his memoir. 95. *Reminiscences,* pp. 302–3.

96. Kempo chosakai jimukyoku [Constitution Investigation Commission Secretariat], "Senso hoki joko to tennosei iji tono kanren ni tsuite" [On the war-renouncing article and its relation to the preservation of the emperor system] (Tokyo: February 1959). This is based on the recollections of Hamuro Michiko, daughter of Ohira Komatsuchi, privy councilor and a close friend of Shidehara. Ohira confided in his daughter the conversations he had with Shidehara. See also Toshiro Iriye, *Nihon koku kempo seiritsu no kei'i* [The circumstances surrounding the establishment of Japan's constitution] (Tokyo: Kempo chosakai jimukyokyu in the prime minister's office, 1960), pp. 96–108. The author was the director of the legal division in the prime minister's office in 1945–46. Both documents are available at the Lou Henry Hoover Library, Stanford University.

97. *FRUS,* 1946, VIII, pp. 395–96. Emphasis added.

98. Whitney, *MacArthur,* p. 248.

99. Arturo M. Tolentino, *The Government of the Philippines* (Manila: R. P. Garcia, 1950), pp. 517–27. The Philippine precedent was brought to my attention by Go Nakagawa, "Nichi-Fi ryokoku kempo ni miru ruien" [The resemblances seen in the constitutions of Japan and the Philippines], *Chuo Koron,* May 1987, pp. 178–89.

100. Takayanagi, I, pp. 322–28.

101. Toshiyoshi Miyazawa, "Nihonkoku kempo oshitsuke-ron ni tsuite" [Was the Japanese constitution imposed?], *Jurisuto,* March 15, 1973, pp. 96–99. Miyazawa thinks Matsumoto is credible. It must be remembered that shortly thereafter Yoshida was put in the position of having to defend the constitution and its legitimacy.

102. At one point the general urged that the people of Japan should take moral leadership of the world with the constitution. Shidehara is reported to have said, "You speak of leadership, but probably no one will be the follower." To which the general replied, "Japan has nothing to lose if there were no followers. The fault lies with those who don't follow." Masumi, I, 125.

103. Ibid., I, 125.

104. Ibid., I, 174–75.

105. Shoyu Kurabu, *Kizokuin ni okeru Nihon kempo shingi* (Tokyo: Shoyu Kurabu, 1977), p. 64.

106. Dower, *Empire,* p. 323.

# Chapter 3

# Kennan Ends Radicalism

Without exaggeration, one can say that in succession the United States had two occupation policies that contradicted each other in basic assumptions. One was in force from 1945 to late 1948. The other originated in the policy of containment conceived by George F. Kennan, the first director of the Policy Planning Staff at the State Department; it replaced wartime U.S. cooperation with the allies with the assumption of balance of power; called for rehabilitation of Japan and ultimately enlisted the country as America's military "ally." In the early, punitive-utopian phase, SCAP enlisted the Communists in the "antifeudal struggle," so to speak, and encouraged the Socialists to become the "center" in the new Japanese politics. But in late 1948, simultaneously with the start of containment in Asia, SCAP abruptly shifted support to Yoshida's conservatives.

Reflecting SCAP's reorientation as well as the polarization of politics in Western Europe, subterranean shifts started in Japan in the fall of 1947, and they turned into a movement for political realignment by late 1948. The Socialist "center" had caved in by the time MacArthur disowned it, creating a drift toward the far Left. SCAP then tried to cut a firebreak between the JSP and the JCP by discriminating against the latter, but SCAP's authority could barely contain the leftward drift. The JCP, the only party that defied the Americans during the occupation, was winning sympathy for denouncing the reversal and rightward shift of American policy. Washington began a debate on limited rearmament of Japan and constitutional revision. That was a threat to MacArthur's constitution, and he began to sabotage the "reverse course" ordered by the National Security Council. The Japanese prime minister was enlisted to play a key role in creating a half-baked reversal.

During the first three years of the occupation, the political scene in Japan was inert and passive—with the exception of hyperactivity on the Left, among the Communists. After the initial introduction to American troops, the country absorbed the seemingly endless series of mortal blows struck at the body politic

*47*

and the old society by SCAP reforms. Destitute, demoralized, and disoriented, people withdrew to the private sphere and sought sheer survival. They behaved as if they did not see the upheaval going on around them.

The Communists were different, because they were the only ones who defied the emperor and the old system. When the entire value system went topsy-turvy, yesterday's pariah had to be at the top. Equally important, the Communists enjoyed the political support of SCAP. Seasoned New Dealers continued to "consider . . . the Communists and the so-called left wing Social Democrats as the only true liberal elements in Japan."[1]

For instance, the Labor Section of SCAP GHQ gave a blessing to the "production control" movement—a union takeover of production and management—that spread like wildfire in 1946. The Communist leaders did the most obvious thing: they organized unions and infiltrated them. By February 1946, scarcely five months after their release from jail, the Communists organized a new labor federation, called Sanbetsu, with 1.6 million members with the Labor Section's blessing.[2] In contrast, Prime Minister Yoshida was "persona nongrata" at GHQ, because of his stubborn resistance to constitutional change,[3] and because he was a conservative. Although SCAP abandoned the republican option in February 1946 with the adoption of the new constitution, the emperor's safety continued to worry the conservatives until the Far Eastern Military Tribunal excluded him from indictments in 1948. It was not until early 1947 that the Japanese could be reasonably sure that SCAP-JCP cooperation was marginal: a nationwide general strike masterminded by the JCP and slated to begin on February 1 was banned by SCAP's order. Though directed at the incumbent government of Yoshida, the aborted general strike may be viewed as a delayed revolt against the Meiji government by those whom it oppressed. The Truman Doctrine followed a month later. SWNCC 150/4 was to be largely reversed with George Kennan's NSC 13/2 in 1948. It was a reflection of the shift in SCAP's view of the JSP and the JCP that they were called "democratic forces" until the "2/1" general strike but renamed "radical-liberals" (*kakushin*) thereafter.

The first two postwar elections were stage-managed for the specific purpose of encouraging the expansion of the Left and pushing the center of political gravity several notches to the Left.[4] The lower house election of April 1946, called by SCAP as a plebiscite on the new constitution, was intended to wipe the slate clean. It was preceded by the first wave of purge as well as a revision in the electoral law, with this result: Of the two prewar conservative parties, the former Minseito party fielded 274 candidates, of whom only 10 escaped the purge. Former Seiyukai had 43 candidates, of whom 33, including Hatoyama, the party leader, were disqualified. The JSP ran 17 candidates but lost 11 to the purge. The Cooperative party, a minor conservative party, had 23 candidates, of whom 21 were disqualified; one survivor was defeated, and another left the party.[5]

Hastily each party replenished their candidates in time for the election, with this result: former Seiyukai, now led by Yoshida, won 140 seats in the 466-seat chamber; former Minseito, of which Shidehara became the leader, 94; the JSP, 92; the Cooperative party, 14; the JCP, 5; and other minor parties and independents, 119. The state of confusion can be seen in the fact that 363 political parties campaigned and 119 independents got elected. Yoshida was named third prime minister since 1945, in spite of his troubles with the Government Section. This was one of the rare instances where SCAP respected the Japanese "free will" that contradicted him (another instance was Yoshida's victory in the 1949 election).

Surprisingly, the grassroots organizations of two prewar parties, based on personal contacts of local notables, were surviving the major surgery of reforms. These two parties shared more or less identical outlooks and policies, and they were to go through many splits, fusions, and realignments under various labels until they merged into the Liberal Democratic party in 1955. These splits and fusions were a vital part of Japan's transformation, as to be shown, but the several names borne by the new conservative entities were unimportant. To avoid confusion, we call them "former Seiukai" and "former Minseito."[6]

When the "2/1" general strike was banned, the JCP, the pied piper, avoided collision with SCAP, but, sensing a shift in the wind, it began to snarl. It unfurled the slogan, Democratic National Front (minshu kyukoku sensen) with the term "national" signifying intense attacks on the Yoshida government as the American proxy. Whether SCAP approved Yoshida or not, he was the lightning rod and whipping boy for MacArthur, who was above Japanese criticisms.[7]

After the "2/1" general strike was averted, MacArthur called another election, not just for the lower house but for the House of Councilors created by the new constitution to replace the House of Peers. The electoral laws were again changed; union membership had roughly doubled to reach five million by then; and the purge was spreading to wider circles. These events had a visible impact on the outcome. In the April 1947 poll, the JSP emerged as the party of plurality in the lower house with 143 seats, an increase from 92. Yoshida's conservative party (former Seiyukai) won 131, a decrease from 140. Shidehara's former Minseito won 121, an increase from 94. The mildly conservative Cooperative party captured 29 seats, an increase from 14. The Communists won 4, for a loss of 1. In the 250-seat upper chamber, the outcome was as follows: the Green Breeze Society (Ryokufukai), a moderately conservative group, 92; former

Seiyukai, 44; former Minseito, 42; the JSP, 47; independents, 20; and the JCP, 4.

Having collided head-on with the first two cabinets, Higashikuni and Shidehara, and having altered the political, economic, and social structure, SCAP had finally produced a party of plurality that met its approval. But the first postelection utterance of the JSP's Christian chairman, Katayama Tetsu—on whom MacArthur rested his hope for a Christian and democratic Japan—was "We're in trouble."[8] Made up of liberal intellectuals and union stewards on the fringe of prewar Japan, the Socialist leadership was simply not ready to run the government. The two conservative parties controlled the majority, and Yoshida tried to work out a coalition with the JSP under his prime ministership. But SCAP adamantly insisted on Katayama.[9] To make him a prime minister, SCAP's Government Section arranged his marriage with former Miseito, which was born again under the new leadership of Ashida Hitoshi, career diplomat and format editor of *Japan Times and Mail*. SCAP seemed to have spared Ashida from purge precisely for this purpose.[10]

In a public statement, MacArthur congratulated the nation for having chosen the Katayama government, the "moderate course."[11] He was signaling the emergence of a postwar tradition in politics. In the end, the JSP did not become the centrist force, but nonetheless the center of gravity in Japanese politics had shifted considerably to the Left and never returned to the prewar position. As the U.S. embassy reported, Yoshida had been at the extreme Left end of politics before the war. But after the shift, he found himself at the extreme Right end of the spectrum: "There is nothing further to the right [of Yoshida]."[12] Actually he could have disappeared in the purge but for the fact that he enjoyed a "safe conduct pass" owing to his record of having resisted the militarists.

Public opinion as reflected in censored media was outwardly placid and bland in early postwar years. The dominant sector of public opinion was the center Left. However, there was an important minority of conservative intellectuals, a chip off the prewar establishment that had neither supported nor opposed war actively, who were gravely concerned about the disintegration of the Japanese civilization under the impact of defeat and radical reforms. They were disturbed by the prevailing assumption that "there was no viable past to which Japan might return."[13] In attempting to counter that assumption, they chose culture (bunka) as their venue, since politics was either discredited or beyond Japan's own control. Later, Yoshida would seize on the economy as his venue for the same reason. In 1948 they began to publish a highbrow journal called *Kokoro* (The Heart). An early and important contribution of this group to public debate was an article by Tsuda Soukichi defending the emperor system as the linchpin of the Japanese civilization.[14]

But the conservative side at this stage was in serious disarray vis-a-vis the Left occupying center stage. The intellectuals spent 1946 debating the new constitution and their war guilt. There was mutual recrimination and self-exculpation. Then, after the suppression of 2/1 general strike in 1947, signs of restiveness began to appear. Marxists began to take up the subject of autonomy (*shutai-sei*) in elliptical, theoretical language. In the fall, with the Marshall Plan underway in Europe, a large number of intellectuals joined the JCP as a schism appeared between the Communists and the Socialists. Desertion by the intellectuals was beginning to weaken the rightwing Socialists who had dominated the party. But caught in MacArthur's bear hug, the JSP was trying to hold the center in spite of the deserters.

As East-West tension mounted, it found its reflection in domestic politics. Yoshida's Liberals, though out of favor with SCAP, was the one pole. Tied to the Comintern, the Communists had to be the other. For the time being, the Communists and their Democratic National Front would be on the defensive against SCAP's new vigilance. The leftwing Socialists seized the opportunity to supplant the JCP. Yamakawa Hitoshi, foremost theoretician of the leftwing JSP, established the Democratic People's Front (minshu jinmin sensen) in March 1947, shortly after the JCP's general strike was put down.[15] It was designed to be a broad union of the Left.

As shown throughout this book, almost all Japanese leaders from the rightwing Socialist rightward were vexed by the emergence of three major political parties in postwar Japan, rather than two, as it made for instability in the governing majority. Their concern became acute as signs of polarization began to appear. From this point on, the Japanese political system would begin the search for an alternating two-party system against all odds. The only workable formula for a moderate, loyal opposition was the center-Left coalition that began with the Katayama cabinet. Ashida Hitoshi would champion this cause by drawing a line between himself and the Democratic People's Front until he was undercut by the advancing Cold War.[16]

Within three months of October 1946, when the Japanese Diet had approved the constitution, George F. Kennan, America's foremost Soviet expert, was honing the concept that would not only make the constitution irrelevant and out of place but put an end to the universalist approach to foreign affairs that had carried the United States through the great war. That concept, containment, was revealed in *Foreign Affairs* magazine in July 1947.[17] Soviet conduct in the Mediterranean, Eastern Europe, and China and its attitude toward Western Europe had undermined the hopes for Great Power collaboration, and forced the United States to withdraw into its own sphere of influence. To replace the

British presence in Greece and Turkey, the Truman Doctrine was announced in March 1947, and the Marshall Plan soon followed. By the summer, Kennan turned his attention to Japan.[18]

Kennan's philosophy of realism was consciously opposed to that of Franklin Roosevelt's, which Kennan called universalism. The two could not be further apart. The shock and tremors caused by Kennan's ideas on the contemporary scene, however, have been almost forgotten since. Somehow, the inclination toward universalism is so innate to America and has such restorative power that it seems always to win out in the end. America paused in the track of Roosevelt's universalism, listened to Kennan for a while, but roared off in the direction of Cold War universalism after the Korean War. The demobilized war machine was rebuilt and the United States became what Daniel Yergin called the "national security state." But if Kennan's impact on U.S. policy was not as great as he might have wished, his ideas served the pivotal role in Japan.

At the core of realism was respect for the dignity of separate nation sates and for the particular histories behind their existence, and a call for diplomacy and statecraft to harmonize their national interests. Realism abhorred legal or moral abstractions that were overdrawn to universal proportions.[19] There can be no final peace, Kennan insisted, though peace is not a chimera. It can be approximated "as a matter of historical equity," through "political expediency," and "with an eye to the given relationship of power." "The task of international politics," Kennan said, "is not to inhibit change but to find means to permit change to proceed without repeatedly shaking the peace of the world."[20]

In the changed international environment, the State Department and the SCAP bureaucracy reversed their roles. Under Kennan's guidance, State leapfrogged MacArthur and abandoned SWNCC 150/4. SCAP GHQ in the meantime had grown into a major bureaucracy of 3,500 men beholden to the original occupation mandate.[21] The isolated and semiautonomous domain was jealously guarded by MacArthur, with his enormous prestige. MacArthur wore two hats—as commander in chief, Far East, reporting directly to the JCS, and as supreme commander for the Allied powers, accountable to the Far Eastern Commission—and he adroitly switched between them to guard his autonomy. He was virtually immune from congressional oversight, and the weak civilian leadership of the army "had not been able to issue a single order to MacArthur," according to Navy Secretary Forrestal.[22] In spearheading the new U.S. policy toward Japan, Kennan collided with MacArthur.

An early indication of the divergence between MacArthur and Washington surfaced in March 1947, when MacArthur discussed the need for a peace treaty in a conversation with foreign correspondents, an event that took Washington by surprise. By this time, MacArthur's defiance of Washington was giving rise to the alignment of such men as Dean Acheson, James Forrestal, William Draper (army secretary), George Marshall (secretary of state), and George Kennan against him. SCAP's belated zeal in *zaibatsu* liquidation, at a time when the Japanese economy was in total collapse, was at issue. MacArthur was accused of undermining Japan's economic recovery, and he was dodging his critics with the argument that recovery was impossible without first having a peace treaty.[23] In early 1948 several important missions visited Japan to recommend a change in policy. The Strike report, made public by the War Department in March, argued against *zaibatsu* liquidation and in favor of relaxing reparations payment.[24] Kennan visited Tokyo in March 1948. Army Under Secretary William Draper came also, with a large entourage that included Percy Johnston, chairman of the Chemical Bank and Trust Company, who produced the Johnston Report for the army in May. It argued for an eight- or ninefold increase in Japan's exports.[25]

Even if we were to discount Kennan for "prejudice" born of State-Defense rivalry, his findings in Tokyo were somber. He was shocked by the radicalism and naivete of the occupation administration that he saw. "The nature of the occupational policies," he said, "pursued up to that time by General MacArthur's headquarters seemed on cursory examination to be such that if they had been devised for the specific purpose of rendering Japanese society vulnerable to Communist political pressures and paving the way for a Communist takeover, they could scarcely have been other than what they were."[26] There were no armed forces, no coast guard, no interior ministry, no espionage law, no counterintelligence function, and "Japan's central police establishment had been destroyed."

The purge program without trial, appeal, or due process was spreading to the business community. Kennan thought the practice was "totalitarian." "I doubt, in fact, whether many persons in SCAP . . . could explain [the purge's] history, scope, procedures and purpose," Kennan wrote. Trust-busting, or *zaibatsu* liquidation, was embraced with "wild enthusiasm" in Tokyo. Its effects converged with those of the purge of businessmen and confiscation of plants and factories for reparations. The result was that the entire Japanese economy was standing still at one third of the prewar (1932–36) level. As American taxpayers propped up the economy, these plants were being shipped to China, rapidly falling under communist control. Kennan was equally critical of SCAP's social-educational reforms, such as changing the family system or the writing system. "All we were doing," he said, "was tearing apart the closely woven fabric of Japanese society. Some of the young officers in GHQ SCAP were outdoing the Russians in their enthusiasm for uprooting traditional structure."[27]

At a meeting of MacArthur, Kennan, and William H. Draper, undersecretary of the army, Draper broached the subject of rearmament but was rebuffed by an indignant MacArthur. "Japanese rearmament," he said, "is contrary to many of the fundamental principles which have guided SCAP ever since the Japanese surrender. . . . Abandonment of these principles now would dangerously weaken our prestige in Japan, and would place us in a ridiculous light before the Japanese people. "He went on to cite additional reasons: (1) Rearmament would "alienate the nations of the Far Eastern basin"; (2) "Even our best efforts" would make Japan merely a "fifth-rate military power" without the former colonies; (3) Japan could not afford the cost of rearmament; and (4) The Japanese themselves were opposed to it.[28] With the exception of item 3, all the arguments are still maintained today by both governments.

And yet MacArthur was insistent that an early peace treaty and independence for Japan were desirable. MacArthur saw "several signs" that the occupation "no longer serves its purpose." He had in mind the sullen mood of workers, intellectuals, and the leftwing parties following the suppression of "2/1" general strike.[29] But in view of Japan's defenselessness, the idea of peace with Japan struck Kennan as "madness."[30]

It was evident that MacArthur was impaled on the horns of the dilemma he had created. The constitution as the capstone of occupation reforms was to be a testament to his greatness. He had to ensure its permanence by concealing its origin and by ending the occupation before the Japanese revolted against it. Yet if the constitution remained in place, Japan was defenseless and had to remain under U.S. control.[31] Thus MacArthur was the first American official to state in May 1947 that the United States had a moral obligation to defend Japan.[32] In the company of Kennan, however, he indicated his preference for demilitarized Japan guaranteed by the United States and the Soviet Union. Kennan did not share MacArthur's trust in Russian good faith and felt he was irresponsible.[33]

There is an episode that sheds light on MacArthur's insistence on keeping the constitution. Back in 1938 he struck upon the idea of mobilizing all the units of the fledgling Filipino army for a grand parade in Manila to boost morale. His aide, Dwight D. Eisenhower, told him "that it was impossible to do the thing within our budget," but was overruled. Upon learning of the scheme and its cost, President Quezon told MacArthur to cancel it immediately. "Visibly upset," MacArthur chastised Eisenhower for actually setting the plan in motion. This was the beginning of their mutual estrangement.[34] According to Eisenhower, MacArthur "had an obsession that a high commander must protect his public image at all costs and must never admit his wrongs."[35]

Kennan's own idea for Japan's security was very different from what later came to pass under the rubric of containment. In Kennan's judgment, Japan, not

China, had the requisite industrial capacity to constitute power in Asia. It was in America's interest to prevent it from falling into hostile hands. He wanted Japan denied to the Soviet Union but also free of American control. An exception was Okinawa, which neither Kennan nor MacArthur was prepared to relinquish. Keeping Japan neutral was also leverage for persuading the Soviets to disengage from Korea. Later, Kennan felt that the Korean War was Moscow's answer to the U.S. preemption of Japan. If the Russians were too unreasonable, however, he was ready for a limited rearmament of Japan and some form of U.S.-Japanese association.[36] Both Kennan and MacArthur were opposed by the JCS, which began to lobby for immediate rearmament preceded by a second constitutional revision under SCAP supervision.

Kennan felt that Japan had substantially fulfilled the terms of the Potsdam Declaration. But because the declaration provided for the allies' security against Japan without guaranteeing Japan's own security, the occupation would continue: not for its original purpose of "punishment," but to "bridge a hiatus in the status of Japan caused by the failure of the Allies to agree on a treaty of peace." Actually the conflict between the State Department and the JCS over a treaty was to blame for the delay.[37] Stability and rehabilitation were the watchwords from here on. Kennan was opposed to reparations, and he demanded an end to the purge and *zaibatsu* liquidation. In general he wanted the tight occupation control relaxed so that a degree of self-government could begin. In early 1948, for instance, 90 percent of Diet bills originated with the SCAP Government Section, and GS officials went to the Diet floor to lobby for their bills.[38]

Upon returning home from Japan, Kennan formulated his recommended changes in NSC 13/2 of October 1948. The peace treaty was temporarily shelved. The United States was to continue exploratory talks with the Allied governments on timing and procedure, but "second only to U.S. security interests, economic recovery should be made the primary [sic] objective," said the NSC paper.[39]

In spite of the difficulties in access to foreign media, members of the Japanese elite kept their ears close to the ground. They were aware of the storm gathering on the horizon, the polarized pull of the two superpowers, the policy debate in the United States over Germany and Japan, and *Newsweek*'s attack on radical economic reforms in Japan.[40] The Japanese elite sensed an opportunity as well as liabilities in the rapidly shifting circumstances: opportunities because Japan was viewed as a potential ally, and liabilities because the Americans were inclined more and more toward an extended stay in Japan. Public opinion began to stir. This was the first time since the defeat that the Japanese showed an acute interest in foreign policy.

In July 1948 UNESCO sponsored a statement by eight distinguished social scientists from around the world, led by Gordon W. Allport, psychologist at Harvard. Though couched in terms that were to become standard fare for peace movements since—berating exploitation of man by man and statist myths as causes of war—the appeal struck home because it articulated the widely shared fear that in a mere three years since 1945 the world was headed for another war. It elicited a surprisingly strong response in Japan. When Yoshino Genzaburo, head of Iwanami Books and founder and editor of a respectable journal of opinion for liberal intellectuals, *Sekai,* issued a call for a meeting to discuss a common response, 55 distinguished scholars and men of letters rallied.[41] They organized themselves into the Peace Problem Symposium (Heiwa mondai danwakai or PPS). Weighted in favor of the political center and center Right *at the time,* PPS chose unarmed neutrality between the two superpowers as Japan's desideratum.

Neutrality was respectable at the time, with MacArthur and Kennan defending it.[42] But the JSP was a governing party, and if pressed for a solution to Japan's security, many Socialist politicians opted for relying on the United States for protection. By the time the Korean War came, however, the center Right would drop out of the PPS and the JSP would embrace neutrality.

But already in 1948 the PPS was a harbinger of things to come. In its opinion, the United States suffered a major loss of its prestige with the policy reversal. Reproaching America for its change of heart was a liberal stance, and it was the only "safe" way of criticizing the conqueror. Said the PPS communique:

> Inasmuch as our constitution stipulates renunciation of war, and inasmuch as our very existence is thereby entrusted to the good will of those nations which have tried our leaders in the name of peace and civilization, the problem of peace and war is manifestly a special concern to us. That is, to us who are so situated as to be different from the nations that are in charge of international crises, the problem of peace has its own distinct significance and imminence.[43]

Here was a kernal of holier-than-thou smugness combined with aloofness from power entanglements, thought to be America's province, an attitude that would gain wider currency later.

Meanwhile, MacArthur's defense of the constitution and neutrality was the major obstacle in the way of the JCS, which had unsuccessfully lobbied to have Japanese rearmament accepted in NSC 13/2. He had to be disabused of this outlandish policy. In early February of 1949, about a month after the Peace Problem Symposium issued its communique, Army Secretary Kenneth C. Royall visited MacArthur.[44] The general probably repeated his thesis that the United States had a moral obligation to defend unarmed Japan. Obviously exercised by this idea, Royall held a conference with American newsmen, a not-for-attribution backgrounder, to be released after his departure.

On February 12 the Japanese press broke front-page stories that curdled the nation's blood. Newspapers quoted an unnamed high American official as saying, "I don't know what our troops could do in Japan in the event of war. I am not certain we could hold Japan, nor am I certain it would be worthwhile as long as we have Okinawa and the Philippines." The quotation went on, "America is not obligated to stay in Japan. We don't owe the Japanese anything, not even a moral obligation. We had the right—and the duty—to disarm them after the war, even though someone else may later cut their throats."[45]

Royall's remarks were seared into Japanese memory. On February 14, *Asahi* carried an editorial, written by Ryu Shintaro, a member of the PPS, entitled "Spiritual Autonomy," which under the circumstances amounted to a protest by a censored newspaper. By autonomy, he meant neutrality. As an obvious riposte to Royall, MacArthur went public in late February with his defense of neutrality calling on the Japanese to be the "Switzerland of the Pacific."[46] MacArthur and the liberal reformers in the Government Section of SCAP GHQ were on the defensive in the shifting winds. The Berlin blockade came in April 1948, and by year's end Kennan's NSC 13/2 had come down the channel from Washington. But their activist zeal was undaunted. Toward the end of the year, they began an attempt to prop up and make a go of the political "center" that they had brought into existence in 1947 with their backing. It appears in retrospect that MacArthur had designated the "center" coalition as the guardian of his constitution.

In spite of generous American help, the Socialist-conservative coalition government of Prime Minister Katayama Tetsu ("Indecisive Tetsu") collapsed in February 1948 from internal squabbling among the Socialists. It would have been normal parliamentary protocol for the opposition to assume power, but the opposition happened to be Yoshida, still persona nongrata. At the insistence of the GS and in spite of much hue and cry about "constitutionalism," an indirect gibe at SCAP, the coalition stayed in power by choosing Ashida, the leader of the conservative coalition partner, as prime minister. MacArthur must have known that, unlike Yoshida, Ashida had earlier supported the constitutional revision by SCAP.

A vital component of MacArthur's efforts to prop up the "center" was his containment of the far Left, which was increasingly attracting the Socialists. He did a somersault vis-a-vis Sanbetsu, the Communist-controlled labor federation, he had earlier brought into existence. Now he decided to isolate it and to steer a moderate reformist group within Sanbetsu toward the "center" coalition. In March 1948 SCAP banned another nationwide strike planned by a front of Sanbetsu. In July, MacArthur followed up with a letter to Prime Minister Ashida banning strikes and collective bargaining by employees of government enterprises.[47] The "MacArthur letter" designed to curtail Sanbetsu was resented roundly as regression by workers of all stripes, including even JSP members. Nonetheless, SCAP's intervention caused a faction of Sanbetsu—called the Democratization League (Mindo)—to break away and establish another federation to the right of the Communists. The Mindo group joined the JSP en masse. For the time being, SCAP's power was able to channel the workers to the Right and out of Communist control.[48] JSP membership increased from 39,199 in September 1946 to 95,333 in January 1948, and kept on increasing.[49] From the outset, Mindo was influenced by the Peace Problem Symposium and its idea of neutrality.[50]

But Mindo turned out not to be as moderate as MacArthur had hoped. Mindo's affiliation with the JSP had an immediate impact on the leadership of the party: at the fourth party congress, in April 1949, Suzuki Mosaburo of the leftwing defeated Asanuma Inejiro of the rightwing to become the secretary-general. This was a major turning point for the Socialists.[51]

Ashida's "center" coalition was illfated from the start—it had to buy votes to win the Diet's confidence. Ashida and his Socialist partners reportedly took political funds from a fertilizer manufacturer called Showa Denko in return for government loan with easy terms. The officials of the GS, as well as the Economic and Science Section of SCAP, which handled the purge of Showa Denko's management, were reported to have been involved in the bribery as well.[52] Arrayed against Ashida's coalition government and its patron, the GS, was the partnership formed between General Charles A. Willoughby, head of G-2 (intelligence), and Yoshida. Willoughby, whom MacArthur once called "my dear fascist" in jest, was a dedicated anti-communist who had been colliding with liberal GS policies almost from the outset of the occupation. When rumors of graft began to circulate, the Ministry of Justice was ordered by Willoughby to investigate while he began an investigation of his own.

The GS officials did their best to shield the Ashida government and restrain the prosecution, but with key cabinet officials—including the prime minister—in jail by September, the government was doomed. The GS granted Ashida permission to resign by early October, but it made another attempt to prevent Yoshida from stepping in. It indicated subrosa that an alternative conservative candidate, Yamazaki Takeshi, secretary general of Yoshida's party, should be nominated for the position of prime minister.[53] Seeing Yoshida's trouble with the almighty GS, his internal enemies smelled blood. They decided to edge him out. They were professional politicians of prewar vintage, earthy and vernacular-speaking, who looked upon the imperial bureaucracy as the enemy of parliamentary democracy. Yoshida fully reciprocated their feeling and had nothing but contempt for the professional pols.

GS officials' interference came to naught when Yoshida called their bluff and appealed directly to MacArthur. A young politician by the name of Tanaka Kakuei—to be a prime minister later—is said to have inspired Yoshida to make that appeal.[54] Yoshida said to MacArthur, "Is it good for you to direct Japanese politics so far? Am I not the president of the Liberal Party? Why do you appoint my secretary-general  Yamazaki prime minister? Is this your order?"[55] At the same time, Yoshida's followers ganged up on Yamazaki and forced him to resign his Diet seat, which disqualified him for any cabinet post. Yoshida barely survived the crisis. The second Yoshida government was installed in October 1948. But Yoshida never forgot his grudge against the party politicians, as we shall see.

Though Yoshida survived the crisis of October 1948, GS harassment against his caretaker government continued—with willfulness that defied explanation and that must have puzzled Yoshida himself. In January 1949 Ichimada Hisato, governor of the Bank of Japan, the central bank, came to see "Ambassador" Sebald to lodge a protest. Sebald, a man of conservative inclination, wrote a sympathetic report to Washington. In Ichimada's view, "recent acts of intervention were deliberately intended to weaken Prime Minister Yoshida's position because of his unpopularity with some sections of General Headquarters." Ichimada reminded Sebald that "political forces operating outside the constitutional framework of the government is [sic] not new to Japan," but that "if it is necessary to take such extreme measures because of critical or emergency conditions, . . . it might be better in the long run and certainly more efficient to suspend temporarily parliamentary processes of government and govern Japan solely through General Headquarters directives." Ambassador Sebald wrote to Washington, "We should avoid weakening the conservative position" when the "broad socialist middle group [is] disintegrating.[56] We return to this strange embroilment between MacArthur and Yoshida after a brief look at Yoshida's biography.

Yoshida Shigeru was born in 1878 as the fifth son of Takeuchi Tsuna, who was a leader of the peoples' rights movement, a movement of dissenters among the samurai class that had engineered the Meiji Restoration. Takeuchi sired 14 children and gave Shigeru up even before his birth for adoption by Yoshida Kenzo. His adoptive father was an enterprising samurai who worked for the firm of Jardine Matheson before going on to found a shipping agency of his own and amassing a fortune. Shigeru grew up like a prince amid wealth and servants.[57] His high regard for the Anglo-Saxons and his view of commerce as a handmaiden of diplomacy may be traceable to his upbringing under an Anglophile business tycoon. His adoptive mother—a highly cultured woman and stern disciplinarian—saw to it that Yoshida was educated in classical Chinese, which was synonymous with Confucian ethics.

Yoshida Kenzo died when Shigeru was nine. Thereafter he lived a "lonely life in a lonely house" with his adoptive mother. "It was a childhood . . . devoid of warmth—and most certainly devoid of that smothering maternal indulgence (*amae*) which contemporary scholars emphasize in the shaping of the 'typical' Japanese personality."[58] It is not surprising that he developed an uncanny knack for ingratiating himself with those whom he needed—without losing his own bristling sense of self-importance. As Eto Jun, a brilliant literary critic, has noted, Yoshida was adopted four times in his lifetime, each time enhancing his fortune further: by the Yoshidas; by the Makinos, his wife's family; by Hatoyama, who installed Yoshida as his successor when purged by MacArthur; and by MacArthur himself.

Upon graduating from Tokyo University in 1906, the year after Japan's victory over tsarist Russia, he entered Gaimusho and was assigned to the China service. He was to spend 11 years in China before 1928. China was neither the most preferred station nor a fast track for the Foreign Ministry elite. However, the years Yoshida spent in China encompassed the rough-and-tumble era of imperialism, from the fall of the Ch'ing Empire through the warlord period. Yoshida fully rose to the occasion and distinguished himself as an imperialist and nationalist second to none.

Yoshida's defense of the empire was part and parcel of his deep and abiding loyalty toward the throne. In 1909 he had the good fortune to be coopted into the charmed circle around the throne by virtue of his marriage to the eldest daughter of Count Makino Nobuaki (Shinken). Makino was the son of Okubo Toshimichi, the Satsuma samurai who had founded the Meiji Restoration government, and Makino later became foreign minister and privy seal. In that capacity, Makino was a trusted adviser to Emperor Hirohito.

Throughout his life Yoshida remained pro-British and regarded the Anglo-Japanese alliance of 1904-21 as Japan's most valuable asset and a benchmark for subsequent Japanese conduct of foreign policy. He opposed a conflict with the Anglo-American powers, and like many sober nationalists he drew a line at the completion of Japan's empire in Manchuria. Thus far, he was convinced, Japan's interests complemented those of the Anglo-American powers. He felt that Japan's case for establishing Manchukuo was "solidly grounded—but poorly executed, and amateurishly presented" because of the strong-arm tactics of the militarists.[59] He parted company with the imperial army when it began to infiltrate into north China. Yoshida was in his element when he was appointed ambassador to the Court of St. James in 1936, where he sought to restore something of the Anglo-Japanese alliance. As the storm gathered over Europe,

British interests beyond Suez were quite defenseless. Yoshida felt Japan's assurances of British security could be exchanged for British support for Japanese position in China, but he was beleaguered.

By this time Yoshida was branded "liberalist" by the military, was kept from ministerial appointments, and lost his freedom of action. He resigned from the Foreign Ministry in 1939. But he met frequently with Robert Craigie, British ambassador in Tokyo, and Joseph Grew, the American counterpart, to explain Japanese decisions and plead for moderation. Grew in turn came to believe that moderate, pro-American leaders like Yoshida and his father-in-law represented the only chance the United States had for peace with Japan. When Henry Stimson and Grew worked for moderate peace terms before Potsdam, they rested their hope for a new Japan on men like Yoshida. Again in 1945, Yoshida, his father-in-law, Konoye, Hatoyama,[60] and a few other men were engaged in a secret move to bring about an early end to the war through a desperate appeal to the throne. Yoshida was arrested by the military police in April and spent ten weeks in jail. The arrest, it turned out, established him as antimilitarist, and that was equivalent to having a safe conduct pass during the occupation.

For all his disagreements with the militarists, Yoshida was free of guilt feeling about Japan's war with the United States.[61] Upon succeeding Shigemitsu when he was dismissed by MacArthur as foreign minister in September 1945, Yoshida went to see Admiral Suzuki, who had been prime minister until the surrender, for advice. Suzuki told Yoshida to be a "good loser."[62] A more accurate translation would be, "know how to lose with style," a phrase Yoshida later used with his reckless sense of humor. "There are instances where you lose a war but win diplomatically," was another remark attributed to Yoshida.[63] It took some finesse for him to survive under the early occupation regime, since he was intensely disliked by the SCAP liberals, who held the power of purge. It also took some duplicity to be the butt of constant meddling and still keep one's temper. Yoshida and the bureaucrats—the *kuroko,* or the faceless men in black tunics who appear on the Kabuki stage—survived better than the political type, such as Hatoyama and Ishibashi, both victims of purge and future prime ministers.

In a moment of serenity, Yoshida recalled how it felt to be under American tutelage:

> In a sense, we might have found the task confronting us considerably easier had we found our own aims to be drastically opposed to those of the Occupation so that we could concentrate our efforts on thwarting Occupation policy at every turn. As events turned out, the difficulties experienced by both sides sprang mainly from the fact that our aims were the same.[64]

When the April 1946 election gave Hatoyama's former Seiyukai a plurarity, Shidehara was ready to resign in his favor. But SCAP, who was about to purge Hatoyama, asked Shidehara to stay on but was refused. Former Seiyukai nominated Yoshida to succeed Hatoyama, and compounded MacArthur's problem: Yoshida was possibly the worst choice because of his opposition to the constitution. As the party leaders settled on Yoshida as successor, he bargained hard for favorable terms: (1) that he be given a free hand in all appointments; (2) that he not be bothered with fundraising; and (3) that he be allowed to resign whenever he liked. Hatoyama consented. Then Yoshida bargained with MacArthur for food. SWNCC 150/4 stipulated that Japan be left to stew in its own juice and not be provided with aid.[65] But the first postwar May Day was at hand and an unprecedented crowd of half a million workers demonstrated in front of the GHQ building. "We'll form a cabinet after MacArthur promises to give us food," Yoshida said, "He'll bring food from America if we wave the red flag all over the country for a month."[66] Yoshida was right.

Yoshida was no yes-man. He gave the Americans hard advice. But he also knew when to back off. He would let the Central Liaison Office, an euphemism for Foreign Ministry, probe SCAP's intent. Where he felt strongly on an issue, he would let either the Foreign Ministry bureaucracy or one of his ministers stake out the ground. If GHQ did not relent, he would dismiss his subordinate and make peace with MacArthur.[67]

But these traits were not exactly the right stuff for a democratic politician. The media nicknamed him "One Man," and along with the expensive cigar he smoked, that epithet became his trade mark. Short-tempered and arrogant, he would never take the trouble to explain his policies to the public. His legendary antics included pouring a cup of water on newspaper photographers and calling a Socialist Dietman a "damned fool" in the lower chamber, which led to the dissolution of the Diet in 1953. As if to slight the party pols, he manufactured cabinet ministers like pancakes during his long tenure—altogether 79 people, some of whom were appointed more than once.[68] Often he could not remember their names. The mass production of cabinet ministers, however, did have a leveling impact. A cabinet post in prewar Japan was lofty station, to which few politicians aspired. After Yoshida debased the coin, it became available to everyone, in accordance with seniority.

George Kennan's alarms about the confusion and instability in Japan was neither exaggerated nor inaccurate. MacArthur's "center" coalition was discredited because of the graft scandal, incompetence, and association with MacArthur and Ashida. The JSP itself was being pulled two ways and coming unstuck.[69] The leftwing JSP felt vindicated in its standing assertion that unprincipled cooperation with the "reactionary forces" was corrupting. Under Moscow's thumb, the Communists reacted with even greater alacrity to events abroad, such as the Chinese Communist victory in wresting Manchuria and the Truman administration's military assistance to Chiang Kai-shek. The JCP began to bare its claws in domestic terrorist acts. East-West tension was reproducing itself inside Japan, but MacArthur was feuding with Yoshida, the only alternative he had.

The federal agencies in charge of Japan became alarmed over the situation and MacArthur's puzzling stubbornness. Although they could not agree among themselves on a peace treaty with Japan or its rearmament for the time being, they stood behind Kennan's NSC 13/2. Toward the end of 1948, the JCS issued to MacArthur a succession of directives calling for a large reduction in SCAP bureaucracy, appointment of a State Department representative not subordinated to SCAP, lifting of the purge, recentralization of police, reduction of Japanese payment for occupation costs (amounting to one-third of the annual Japanese budget), etc.[70] The State Department was particularly disturbed by "General MacArthur's refusal thus far to moderate the purge in any substantial degree, in the face of virtually unanimous opinion in Washington."[71] But MacArthur succeeded in stymieing Washington with the argument that he was not merely the CINCFE but the supreme commander for the Allied powers. In desperation the Army Department decided on a compromise that would preempt MacArthur's economic power only. In December 1948 Army Undersecretary William Draper sent the so-called Nine Point Program to MacArthur. He followed it up in early 1949 by dispatching Joseph M. Dodge, president of the Detroit Bank, who had recently worked on currency reform in occupied Germany, to Tokyo to oversee the program. At least the economic half of Kennan's NSC 13/2 was getting implemented.

The Dodge Line, as it came to be popularly called in Japan, was strong medicine, calling for a "super balanced budget" and deflationary policy. Most conspicuously, Dodge called for a retrenchment of government bureaucracies through elimination of 264,000 jobs, a 16 percent cut. The gross national product still stood at 30 percent of what it had been in 1930. Government workers in the newly established Japan National Railway Corporation, slated to be dismissed, fought back under Communist leadership. Sabotages and train wrecks suddenly mushroomed, with 1,574 incidents reported in July and 488 in August.[72] The president of the Railway Corporation died under mysterious circumstances, still unresolved. These acts were a declaration of war against SCAP's attempt to liquidate Sanbetsu. MacArthur began to receive blackmail threats from the radical underground.

Yoshida managed to call a lower house election in January 1949 in spite of another GS objection, and the result vindicated Sebald's plea against SCAP's meddlesome conduct. Yoshida's former Seiyukai won a stunning victory, with 264 seats, an increase from 131; Ashida's former Minseito was reduced from 132 to 69; the JSP declined from 144 to 48 and the Cooperative party from 31 to 14; but the Communists jumped in strength from 4 to 35 seats! Max W. Bishop, chief of the Division of Northeast Asian Affairs, wrote that the election was "a protest vote—protest against the occupation. Mr. Yoshida has become a symbol of Japan's ability to stand up to the occupation."[73]

In the wake of the January poll, MacArthur took Yoshida into his confidence, and with that patronage on top of his electoral victory, Yoshida's rule became absolutely stable. Adenauer in the West and Yoshida in the East began to align the former Axis powers with the United States. An easy camaraderie began between MacArthur and Yoshida, enabling Yoshida to go over the heads of lower SCAP officials to the supreme commander. Dismayed by the end of liberal reforms, many of them headed home. Colonel Kades, deputy director of the GS, was quietly dismissed. Yoshida was to stay in power for six years, longer than any other prime minister since 1945, and Japanese observers are unanimous in the judgment that he owed his longevity in office to his ability to "get along" with the Americans.

This much was obvious even to a casual witness. Actually, this observation, culled from standard history, does not go far enough, for it passes over two puzzles. One was the strange reversal of MacArthur's role when he received NSC 13/2. Earlier, when he received SWNCC 150/4, the initial occupation directive, he disagreed with its harsh punitive character and watered it down. But when the State Department more than met MacArthur's preferences in NSC 13/2, he was to insist on reversing the reverse course. A second puzzle was SCAP's imbroglio with Yoshida. Why?

I maintain that MacArthur was quite consistent in his own mind. It seems that when he wrote his constitution, it became his overriding personal goal, almost an obsession, to preserve, protect, and perpetuate it by whatever means and at whatever cost. It may be recalled that just before the 1946 election, which was to be a constitutional referendum, a heated debate took place at the SCAP GHQ over the scope of the purge.[74] The New Dealers in the GS advocated an extensive social engineering, and MacArthur sided with them in order to insure the constitution's survival (the second intervention). The constitution passed the plebiscite, but the government was still in the hands of Yoshida with the record of having fiercely resisted the constitution. The purge and other reforms went on, and at last the election of 1947 gave MacArthur a "center" coalition government that could be entrusted with the constitution.

In order to protect the wobbly Socialists, he cut the firebreak between them and the Communists. This was as far as he would go in reversing himself. He vetoed the political side of reverse course including two requests by Yoshida to recentralize the police apparatus.[75] By late 1948 both the State and Defense departments completely reversed themselves and began discussing constitutional revision and rearmament as the precondition of a peace treaty. In addition, State and Kennan were very strongly in favor of lifting the purge and reinstating a U.S. "ambassador" independent of SCAP. The purge was evidently very important in MacArthur's mind for the preservation of his constitution, and in 1948 the GS was even proposing to perpetuate it by writing it into the prospective peace treaty with Japan.[76] An independent U.S. "ambassador" would interfere with MacArthur's constitutional scheme, as POLAD did earlier. Therefore, the "reverse course" promoted by the Washington bureaucracies represented a threat to MacArthur's constitutional scheme.

So did Yoshida, the only alternative to the Socialist-Ashida coalition. That coalition had to preside over the forthcoming peace conference if the constitution was to survive in the postindependence Japan. Hence the enormous pressure to undermine and retire Yoshida. But the pressure backfired, and Yoshida was returned with an impressive majority in the January 1949 poll. By then both men were presumably inclined to say, "If you cannot beat him, join him." I must posit the secret MacArthur-Yoshida compact (or MacArthur's third intervention) to defend the constitution at this juncture. Although it is an inference, there is no doubt whatever that it took place. Suddenly MacArthur's harassment of Yoshida gave way to unshakable confidence in him. Lest Yoshida should become the target of terrorist attack, he ordered a bloodtype test for Yoshida.[77] It so happened that Yoshida's concept of Japan's future, already hammered out independently by 1947, was predicated on American protection, and the constitution would provide a convenient cover.

I must pause here to inquire into additional matters of major importance. It has been shown that the constitution and the purge were intimately related with each other. So were the establishment of the JSP and the purge. These links must be analyzed more precisely. The Potsdam Declaration did envisage some sort of purge for demilitarization purpose. But SWNCC 150/4 enormously expanded its scope by adding "democratization" as a collateral goal. "Democratization" rested on E. H. Norman's theory that social structure determines the political will, either toward war or democracy, and it called for large-scale social engineering including forcible redistribution of "the means of production." Thus the "democratizing" purge lent itself to MacArthur's dearest wish to remove the potential opposition to his constitution, to nurture a vibrant political center that could defend it, and to see to it that the center government would preside over the future peace conference.

But there were dangerous flaws both in the conception and execution of the purge. "Democratization" as such cannot justify purging of men from public life nor confiscation of private property. All purges including economic ones could be justified only as punishments against "militarism." But the social engineering goal called for a massive turnover in public life. The Japanese administrators were frequently told to "come up with a round number" to be purged. General Whitney, director of the GS, was trying to emulate the figure of 300,000 denazified in Germany.[78] The Japanese plea for screening individual cases was brushed aside because it was suspected—correctly, in my view—of being subterfuge for creating interminable delays. "Individual 'guilt' . . . is irrelevant," said Whitney in January 1946, just prior to the constitutional plebiscite.[79] In this fashion, a large mass of Japanese were branded "militarists" without cause, to make room for the Socialists, the constitution, and other engineering projects.

There was another group whose perpetuation and enhancement in power in postwar Japan was insured by the purge: the central-ministry bureaucracies. The power, recruiting pattern, esprit de corps, competence, and practices of the imperial bureaucracies were carried over to their postwar successors primarily because of the purge and the so-called indirect rule.[80] At the very outset, I presume, the attempt to implement the extravagant goals of the purge gave rise to an urgent question, how far to go? Ideally the bureaucratic elites had to be purged. But the administrative needs of the occupation stood in the way. So a third, operational goal of the purge emerged: save the bureaucracy.

The same result was insured by another factor, the nature of the occupation government. Given the depth and scope of reforms called for in SWNCC 150/4, the power of SCAP was and had to be absolute, as previously noted. The occupation of Japan was indirect in form only, the Japanese government, both the political and administrative branches, being confined to purely administrative role for the most part. The plenary and unbounded power was exercised by SCAP and its bureaucracy, either directly through SCAPINs or indirectly through Diet legislations. SCAP officials drafted most of the bills, often in consultation with the relevant Japanese bureaucracies; took the bills to the Diet floor to lobby for them if necessary; and always secured the consent of the Diet.[81] The principle of Diet supremacy, proclaimed in the constitution, was suspended—MacArthur was the real sovereign. Nevertheless, MacArthur personally insisted on rigidly maintaining the facade of self-rule or democracy. One reason appeared to be his desire to perpetuate the constitution.[82] Again the only practical solution was to save the bureaucracy.

The central ministries were retained almost intact with this exception: the Justice Ministry was reformed, the Imperial Household Ministry was reduced to an agency, and the Interior Ministry was disbanded, with its personnel being transferred to other ministries, some to the latter-day Defense Agency. The impact of demilitarization, constitutional defense, and "indirect rule" can be shown graphically in the purge and its result. Table I shows the effect of the purge by categories of elite, and Table II the purge within the bureaucratic elite. In the ministries of foreign affairs, finance, and the like, many administrative vice-ministers and bureau chiefs remained at their jobs.[83]

It is likely that SCAP's dependence on Japan's central ministries began practically on day one of the occupation. With the language barrier being so great, but lacking in expertise of its own, SCAP's staff of several hundred officials could hardly run the country, let alone shake it upside down, without the assistance of at least one branch of the native government. The critical liaison function was naturally filled by the foreign ministry bureaucrats, who produced three prime ministers, Shidehara, Ashida, and Yoshida, who governed nearly the whole length of the occupation period (the remainder were Higashikuni and Katayama). In the occupied Japan, the hierarchy of power consisted of SCAP at the top, the Japanese bureaucracies second, and the professional politicians at the bottom.

In prewar Japan the professional politicians in the Diet and the imperial bureaucracy had a long history of contention, with the latter (e.g., Interior) enjoying the upper hand. Given that history, the bias in the purge was bound to rekindle a fire. The Yamazaki affair was a sign of that. But things did not stop here. The nature of the occupation government tended to blur the locus of authority as between SCAP and the Japanese government. To the extent that Japan was under the military rule, the native government, handling most of

**Table I**
Purges by Elite Categories

| Category | Number | Percent |
|---|---|---|
| Military | 167,035 | 79.6 |
| Political | 34,892 | 16.5 |
| Ultranationalist | 3,438 | 1.6 |
| Business | 1,898 | .9 |
| Bureaucratic | 1,809 | .9 |
| Information media | 1,216 | .5 |
| Total | 210,288 | 100.0 |

**Table II**
Purge of Bureaucratic Elite[a]

| Category | Number | Percent |
| --- | --- | --- |
| Number screened | 42,251 | 100.0 |
| Number purged | 830 | 1.9 |
| Shinninkan screened[b] | 87 | 100.0 |
| Shinninkan purged | 42 | 48.3 |
| Chokuninkan screened[c] | 1,974 | 100.0 |
| Chokuninkan purged | 164 | 8.3 |
| Soninkan screened | 40,190 | 100.0 |
| Soninkan purged | 624 | 1.55 |

[a]These statistics include only those screened and not those who retired or resigned and subsequently were provisionally designated. Hence the discrepancy between the total number of bureaucrats purged in Table I and the total number here.
[b]Ministers and privy councilors by imperial appointment.
[c]Vice ministers and senior civil servants by imperial appointment.
From Hans H. Baerwald, *The Purge of Japanese Leaders under the Occupation* (Berkeley: Univ. of California Press, 1959), pp. 80, 82.

administration, was absolved of responsibility; but to the extent that it was supposed to be a democracy, SCAP was largely free of responsibility. This blurred responsibility in turn gave rise to collusion between the SCAP officials and the Japanese government, to corruptions and abuses.[84] Some of the purge administration was transferred to the native civil service. So, Japanese career bureaucrats, charged with reviewing purge cases, it is said, "was in an excellent position to protect a group in which they had a vested interest, namely, the bureaucracy."[85] From the beginning the purge was controversial and gave rise to many rumors and allegations of irregularity and collusion because it was "used to remove the political opponents of [American or Japanese] individuals empowered to administer the purge.

The pro-bureaucratic and pro-Socialist bias built into the purge invited suspicion and resentment to begin with. But that was a price for saving the emperor. In 1948, however, MacArthur launched himself on a course that would mortgage Japan's future policy, foreign as well as domestic, to his constitution. And he and Yoshida began to use the purge or, to be precise, the delay of depurge for that purpose. On his own MacArthur had decided in late 1948 to freeze the purge, and it would go on for two and a half years thereafter. With this one secret stroke, he succeeded in keeping out the purged politicians from the peace negotiations, thus tilting Japan's and the United States' future foreign policies in the direction of his choice. MacArthur went on meddling in the process of peace negotiation for the sake of saving his constitution until his dismissal in April 1951. Thereafter Yoshida began to use the purge for the same purpose.[87] In the course of these events, the fact of MacArthur's collusion with Yoshida became public knowledge.

When that happened, the constitution, the purge, the Socialists, and the bureaucrat-politician struggle turned into political issues with a nasty edge. Yoshida was at the point where all the four issues intersected each other. They would poison and complicate the subsequent politics of Japan and the U.S.-Japanese relations. Understandably the professional politicians began to resent the United States, the constitution, the bureaucrats, and, to a lesser extent, the Socialists, the latter two being perceived as American stooges. Deep political fissures began to separate the three groups from each other.

After the hair-raising experience in the hands of the GS and the politicians in the Yamazaki affair, Yoshida drew a political line around himself first. In the 1949 election, he encouraged talented bureaucrats to run for Diet offices, so as to insure himself against the day when the purged politicians would return. Still small in number, the new breed of politicians came to be called—somewhat pejoratively—the "disciples of the Yoshida School."[88] He also instructed Ikeda Hayato, his disciple, a former finance official, and incumbent finance minister, to work closely with Joseph Dodge on fiscal retrenchment, in an attempt to cultivate a direct link to Washington.[89] The foreign and finance ministries became important tools of Yoshida's politics, both domestic and international.

## NOTES

1. Max Bishop in the office of POLAD speaking in April 1946, in *Foreign Relations of the United States* (Washington, DC: GPO, 1971) 1946, VIII, 192. George Atcheson reported in September 1946: "The feeling became widespread in Japan that General Headquarters was giving both direct and indirect support to communistic activities in this country." Ibid., p. 315.

2. Theodore Cohen, *Remaking Japan: The American Occupation as New Deal* (New York: Free Press, 1987), pp. 209–10.

3. Hitoshi Ashida, *Ashida Hitoshi nikki* [The Ashida Hitoshi diary] (Tokyo: Iwanami Shoten, 1986), II, 130. According to a State Department source, he received "neither approval nor disapproval"; cited in *FRUS*, 1947, VI, 158.

4. The best reading on this point is Government Section, SCAP, *Political Reorientation of Japan, September 1945–September 1948* (Washington, DC: GPO, 1949), 2 Vols.

5. Junnosuke Masumi, *Sengo seiji, 1945–1955* [Postwar politics, 1945–1955] (Tokyo: Tokyo University Press, 1983), I, 174–75; Hans H. Baerwald, *The Purge of Japanese Leaders under the Occupation* (Berkeley: Univ. of California Press, 1959), pp. 83–85.

6. See the diagram in the appendix I showing their genealogy and different labels.

7. All political parties followed the pattern: criticizing the government but not SCAP. See the official JSP history, in Nihon Shakaito, *Nihon Shakai-to no sanjunen* [Thirty years of the Japan Socialist Party] (Tokyo: Japan Socialist Party, 1975), I, 254.

8. Masumi, I, 235.

9. Ashida, II, pp. 188–202; Masumi, I, p. 240.

10. Masumi, p. 231; Hans H. Baerwald, *The Purge of Japanese Leaders under the Occupation* (Berkeley: Univ. California Press, 1959), pp. 95–96.

But note that Yoshida is alleged to have purged Ashida's friends so as to bring about his own prime ministership. Ibid., pp. 84–85.

11. *Political Reorientation of Japan*, II, 767.

12. *FRUS*, 1949, VII, 747.

13. Cited in John W. Dower, *Empire and Aftermath: Yoshida Shigeru and the Japanese Experience, 1878–1954* (Cambridge: Harvard Univ. Press, 1979), p. 278.

14. "Kenkoku no jijo to bansei ikkei no shiso" [The circumstances of the nation-founding and the idea of uninterrupted imperial rule], *Sekai*, April 1946, pp. 29–54. For the best summary of the Kokoro group's activities, see Osamu Kuno, *Sengo Nihon no shiso* [Postwar Japanese thoughts] (Tokyo: Keiso Shobo, 1966). Michio Takeyama, *Showa no seishinshi* [The spiritual history of Showa] (Tokyo: Fukutake Shoten, 1983) may be regarded as the keynote statement of the Kokoro group. In the 40 years since the war, it has been not Marx but the Japanese culture that won the hearts of the intellectuals. See Shunsuke Tsurumi's open confession of his change, in *Sengo Nihon no taishu bunka* [Popular culture of postwar Japan] (Tokyo: Iwanami Shoten, 1984).

15. Seizaburo Shinobu, *Sengo Nihon seijishi*, I, 291–93, 335, 338, 362; II, 417, 571.

16. See Vols. II and III of his *Ashida Hitoshi nikki*.

17. George F. Kennan, *Memoirs, 1925–1950* (Boston: Little Brown, 1967), p. 355.

18. Ibid., p. 375.

19. *Realities of American Foreign Policy* (Princeton, NJ: Princeton Univ. Press, 1954), pp. 22–23.

20. Ibid., p. 36.

21. Kennan, *Memoirs*, pp. 382–83.

22. Michael Schaller, *The American Occupation of Japan: The Origins of the Cold War in Asia* (New York: Oxford Univ. Press, 1985), p. 94.

23. Ibid., pp. 95–96. MacArthur declared that the first two stages of occupation, disarmament and democratization, had been completed, and that the third stage, that of economic reconstruction, must begin, but that it must be preceded by a peace treaty. Chihiro Hosoya speculates that Hugh Borton's peace plan at the State Department prompted MacArthur to come up with his own, in *San Furanshisuko eno michi* [The road to San Francisco] (Tokyo: Chuo Koronsha, 1984), p. 11.

24. Schaller, pp. 108, 120.

25. Ibid., pp. 127–31.

26. Kennan, *Memoirs*, p. 376.

27. *FRUS*, 1948, VI, p. 804. When Kennan brought this fact to the general's attention, he allowed that "to some extent our occupation policies had been influenced by academic theorizers of a left-wing variety." *FRUS*, 1948, VI, 699.

28. *FRUS*, 1948, VI, pp. 708–9.

29. *FRUS,* 1947, VI, 233, 450.
30. *Memoirs,* p. 376.
31. When the Far Eastern Commission tried to review the constitution one year after its passage, this is what MacArthur said: "Throughout the development of the new constitution, action has been largely avoided which might be construed as compulsory process in order that nothing might negate or compromise the free character essential if the instrument is to live. . . . [A review of the constitution by the Far Eastern Commission] would reduce the very essence of durability upon which the instrument has been built to a frail skeleton of temporary expedience overshadowed by the threat of forced abrogation or revision at the point of Allied bayonets." *FRUS,* 1946, VIII, 353.
32. William J. Sebald, *With MacArthur in Japan: A Personal History of the Occupation* (New York: W. W. Norton, 1965), p. 80.
33. That the State and Defense departments "viewed the Supreme Commander as the greatest single danger to Japan's security" seems a hyperbole. But that was how MacArthur was perceived by the Washington bureaucracy at the time. Schaller, p. 121.
34. D. Clayton James, *The Years of MacArthur, 1880–1941* (Boston: Houghton Mifflin, 1976), I, 525–26.
35. Ibid., p. 413.
36. *FRUS,* 1948, VI, 691.
37. *FRUS,* 1948, VI, 704.
38. According to Ambassador Sebald, in *FRUS,* 1948, VI, 674.
39. *FRUS,* 1948, VI, 858–62.
40. *Newsweek*'s foreign editor, Harry F. Kern, and its Tokyo correspondent, Compton Packenham, started a blistering attack on SCAP's economic policy in January 1947. Schaller, pp. 93–94. Kern befriended Hatoyama Ichiro and Kishi Nobusuke, and acted as an intermediary between Hatoyama and Dulles. See Chapter 4 of this book. See also Sebald, p. 75.
41. Among them were 12 professors of Tokyo University, 11 professors of Kyoto University, the chancellor of the Peers' School College who later became minister of education, another future education minister, a member of the editorial board of *Asahi,* Japan's most prestigious daily, 2 members of the House of Councilors, and one future chief justice of the supreme court.
42. See the discussions by the PPS organizers in *Sekai,* July 1985 (40th anniversary issue), pp. 2–97. See also Takeshi Igarashi, "Sengo Nihon gaiko taisei no keisei" [The formation of the postwar Japanese foreign policy system], Part I, *Kokka Gakkai Zasshi,* June 1948, pp. 343–409; Part II, ibid., September 1949, pp. 463–507.
43. *Sekai,* July 1985, p. 103.
44. See Sebald, pp. 247–48; Seigen Miyazato, "Amerika gasshukoku seifu to tai-Nichi kowa" [The United States government and peace with Japan], in Akio Watanabe, ed., *Sanfuranshisuko kowa* [The San Francisco peace treaty] (Tokyo: Tokyo Univ. Press, 1986), p. 119; *FRUS,* 1948, VI, 692; *FRUS,* 1949, VII, 671–73.
45. Sebald, p. 81. The impact of this statement can be gauged from the fact that it is quoted by many Japanese leaders and writers.
46. Seizaburo Shinobu, *Sengo Nihon seijishi* (Tokyo: Keiso Shobo, 1967), III, 932.
47. *Nihon Shakaito no sanjunen,* I, 174–83.
48. A leader of the switch put the motive this way: "We are going to unite with the right to strike the left, and after striking the left we will strike the right, in order to find

72                  *The Price of a Constitution*

the center of gravity for the labor movement." Cited in *Nihon Shakaito no sanjunen,* I, 172.

49. Ibid., I, 203.

50. *Sekai,* July 1985, p. 63.

51. *Nihon Shakaito no sanjunen,* I, 215; Shinobu, *Sengo Nihon seijishi,* III, 957.

52. Masumi, II, 251–57.

53. Just before the GS suggested Yamazaki as successor, MacArthur also called in Miki Takeo, a conservative leader in the Ashida coalition, to see if he could form a cabinet. Miki declined on the ground that his faction was too small. Yuzo Tamura, *Sengo Shakaito no ninaite-tachi* [Those who bore the postwar Socialist Party] (Tokyo: Nihon Hyoronsha, 1984), p. 157.

54. Isamu Togawa, *Shosetsu Yoshida gakko: hoshu honryu* [The Yoshida school, a novel: the conservative mainstream] (Tokyo: Kadokawa Shoten, 1980), p. 37.

55. Masumi, I, 262–63.

56. *FRUS,* 1949, VII, 605–7.

57. Dower, *Empire,* p. 29.

58. Dower, *Empire,* p. 21.

59. Dower, *Empire,* pp. 96–97.

60. Masataka Kosaka, *Saiso Yoshida Shigeru* [Prime Minister Yoshida Shigeru] (Tokyo: Chuo Koronsha, 1968), p. 21.

61. Dower, *Empire,* pp. 277–78, 296–98, 399, 322, 329–30, 332.

62. *The Yoshida Memoirs,* p. 58.

63. Kosaka, *Saiso Yoshida Shigeru,* p. 5.

64. *The Yoshida Memoirs,* p. 128.

65. *FRUS,* 1945, VI, p. 731.

66. Yoshida, *Kaiso junen,* IV, 124–25.

67. Kosaka, *Saiso Yoshida Shigeru,* pp. 41–42. The extension of compulsory education by three years, a task that strained fiscal resources to the limit, was agreed to after Yoshida dismissed the education minister, Tanaka Kotaro, in this fashion.

68. Dower, *Empire,* p. 316.

69. See report by Sebald, cited above. See also *Nihon Shakaito no sanjunen,* I, 194.

70. Igarashi, *Tai-Nichi kowa to reisen: sengo Nich-Bei kankei no keisei* [Peace with Japan and the Cold War: the formation of postwar Japan-U.S. relations] (Tokyo: Univ. of Tokyo Press, 1986), pp. 121, 125, 128, 131, 135, 137, 150; see also Schaller, pp. 86–87.

71. *FRUS,* 1948, VI, p. 878. This memorandum was written in October 1948.

72. Shinobu, *Sengo Nihon seijishi,* III, 995–96.

73. *FRUS,* 1949, VII, 660.

74. Mark Gayne, *Tokyo Diary* (New York: William Sloan, 1948), pp. 162–64.

75. Igarashi, *Tai Nichi kowa,* p. 153. This must have taken place after the compact mentioned below. My guess is that MacArthur could not afford to give Yoshida all the police power he wanted lest he should pounce on the Socialists.

76. *FRUS,* 1948, VI, 786.

77. Igarashi, *Tai-Nichi kowa,* p. 170.

78. Taizo Kusayanagi, Nihon kaitai [Japan liquidated] (Tokyo: Gyosei, 1985), p. 83.

79. *Political Reorientation of Japan,* p. 18. He went on to say, there is "no objection to the establishment of a Commission of Inquiry, . . . providing that the individual is first removed from public office" and screened later.

80. Chalmers A. Johnson mentions only the latter, in *MITI and the Japanese Miracle: The Growth of Industrial Policy, 1925-1975* (Stanford: Stanford Univ. Press, 1982), chapter 2. See also Hiroshi Masaki, "Kanryo konjo" [Bureaucratic habit], *Chuo Koron,* January 1949, pp. 44–48.

81. "Puppet government" was the phrase used, in *Ashida Hitoshi nikki,* II, 17.

82. The best place to see this point is in Whitney's introduction to *Political Reorientation of Japan.*

83. Hans H. Baerwald, *The Purge of Japanese Leaders under the Occupation* (Berkeley: Univ. of California Press, 1959), p. 82. Baerwald says, "The purge left the bureaucracy almost unchanged in the composition of its personnel."

84. Ibid., p. 102.

85. Ibid., p. 46.

86. Ibid., p. 20. Masumi, a foremost expert, says that the purge of Ken Inukai, Wataru Narahashi, and Takeshige Ishiguro, all of former Minseito, in 1947 "might have been directed by Yoshida." Masumi, I, 239. Baerwald merely reports "the widely held contention that these removals were motivated by political considerations . . ." Baerwald, p. 84. But I am inclined to discount allegations of Yoshida's influence over the purge prior to his compact with MacArthur.

87. See the next chapter.

88. Shinobu, *Sengo Nihon seijishi,* III, 823.

89. Yumi Watari, *Sengo seiji to Nichi-Bei kankei* [Postwar politics and the Japan-U.S. relations] (Tokyo: Tokyo Univ. Press, 1990), section 1, chapter 1. In spite of its title, this is virtually a biography of Ideda.

# Chapter 4

# Toward The San Francisco Peace Conference

In 1949 a peace treaty with Japan was placed on the agenda. Intense debate and political maneuvers in both Washington and Tokyo culminated in the peace and security treaties signed in San Francisco in 1951. Because of their unhappiness with U.S.-Japanese relations as codified in the security treaty, the Japanese would debate alternative arrangements after San Francisco, but they ended up reaffirming the outline of the "San Francisco system," as they called it, nine years later. Thus with some modification, today's Japan is still moving in the orbit decided in 1949–51.

It was the Korean War and NSC 68—the Truman administration's basic security policy—that decided Japan's place in the American orbit. The modus operandi of the bilateral relations was shaped by collisions and settlements between three actors. The JCS and the Defense Department wanted to continue the military occupation of Japan to protect it and to protect the United States against it. But they also insisted on limited rearmament by Japan. The State Department, represented by John Foster Dulles in the final negotiation, defended a position that was ambivalent, a fact of some importance. On the one hand, State argued strenuously for Japan's equality in a nonpunitive peace and showed a strong solicitude for Japanese consent to any arrangement. On the other hand, State's concern for Japan's independence concealed its bureaucratic interests in wresting control over the country from the JCS, by terminating the "military government" under SCAP. Hence, to what extent State was interested in Japan's independence outside of this context remained to be seen. Dulles's talk of "mutuality" meant that if Japan refused to honor it through rearmament, he could penalize it by siding with the JCS.

MacArthur and Yoshida wanted unilateral U.S. protection for Japan without an injury to its "amour propre" (Yoshida) if possible. The massive, unbridled U.S. military presence the JCS demanded, Yoshida felt, made it meaningless to speak of self-help, mutuality, or collective security.

For the purpose of our analysis and to better understand the dispute that was to unfold after San Francisco, we can conceptualize four grades of U.S.-Japan relations on a scale ranging from equality to inequality. First is the relationship of full equality and mutuality, which may be termed the Gaullist option. Nuclear-armed Britain and France in NATO are the model. A Soviet attack on the United States is an attack on Britain and France, and they are bound by the rule "all for one, one for all." Without an offensive arm, America's allies cannot act on full mutuality. The second grade is represented by Adenauer's Germany, which is fully, conventionally armed and which can exchange "mutual help" with all of its NATO allies *within the European theater*. This is made possible by the multilateral character of the Atlantic treaty. The United States has been trying to replicate this condition within the bilateral treaty with Japan—without success.

The third grade is represented by Japan since 1960, when the original treaty was revised: This Japan is conventionally armed also but confines its military operations solely to its territorial space, on constitutional grounds. Thus it refuses to undertake any collective security measures with the U.S. armed forces beyond that space. At the bottom is the protectorate arrangement Yoshida and MacArthur both asked for in 1950–51. Japan may or may not possess armed forces in this instance, but they are irrelevant to its status because they are more or less constabulary in nature. The basic exchange here is between Japan's base lease and unilateral U.S. protection. Washington has regarded the third and fourth grades as unequal to itself. Japan accepted the fourth in San Francisco and sought an upgrade to the third thereafter. Only the third and fourth grades conform to Japan's constitution.

The peace treaty scheme for Japan evolved in three major stages, depending on the state of U.S.-Soviet relations. In 1946–47 the State Department under Secretary Byrnes prepared a draft peace treaty of punitive character. Japan's neutrality and disarmament were to be supervised by a regime of Allied inspection, which was to last 25 years. But this presupposed the continuation of the wartime Allied unity. In the second stage, 1947–48, George Kennan sought a modus vivendi between the superpowers that mistrusted each other but that refrained from dividing up the world. Neutrality, including armed neutrality, was in vogue at this stage. The minimum American condition was that Japan not fall into hostile hands, Japanese or foreign.[1] Kennan was prepared to neutralize Japan if the Soviets could be persuaded to disengage from Korea in return. MacArthur's Switzerland scheme, also born of the second stage, simply assumed a rather benign Soviet intention in return for a U.S. presence confined to Okinawa. That suited most Japanese who wanted to recover from the war on the periphery of the American sphere. But they faced a dilemma; a non-punitive peace rested on a degree of tension between Washington and Moscow, but if the tension grew excessive Japan would face a military integration into the American alliance. That began to happen in late 1949, as the superpower push came to a shove in the third stage.

Kennan's policy in NSC 13/2 placed Japan's rehabilitation ahead of the peace treaty because the United States could not find an alternative to status quo for Japan's security; Japan could not be left defenseless; but there was no support for its rearmament; nor for postoccupation U.S. presence. But by the time the Berlin blockade was lifted in May 1949, State began to lobby for peace again. George Marshall was succeeded by Dean Acheson at State in January, and Kennan retired. In April the North Atlantic Treaty Organization (NATO) got off the ground, and the new secretary of state was preoccupied with Germany and Europe through the summer. Next on his agenda was Asia. The People's Liberation Army had crossed the Yangtse in April and the fall of China seemed imminent. But in Japan the January election had returned Yoshida and the 35 Communist members to the Diet on the wave of hostility toward the United States. A series of spectacular acts of sabotage carried out by the Japanese left served as a riposte to the ''reverse course'' and the Dodge Line of retrenchment policy.

The immediate antecedent to the latest peace move by Acheson was the British inquiry on the matter in September.[2] But the main concern of the State Department was to avoid having to veto a Soviet peace initiative. That would certainly create even greater restiveness among the Japanese.[3] Already, at the four-power foreign ministers' conference in Paris in May, the Soviet Union had broached the subject. On October 3 Acheson wrote to Louis Johnson, defense secretary, asking for the Pentagon's conditions for peace with Japan. To commit Johnson and his ponderous bureaucracy to an early action, Acheson publicized that he was preparing a treaty draft, news that stimulated Japan.[4]

With that, the peace treaty became embroiled in the running bureaucratic war between the State and Defense departments. Unlike State, preoccupied with Japan's internal politics, the JCS and the Pentagon were naturally concerned with military security of the United States against both international communism and Japan. As championed by the under secretary of the army, Tracy Voorhees, Draper's successor, the military demanded ''total peace'' that encompassed the Sino-Soviet bloc (so as to lesson communist menace to Japan, allegedly) and exclusive U.S. military control over Japan. Since these demands were incompatible, an indefinite continuation of occupation was the only conclusion. Voorhees ''fanatically oppose[d] any treaty'' and maintained ''[W]e can dictate Japanese behavior'' under military rule, including, presumably, their acquiescence in the use of Japanese bases for strategic strike against the Soviet Union.[5] But at the same time the military was already on record demanding Japan's limited rearmament and constitutional revision, the latter to be forced on Japan while still under occupation.[6]

MacArthur felt that the Pentagon was "imperialistic."[7] Truman was opposed to the Pentagon, too, but evidently it was difficult to overrule it on military matters. Faced with Johnson's objection, State prepared two alternative plans: a de facto peace, involving domestic autonomy for Japan, and a Pacific pact, a regional military alliance that would keep Japan's rearmament under international control, as was done vis-a-is Germany in NATO. A regional alliance never materialized, but the idea of guaranteeing Japan's neighbors against it survived in a series of bilateral pacts between them and the United States.

The State Department had lost a large measure of influence over Japan to the military once the occupation began. Its influence was further curtailed by Mac-Arthur when he discovered that George Atcheson in the office of political adviser (POLAD), a functioning ambassadorship in the occupation, was involving himself in the scheme against the emperor. An attempt to reassert State's control over the occupation began with Kennan's policy reversal. Capitalizing on Washington's discontent with MacArthur's independence, State succeeded in preempting the economic side of rehabilitation by appointing Joseph Dodge, but MacArthur managed to keep control over the political half. It was evident that as long as the occupation continued, the department would play second fiddle to the military over policy toward Japan and that an ambassador could not be posted to Tokyo.[8] The JCS and the Pentagon, too, I infer, understood this proposition well: hence their adamant defense of continued occupation. The State Department's increasingly vocal demand for Japan's independence and equality must be seen in this context.

The State-Defense impasse placed MacArthur in a position to mediate between them on peace with Japan. Knowing his influence, both departments dispatched their respective officials to Tokyo to woo him. MacArthur's influence was enhanced also by the fact that he was popular among the Senate Republicans who were to sit in judgment of any treaty with Japan. MacArthur's starting point was the constitution, and he was still struggling with the dilemma he had created. The best solution for his Japan was semineutralist dependency recouperating on the outer fringe of America's backyard. He wanted an early and benign peace, and he felt that State was making too much concessions to Defense with either of its plans, de facto peace or a Pacific pact.[9]

China fell in November. Recovering from Truman's surprise victory in the 1948 election, the Republicans went on the offensive over the "loss of China." It was becoming a political impossibility to "throw Japan away after China." Still, MacArthur was adamant on Japan's neutrality. As late as May 1950, one month before the hostilities commenced in Korea, he was calling for Japan to be the "Switzerland of the Pacific."[10] By then he was all alone with the quixotic idea. But in both MacArthur's and Yoshida's case, neutrality was a bargaining chip to strengthen Japan's position in the forthcoming peace negotiation. Ostensibly, MacArthur's neutrality plea was based on the judgment that the Soviet Union also wanted a neutral Japan because its aim in Asia was "defensive."[11] The United States in May 1949 decided to remain in Okinawa indefinitely (NSC 13/3), and MacArthur felt that was adequate for Japan's security *and neutrality*.[12] He was strongly opposed to a posttreaty regime of control over Japan.

Before the downfall of the Socialist-Ashida coalition government in late 1948, that is, during the period that roughly corresponded to the second stage mentioned above, Japan's political parties—with the exception of the JCP—had a rough consensus on the form of peace treaty and posttreaty foreign policy. The consensus jelled around a peace plan study that Yoshida as foreign minister ordered into being in 1945. It was endorsed by the Socialist-Ashida coalition, and Yoshida resumed stewardship over it in his second cabinet. Its wisdom aside, Yoshida's sheer tenacity in sticking to his idea through all the sea changes in domestic and international environment from 1945 on, and in seeing to it that the Americans bought the idea, may deserve grudging admiration.[13]

The early postwar origin of Yoshida's concept must be stressed here. At that stage the U.S. peace plan was shifting from a 25-year punitive occupation to Kennan's idea of merely denying Japan to the Soviets without fortifying it. Contemporary American media would raise eyebrows even at a casual mention of Japanese constabulary, and few, if any, thought of the U.S. presence as giving Japan a free ride. Yoshida made a virtue of necessity by calling on Japan to take a few decades of semiretirement from international public life to seek recovery from the devastation and trauma of defeat. A strong Anglophile and anticommunist, he had no doubt whatever that Japan should seek an association with America, but he was strongly opposed to the "postoccupation regime of control." In the Ashida memorandum of 1947, which was an outgrowth of Yoshida's concept, Japan asked to have its "security guaranteed by the United States" through the maintenance of its "armed forces in the areas adjacent to Japan [Okinawa]" though additional bases would be made available in Japan proper in an emergency. In addition, Japan would also maintain a constabulary force to look after the domestic order.[14] He felt the exchange—of protection for bases—deserved to be honored in an equal and mutual treaty.

He was also quite insistent in private on U.S. retention of South Korean salience. Yoshida's neutrality scheme, for instance, included neutralization of the Korean peninsula.[15] But his concern became superfluous when fighting the Korean War became the operational purpose—though nowhere stated—of the U.S.-Japan security arrangement for the JCS and the Pentagon. In addition,

Yoshida was hoping to get a sizable American assistance to restore Japan's economic health.

Yoshida appeared to hope that the rising superpower tension, which had already aborted a punitive peace, would play into his hands by making Japan almost indispensable to Washington. But it remained to be seen whether excessive tension would compel Washington to make demands on Japan that he preferred to avoid. He was walking the tightrope, balancing the superpower tension against his desire for an American protection.

In late 1948 the Japanese Diet began for the first time to interest itself hesitantly in the peace treaty and Japan's future in the world. The Peace Problem Symposium was already in action, as noted previously. The JCP, acting in concert with Moscow, had determined by August that Japan should demand an early, total peace. The Socialists had been rather passive during the Diet debate on the constitution in 1947. They were torn between loyalty to the throne and the egalitarian impulse to grasp popular sovereignty. The JSP was equally unsure in formulating a foreign policy stance. In November 1948 it sponsored jointly with other parties a resolution calling for early peace, but the party had nothing to say on the content of the treaty.[16] When Kennan's recommendations in NSC 13/2 put rehabilitation ahead of a peace treaty, peace discussions lapsed for a while.

In September 1949 news stories of revived American interest in peace began to circulate. Until the fall of 1949, the opposition parties demanded an "early peace"; Yoshida's stand for "de facto peace" was an echo of MacArthur and the State Department.[17] Diet debate on peace began in earnest in the sixth regular session, which started in November. At this point, Yoshida shifted from "de facto peace" to "early peace" with only the Anglo-American powers. The JSP, in contrast, shifted from "early peace" to "total peace" on the basis of the so-called Three Principles of Peace: total peace, neutrality, and opposition to military bases. The no-war constitution was cited as the premise for the thesis that Japan should avoid conflict with any power or group of powers, but the party—still under the influence of the rightwing on foreign policy matters—was unsure of what to do with Article XI.[18] From this point on, the Socialists became interested in defending the early occupation reforms of domestic institutions against the "reverse course," and their foreign policy stance was affected by that domestic concern. The rightwing Socialists, still the mainstay, were hedging in the face of the increasingly unpleasant choice between another coalition with the conservatives and the people's front with the Communists. The JSP's pacifism had not yet hardened, and it was open to reasonable arguments.

Meanwhile the process of political realignment that commenced with the

U.S. policy reversal and the January 1949 election was proceeding, in less obtrusive ways for now. It was fueled by superpower conflict, which posed the issue, total peace vs. separate peace. Though Yoshida had a comfortable majority in the lower house, he wanted to expand it further in order to insure a safe passage of the treaties he was about to negotiate. Beside, another election was coming up in June 1950 for the upper house, in which his party held a mere 61 out of 250 seats. So Yoshida began to entice the Inukai faction of former Minseito in the opposition to switch allegiance to his party as soon as the January 1949 lower house election was over. Miraculously Inukai had been depurged by July 1948.

Yoshida was probably aware that he was accelerating the polarization by breaking up and undermining the center. Ashida held out in former Minseito, arguing for the continuation of the centrist option that encompassed the rightwing Socialists. Anticipating the argument of John Foster Dulles, U.S. peace negotiator, Ashida felt "bipartisanship" that carried the Socialists was indispensable for treaty negotiations.

The JSP's polarization proceeded on two levels after the demise of the Ashida-Socialist coalition. At this stage, the primary issue was social democracy vs. Marxism in domestic politics, not foreign relations. At the party headquarters, the middle faction led by Wada Hiroo defected to the leftwing in 1949, thereby isolating the rightwing headed by former prime minister Katayama. Katayama's isolation resulted also from the rapid change in party membership that had taken place in 1948–49—the party was innundated by a sudden infusion of more radical union members, who switched allegiance from the Communist-dominated federation to the JSP.

Japan was formally in a state of unconditional surrender, and the American media jealously guarded the fiction of "dictated peace."[19] But de facto Japan was negotiating from considerable strength because Yoshida and MacArthur were agreed on the basic Japanese stance. Although Yoshida was known to play cat and mouse with the general, it is difficult to see anything but identity of minds on peace after their secret compact of early 1949 in defense of the constitution. In September MacArthur made up his mind to abandon U.S.-Soviet guarantee of Japan's neutrality in favor of indefinite U.S. presence in Japan. He would nonetheless keep on talking of neutrality, but that was a bargaining chip. He also decided to abandon postoccupation control in favor of Japan's independence. I take this to mean that, now that Yoshida was his ally, MacArthur did not need to write such controls—e.g., a perpetual purge—into the peace treaty.[20] He wanted the peace conference held in Tokyo under his chairmanship.

In late 1949 in the Diet, Yoshida parried opposition interpellations by saying that the conditions of peace were for the allied powers, not Japan, to decide. But he kept moving closer to the American option by pointing out that total peace presupposed U.S.-Soviet cooperation, which no longer existed. Yoshida argued that an early peace with a few countries was better than none. But, the opposition queried, if Japan were to take the American side in the Cold War, would that not endanger its security? In contrast, the opposition was divided over whether Japan should endure more occupation until a total peace was realized. The government drove home that point.

Under the opposition parties' scrutiny, Yoshida's earlier disavowal of even the right of self-defense under Article IX of the constitution was becoming a sticking point. Refusing to answer "hypothetical questions," Yoshida nonetheless referred to historical precedents in which a foreign military force had remained to observe the vanquished nation's compliance with treaty terms.[21] While formally rejecting a "posttreaty regime of control," he was signaling his willingness to perpetuate the U.S. military presence, two months after MacArthur's decision to that effect. Japan, he began to say in November 1949, possessed the inherent right of self-defense "by diplomatic and other means."[22] He was implying that the constitution sanctioned the U.S. military presence. With the civil war in China ending in the Communist victory in October, Yoshida's predicament became more difficult, as the radical-liberals' demand for total peace and neutrality became popular. They maintained that to continue the state of war with China was to court disaster.

In his New Year's message of 1950 to the Japanese nation, MacArthur seconded Yoshida's interpretation of Article IX of the constitution: he emphatically denied that it deprived Japan of the right of self-defense. Contemporary Japanese reaction was that the general was signaling his consent to rearmament. But his real intent was to ready the Japanese for continued U.S. military presence in Okinawa.[22] Combined with his call for a "Switzerland of Asia," a rejoinder to the JCS and Pentagon, his message seemed to be that if Japan exercises its "right of self-defense" by accommodating the U.S. presence in Okinawa, it can remain unarmed.

In February 1950 the People's Republic of China, scarcely four months old, announced the conclusion of a treaty of alliance with the Soviet Union that was directed specifically at Japan. But by now a willfully ideological solution that bore surface resemblance to "Switzerland of Asia" was winning public acceptance. In early 1950 the Peace Problem Symposium went public for a second time with a communique demanding total peace. The communique rejected "peace in form only, which on the contrary increases the danger for war" by aligning Japan with one side in the Cold War. Avowedly "fundamentalist," the PPS adduced two additional reasons for neutrality: Japan's duty under the constitution; and the need to trade with China for Japan's economic independence, a condition for avoiding political "subservience." Japan's neutrality was to be protected by the United Nations.[24]

In early 1950 the State and Defense departments were still divided over the issues of early peace (or de facto peace) vs. continued occupation. In April Yoshida decided to sound out Washington directly with an offer designed to break the deadlock in his favor. In exchange for early peace, Japan would volunteer to lease bases to the United States and ask the U.S. armed forces to stay. Yoshida's finance minister, Ikeda Hayato, was the emissary to broach the subject to Joseph Dodge, the Detroit banker who had earlier laid down the belt-tightening Dodge Line budget. Dodge, ever since he was dispatched to Tokyo to sidestep MacArthur's chain of command, was Japan's only window on Washington. Ikeda's additional goal was to ask for Dodge's intercession in loosening the budget straightjacket and probe the chances for substantial American aid. The mission was the first of a long series of Yoshida's maneuvers, seeking economic aid for leasing bases.[25]

Ikeda's meeting with Dodge was arranged allegedly without SCAP's knowledge. So when MacArthur discovered the breach in the military chain of command, all hell broke loose at GHQ, and Ikeda had to give a profuse apology.[26] Why did Yoshida take such an obvious risk? I can offer only a speculative answer: Yoshida had been watching MacArthur, by now a good friend, with a mixture of grim satisfaction and pity. The general had impaled himself on the constitution and neutrality and was quite immobilized, while all the Washington bureaucracies, even the State Department, were coming around to accepting a U.S. presence in Japan in some form. Yoshida still needed MacArthur's influence in the tough negotiations ahead and might have decided to give him a chance to back off from neutrality gracefully.[27]

Meanwhile, in June, MacArthur announced the so-called red purge. It was preceded by the Cominform's move to step up subversive activities. In January Cominform (which had succeeded Comintern in the fall of 1947) suddenly launched a campaign of open criticism against the JCP leadership by accusing it of "deceiving" the Japanese people about the true intention of "American imperialism" and of naively believing in the possibility of building a people's democratic government under U.S. occupation through peaceful means.[28]

Cominform was joined shortly thereafter by the Chinese Communist party. Moscow's open criticism shook the JCP, which went into a protracted internal squabble. It was MacArthur who decided the issue for the Japanese Communists, by purging 24 leaders and banning *Akahata* (the Red Flag), the party newspaper, in June. In the red purge that followed, 10,972 civilians and 1,177 government officials, including the leadership of the Sanbetsu federation were

driven from their jobs.[29] The Communists began to fight back with urban guer-
rilla war. At an underground plenary session in October, the JCP formally
declared war and organized an army of partisans, which took its cue from Mao
Tse-tung's strategy and tactics.[30]

MacArthur was notified that in mid-June he was to receive two parties of
Washington VIPs to confer with him on peace. John Foster Dulles, a special
consultant to Secretary of State Dean Acheson, accompanied by John M. Allison, head of the State Department's Office of Northeast Asian Affairs, was one
party. The other consisted of Louis Johnson, secretary of defense, and General
Omar Bradley, chairman of the JCS. The appointment of John Foster Dulles as
special consultant to the secretary of state was made in April by President
Truman. On May 18 Truman placed Dulles in overall charge of the Japanese
peace treaty negotiations. Dulles was a highly visible international lawyer and
an Eastern Establishment Republican. His appointment was intended to
strengthen the Democratic administration's efforts to work out a bipartisan foreign policy with the acrimonious GOP. Simultaneously, the president placed the
State Department in overall charge of peace negotiations with Japan, thereby
subordinating the Pentagon to it. Dulles volunteered for the Japan assignment, a
duty equivalent to that of assistant secretary.

Like Douglas MacArthur, John Foster Dulles came to regard his work
connected with Japan as his greatest achievement. Indeed he worked tirelessly
to offer Japan a generous peace treaty—on the condition that Japan rearmed.
He used MacArthur's influence to restrain Pentagon "imperialism" and then
used the latter as a stick with which to goad Yoshida into rearming. But there
was a serious ambivalence in him, which caused him to alienate all three
political groups in Japan: he was not the sort to take a liking to the Socialists; he
put considerable pressure on Yoshida to have him agree to a constitutional
revision and rearmament; and he ended up undermining the revisionist prime
minister Hatoyama's peace treaty with the Soviet Union. Regarding him almost
as a synonum for the Cold War, the Japanese have refused to give him credit for
his efforts. Standard history that speaks for Yoshida's point of view ignores
him.

Son of a Presbyterian minister, Dulles was a devout Christian, and in his
dying days he would find solace in listening to recorded hymns such as "The
Spacious Firmament on High" and "Through the Night of Doubt and Sor-
row."[31] He shared a peculiar American inclination to moralize foreign relations
("Neutralism is immoral"). For better or worse, it was part of his personality
to view international communism in moral terms. But his Christian universalism was the warp and woof of good internationalism. It showed in his efforts to
enlist Japan as an ally over the objection of the Defense Department. He had

been a member of the American delegation at the peace conference in Versailles and a U.S. representative on the Reparations Committee, but left Paris in disgust after unsuccessfully trying to overcome the Allies' rapacity toward Germany. He was thoroughly convinced of the thesis that the Great Depression and beggar-thy-neighbor protectionism had been the major cause of World War II. In drafting the peace treaty with Japan, he tried consciously to end what he called the "vicious cycle of war-victory-peace-war."

Dulles repeatedly expressed his worries over the prospect of tearing Japan away from Asia and of integrating it with the West, and he entertained the idea of inviting Japan to join what he called an "elite Anglo-Saxon Club":

> I have a feeling that the Japanese people have felt a certain superiority as against the Asiatic mainland masses. Perhaps not a superiority as against the ancient cultures of China, from which they have drawn very heavily. But they have felt that the Western civilization represented by Britain, more latterly the United States, is perhaps sharing in that, represents a certain triumph of mind over mass which gives us a social standing in the world better than what is being achieved in terms of the mainland human masses of Asia, and that they think that they have also achieved somewhat the similar superiority of mind over mass and would like to feel that they belong to, or are accepted by, the Western nations. And I think that anything we can do to encourage that feeling will set up an attraction which is calculated to hold the Japanese in friendly association with us . . . [32]

In Dulles's mind such an elite club was a cultural analogue of the Anglo-Japanese alliance. He knew it was out of the question to replicate that type of alliance between the United States and Japan. This was the dilemma that would haunt him (and those Japanese who agreed with him) from here on. As an individual, he was free of MacArthur's sort of particularism based on race. It was inconceivable that a sovereign nation should forgo the right of self-defense, the sine qua none of independence and autonomy. Yet, Japan's arms of limited capability would be under tight American control. On the U.S.-Japanese tie he was trying to construct, he said he wanted

> the relationship of mutual security . . . under which presumably the military power would be so apportioned that *Japan could not itself be an offensive military threat* and the relationship between the victor and vanquished would be so intimate and integrated as *to make incredible a war of revenge*. [33]

Japan was made to depend on and to integrate itself with the United States to the point where revanchism may be preempted. But whether such integration would leave room for autonomy was open to doubt. Therefore, it was difficult to say who was the fairest: Defense Secretary Louis Johnson, with his unabashed

"imperialism"; MacArthur who postulated a comfortable dependency status; or
Dulles, with his formal equality in a limited rearmament. One thing was certain. Peace or no peace, Japan was starting from a very low standing. This
point was the strongest defense for Yoshida's policy of "realism."

As Dulles and Johnson arrived in Tokyo, neither State nor Defense was
giving an inch, and MacArthur had reason to believe that he could shape the
final American decision through his mediation. He wrote his position on peace
in two memoranda and handed them to Johnson and Dulles.[34] In the memoranda
MacArthur still paid lip service to neutrality but in fact accepted a permanent
U.S. military presence in Japan, the idea Yoshida had broached in Washington.
The military would have far-reaching, unrestricted freedom in all of Japan with
no time limit. There was little give on this point at the Pentagon, and it was the
bottomline of the U.S. position. MacArthur found a justification for the garri-
soning in a novel interpretation of the Potsdam Declaration, which demanded
that "irresponsible militarism" be "driven from the world." MacArthur found
that Japanese militarism had indeed been driven out in fulfillment of the declaration, but that a new militarism had raised its head elsewhere. Therefore the
declaration empowered the United States to remain in Japan![35]

MacArthur tried—not very successfully—to split the State-Defense difference in the bureaucratic war. Dulles would write a peace treaty respecting
Japan's formal equality. After its conclusion, an "independent" Japan would
enter into a security treaty of its own accord. The two treaties would make a
package. Japan would get independence and protection and the United States
military bases. Although Japan would rebuff the demand of Dulles and the JCS
for rearmament, they cannot penalize it because MacArthur would write the
security treaty respecting Japan's "free ride" and its sensibilities. I also suspect
that it was MacArthur's bureaucratic desire to let the Pentagon write its own
status-of-forces agreement as a separate document, so that his treaty would be
free of odium.

While in Tokyo, on June 22—three days before the Korean War started—
Dulles had his first encounter with Yoshida at the home of William Sebald,
POLAD, who left this memorable record:

> Yoshida arrived precisely on time, nattily dressed as always and completely at
> ease. But he was in one of his puckish moods, when in Western terms he refused
> to talk "sense." Dulles, a man not given to small talk under any circumstances,
> tried to steer the conversation toward a discussion of Japan's security. Yoshida
> would have none of this. Smiling and with chuckles, he spoke with circumlocu-
> tory indirectness, with vagueness, and with an astute use of parables. He refused
> to commit himself in the slightest way. "Yes," he said, "security for Japan is

possible, and the United States can take care of it. But Japan's *amour propre* must be preserved in doing so." In any event, the prime minister said, Japan could have security through her own devices, by being democratic, demilitarized, and peace-loving and by relying upon the protection of world opinion. Dulles was flabbergasted. He refused to follow this line of reasoning, and finally abandoned all attempts to discuss other matters. Later he told me he felt very much like Alice in Wonderland. I counseled patience, for this was only a "get acquainted" meeting, making the first round. I did not point out that Yoshida's rationale for security used the very words so often employed in Far Eastern Commission policy decisions.[36]

Yoshida was parrotting back to Dulles the Allies' lectures and reproaches to the vanquished Japan. This was just the beginning of what Dulles was to call Yoshida's "puff ball performance."[37] With Douglas MacArthur in his pocket following the secret compact, the prime minister of occupied Japan had nothing to fear from the U.S. Department of State. For Yoshida the constitution had already served the purpose of saving the throne; he was now using it to protect Japan's "amour propre." He seemed to imply that the proud Japanese nation would rather remain aloof from military entanglement with the United States and do its own thing. Later, he told a bemused American official in the course of conversation on the peace treaty, "When it is objected that Japan will become a colony of the United States, [I] always repl[y] that, just as the United States was once a colony of Great Britain but now is the stronger of the two, if Japan becomes a colony of the United States, it will also eventually become the stronger!"[38]

On June 25 the world was shaken with the news of war in Korea. The most intense phase of the Cold War had begun. Washington braced itself for the possibility that Korea was a feint to draw American forces away from a full-scale assault on the NATO front. But President Truman acted on the lesson of Munich, approving NSC 68, a major decision marking a departure in containment. Reversing himself on both Korea and Taiwan, he ordered MacArthur's forces into Korea under UN auspices. A de facto American guarantee of Japan's security was now in place. Yoshida felt the war was a "godsend."[39] In late October the Chinese People's Volunteer units began to make contact with the UN forces. American public opinion, which had been shifting lately in Japan's favor, completed the swing. China and Japan swapped places, as the American public resented the Chinese "betrayal." It was not uncommon in those dark days for an American to take a Japanese by the arm and say, "We fought the wrong enemy." In the high tide of new globalism occasioned by the war, George Kennan was losing his influence at the State Department. He took his case to the public. At the University of Chicago he lectured as follows:

It is an ironic fact that today our past objectives in Asia are ostensibly in large measure achieved. The Western powers have lost the last of their special positions in China. The Japanese are finally out of China proper and out of Manchuria and Korea as well. The effects of their expulsion from those areas have been precisely what wise and realistic people warned us all along they would be. Today we have fallen heir to the problems and responsibilities the Japanese had faced and borne in the Korean-Manchurian area for nearly half a century, and there is a certain perverse justice in the pain we are suffering from a burden which, when it was borne by others, we held in such low esteem. What is saddest of all is that the relationship between past and present seems to be visible to so few people. For if we are not to learn from our own mistakes, where shall we learn at all?[40]

Kennan's book became reference material at Gaimusho and circulated widely. If Yoshida read it, as undoubtedly he did, it must have struck the imperialist in him with bittersweet irony. America had come full circle, back to Theodore Roosevelt's position and was embracing Japan, fulfilling Yoshida's wish. But Yoshida's troubles in his balancing act was only beginning. To make a partner out of Japan, U.S. pressure for rearmament was stepped up immediately after the North Korean invasion.

In a letter dated July 8, 1950, MacArthur had ordered the National Police Reserve of 75,000 men into existence to fill the vacuum left by the wholesale dispatch of American troops to Korea. This was done on his own initiative and without prior instruction from Washington. Justin Williams, a GS official, called in the leaders of two opposition parties, the JSP and former Minseito, and told them that the Diet had no power to discuss the Police Reserve issue, and that any violation of his order would be punished.[41] A mere executive order seemed to override the constitution and founded what everyone thought was a new Japanese army. Later, in October 1950, another SCAP order—this time secret—had created minesweeper units manned by former Japanese naval personnel, and they were deployed around the Korean coast.[42] Here was the origin of Japan's illegitimate army and the never-ending controversy over it. The opposition leaders quietly resolved to defy the decision when they regained freedom. But in retrospect, the supreme commander intended to create nothing more than an armed police force.

In the summer of 1950 the fighting in Korea was a rout for the UN forces. The combined U.S.-South Korean forces, driven into a tiny perimeter around Pusan on the southern tip of the peninsula, were ordered to "hold or die." Another Dunkirk seemed imminent. A rumor began to circulate that the United States was going to deploy Japanese "volunteers" in Korea.[43] Syngman Rhee, the president of South Korea, vowed that if the Japanese troops were thrown in, he would join the North Koreans and turn his guns against the Japanese.

The idea of Japanese volunteers no doubt turned Yoshida's stomach also, for he had presided over Japan's eviction from the empire a mere five years ago.[44] Korea was not Japan's war as far as he was concerned. Even though a defeat seemed imminent in the summer, Yoshida did not blink. In fact he raised the ante against the Americans. During an interpellation in the Foreign Affairs Committee of the lower house in July, he reneged on his earlier offer to volunteer base-leasing rights. "I am against leasing military bases to any foreign country," he said, "Allied powers do not intend to present such a demand, as it is the desire of the Allied powers to keep Japan out of war." Apparently, this was a very important move on Yoshida's part, for he instructed the vice minister of foreign affairs to call the attention of all foreign missions to his stand.[45]

The idea of sending Japanese troops to Korea enjoyed wide circulation at the time. The American military talked of it; Ashida in the conservative opposition championed the idea of Japanese volunteers for the UN forces.[46] Is it possible that Yoshida's objections to rearmament rested on his objections to seeing Japanese blood spilled in Korea? If that was so, he could well have been a hero to the entire spectrum of Japanese from the right to left. But he was mute on his motive, and, in any case, MacArthur scotched the idea of volunteers on August 8.

The Japanese did not know of Yoshida's secret offer of bases to begin with. All they could see was that the prime minister was acting like the Socialists. This was ironic. The Korean War did awaken the Japanese from what Dulles called "postwar stupor." A nationwide *Asahi* poll of September showed 21.4 percent in favor of "total peace," 45.6 percent in favor of "partial peace," and 33 percent undecided. On the keeping of U.S. bases beyond the peace treaty, 29.9 percent said yes and 37.5 percent no. On rearmament, 53.8 percent was in favor, 27.6 percent opposed.[47] Though the JSP's pacifism was already quite advanced, it was trying to distinguish itself from the JCP by stressing its even-handedness between the two superpowers: it denounced the North Korean invasion.

The Korean War's immediate consequence on domestic politics was that Ashida Hitoshi, former prime minister and leader of former Minseito, became an advocate of rearmament. Always in constant contact with SCAP officials including "Ambassador" Sebald, he was quick to see the shift in Washington's policy and the gap between that and Yoshida. It would not be surprising if Ashida saw a political chance for himself in taking up Washington's cause against Yoshida. Ashida went public with the idea of Japanese volunteers for the UN forces, as noted above. In short order, he began advocating rearmament, moving further to the Right. For the first time, Japan acquired an organized lobby for rearmament, which would be later reinforced when the purged leaders returned. Ultimately, Ashida would carry former Minseito with him on the rearmament issue.[48] That meant he was finally abandoning the idea of centrist coalition with the Socialists as a whole, although he kept close liaison with Nishio Suehiro of the rightwing.

Once hostilities began, the Defense Department and the JCS became even more adamant in opposing peace with Japan—for the duration of the war. In contrast, State agreed to Japan's rearmament at last. Dulles saw in Japan's awakening a golden opportunity for forging an alliance. Truman repudiated the Pentagon by replacing Louis Johnson with George Marshall[49] and authorized a go-ahead on peace negotiations on September 14, the day before the Inchon landing. The understanding was codified into the Seven Point statement Dulles distributed to Allied powers in October, but neither the Soviets nor the Chinese were expected to support it.

With minor modifications, this was to be the shape of peace at San Francisco. The United States placed no formal restrictions on Japan's rearmament and desired to waive further reparations.[50] In spite of Yoshida's strong objections, Japan would be compelled to agree to trusteeship status for the Ryukyus (Okinawa) and Bonin Islands, to be used as U.S. military bases. The Pentagon was adamant on getting unrestricted use of these islands. Japan would renounce its claim to Sakhalin, the Kurile Islands, the Pescadores, and Formosa without naming the claimant.[51]

The trouble was with the bilateral defense treaty that Japan accepted, in its own mind, as a price of peace and independence. The crisis in Korea vastly strengthened the Pentagon's hands. For instance, there were some 1,300 military installations in Japan, a country no larger than Montana, and, using the right of eminent domain, the U.S. forces expanded them because of the war. The war in Korea, Yoshida's "godsend," turned out to be doubled-edged. That in turn, I infer, fortified Yoshida's resolve to add nothing to his offer of bases. With the announcement of the Seven Point statement, Yoshida and Foreign Ministry officials began drafting their own counterproposals. As a bargaining ploy, he ordered a draft of a four-power pact guaranteeing Japan's neutrality and demilitarization of Korea and the western Pacific.

Negotiations began with the arrival of Dulles, now formally ambassador, in Tokyo on January 25, 1951. It was a grave moment for the United States in Korea. The Chinese Communist forces, which had been nibbling around the edges of the UN forces that had reached the Yalu River, had launched a general counteroffensive on November 25 with a force estimated at 200,000. The UN forces retreated south, and MacArthur recommended extension of the war to the Chinese rear in Manchuria. Truman had declared a national emergency on December 17; Washington braced for World War III. A National Security Council paper in May was to order abandonment of Korea in the event of general war with the Soviet Union.[52]

Yoshida remained cool, collected, and calculating through the crisis. He was secretly in contact with two leaders of the JSP leftwing, Katsumada Seiichi and Suzuki Mosaburo, to request their agitation against rearmament.[53] Yoshida needed a cheering section to back up his neutrality option in negotiations with Dulles. This was the only instance of the kind that can be documented, but it was undoubtedly the tip of the iceberg. We must note that only the leftwing Socialists, with their adamant stand on the constitution and rearmament, would serve as Yoshida's proxy.[54]

During the first session, on January 29, Dulles seized on Yoshida's demand for independence to ask what sort of "contributions" he was prepared to make as "a member of the free world." Yoshida understood what that meant but refused to commit himself to rearmament. It may be recalled that during their first meeting the previous June Yoshida managed to evade Dulles with a "puff ball performance," as Dulles called it. But this time Yoshida was emphatic and specific about his reason for objecting to rearmament: "the danger that any pricipitate rearmament would bring back the Japanese militarists who had now gone 'underground.' "[55] The economic risk of rearmament was relegated to a secondary place.

We must make a digression here to explain what Yoshida was saying. It appears that, knowing Yoshida's and MacArthur's refusal to rearm, Dulles had been looking for a Japanese ally. An intermediary to bring them together was forthcoming in the persons of Harry F. Kern and Comton Packenhem, *Newsweek* magazine's foreign editor and Tokyo correspondent, respectively. The two had earlier attacked SCAP's *zaibatsu* liquidation as too radical; then criticized the purge of Ishibashi Tanzan, Yoshida's finance minister, as unfair. Seeking reentry to Japan after a vacation at home, Packenhem was denied permission by General Whitney, director of the GS, and he had to ask Kenneth Royall, army secretary, to overrule Whitney. By an arrangement made prior to Dulles's arrival, the two newsmen were to introduce him to a group of Japanese leaders under purge ("underground"). This was doubly difficult. Dulles was extremely fearful of offending MacArthur, but his need for an ally overcame that fear. MacAuthur and Yoshida obviously had reasons to suspect that Kern and Packenhem were up to something, for MacAuthur kept all three parties— the Dulles mission, the American newsmen, and the prospective Japanese leaders—under close surveillance of MPs. One planned meeting was aborted when military policemen intruded. But a meeting of Hatoyama Ichiro, Ishibashi, and one more Japanese with Dulles took place on February 6. Hatoyama told Dulles that the Japanese must defend their country against "red" influence and they must be more self-reliant militarily, although he declined to send Japanese troops to Korea.[56] Dulles was pleased to have met Hatoyama. The meeting was reported, just after MacAuthur's dismissal as SCAP in April, in a UP dispatch quoting Dulles as saying that Japan needed a "strong man."[57]

Though Dulles's meeting with Hatoyama was one week into the future when he met Yoshida, both he and Yoshida presumably understood what each other was saying and doing. It is doubtful that Hatoyama's "militarism" shocked Dulles, for Dulles was extremely displeased with Yoshida.[58] Having wasted their appointed hour, the two men went to see MacArthur as scheduled. Upon hearing from Yoshida that Ambassador Dulles had been torturing him, Mac-Arthur smiled and volunteered the suggestion that Japan's old arsenals and idle facilities belonging to the imperial army and navy be used in lieu of rearmament. But this first session might as well have been theatre, played according to a script. The day after the Dulles mission arrived in Tokyo, or three days before Dulles met Yoshida, a staff meeting of the mission was held, from which the following was recorded:

> Ambassador Dulles said that he had relied on General MacArthur's judgment as to the type of peace which could be made, and that the proposals which he would be trying to sell to the Japanese were basically General MacArthur's. If he failed he did not want to have placed himself in a position where it could be charged that the failure was due to the fact that General MacArthur had not been present to express his own views. His help was important particularly in connection with the bilateral [defense treaty]. Do we get the right to station as many troops in Japan as we want where we want and for as long as we want or do we not? *That is the principal question*, and we have proceeded blindly on that basis. *Any government which does give us such privileges, however, will be vulnerable to attack as having permitted a derogation of Japan's sovereignty.* Our proposal is going to be difficult to put across. General MacArthur's influence is likely to be decisive; it is doubtful if the Mission can succeed without his help.[59]

The meeting also heard from Sebald that MacArthur met with Yoshida a week before the mission's arrival and that at this meeting the general "laid the groundwork for the Mission's task." The staff meeting agreed that "Ambassador Dulles would not endeavor to persuade General MacArthur to change his conception of his basic role."[60] Dulles was at the mercy of MacArthur for the Senate passage of his two treaties. Out of power for nearly two decades, the disgruntled Republicans had seized on America's recent setbacks as an issue with which to attack and supplant the Democrats. Yalta, the "loss of China," and the alleged menace of international communism at home all played into their hands. But MacArthur's stock reached an all-time high with the Inchon landing, and powerful Senate Republican lawmakers were rallying behind him as a presidential candidate in the 1952 race. On the morning of January 29, several hours prior to the meeting with Yoshida, Dulles observed: "General MacArthur must be one hundred percent behind the treaty. If he were to indicate that it did not exactly reflect his thinking or that he had been left out the treaty would be attacked by the Hearst-McCormick press and might be defeated in the Senate."[61]

The foregoing is the major evidence that leads me to posit a fourth MacArthur intervention on behalf of his constitution. Dulles complained of "localitis" among occupation administrators, but he bowed to the need to have MacArthur's endorsement by accepting the constitution as the premise of U.S.-Japanese relations.[62]

However, Dulles did badger Yoshida to see if he could get a "commitment to a general cause of collective security" and "a token contribution."[63] He rested his case on the Vandenburg Resolution, passed by the Senate in June 1948, as the basis for U.S. participation in NATO and calling for regional collective security, self-help, and mutual aid. Dulles's forcefulness took Yoshida by surprise. Yoshida hastily ordered a draft entitled "Initial Steps for Rearmament Planning" and presented it to the Dulles mission on February 3. The draft called for a 50,000-man force, to be called Hoan-tai (Security Forces), still constabulary in nature. With this move, Yoshida agreed to Japan's rearmament against direct external threat in the near future. Presumably what Yoshida had in mind was an army that can fight only on Japan's soil.[64] Yoshida also verbally promised to Dulles on this occasion that Japan would establish some equivalent of a defense department and a general staff. The agreements left out the constitutional question for the time being. Dulles felt that "the US cannot press the Japanese to assume military obligations until they have dealt with their constitutional problem."[65]

The treaty draft that resulted from this round of sessions stated that Japan has the right to enter into collective security arrangements when she is fully rearmed in the future, that Japan grants and the United States accepts the right to maintain armed forces of its own in and about Japan so as to deter armed attack upon Japan, and that the sole purpose of this measure is to defend Japan from external attack and not to interfere in Japan's domestic affairs.[66] These terms were very generous to Japan and in stark contrast to the treaty that was actually concluded, as will be shown. Yoshida sent the Dulles mission off in a jovial mood.

On April 11, scarcely two months later, President Truman announced the dismissal of General MacArthur. Immediately, Ambassador Sebald called on Yoshida to inform him of the event. "Prime minister was visibly shaken,"

Sebald recalled, "and said that the departure of General MacArthur would come as a tremendous shock to the Japanese people. He added he feels personally indebted to MacArthur to whose guidance he attributes his political success and to whose influence he attributes preservation of the Emperor institution."[67] Five days later MacArthur was gone.

Immediately upon the dismissal, the Yoshida government was notified that Dulles was to return in order allegedly to reassure it of the continuity of U.S. policies. Reflecting the government's apprehension, *Asahi* headlined, "No change in the peace terms: the government's hopes for Mr. Dulles."[68] What transpired in the mid-April meeting of the two sides has been a closely held secret. Judging from what happened to the treaty, Dulles seems to have reopened the rearmament issue—to renegotiate the whole treaty. Could it be that Dulles could not control the JCS in the absence of MacArthur? In any case it was politically impossible for Yoshida to make a turnaround on such a major policy. MacArthur's fourth intervention as well as all the troubles Yoshida endured in order to earn it came to naught. This was a second time since the Potsdam Declaration, Yoshida might have felt, that an American promise turned sour. Although this is strictly an inference, it would be difficult to explain Yoshida's subsequent conduct on any other basis.

Because of the two-China problem, neither the Taipei nor the Peking government was invited to the negotiations or to the peace conference. Japan had to conclude peace with one or the other. Dean Acheson was willing to leave the choice to Japan, but Dulles insisted on Taipei over Peking withholding Senate ratification unless Japan chose Taipei. Yoshida agreed to this arrangement in a letter of May 1951 to Dulles.[69] The loss of the China market and diplomatic autonomy would put him in a major difficulty later.

There was a fourth party to the negotiation of the peace and security treaties—the opposition parties and the people of Japan. "Bipartisanship" was proposed first by former Minseito just before Dulles's arrival in Tokyo in June 1950. (I put bipartisan in brackets because there were four parties at the time.) This party was in favor of "early" and "separate peace" with the United States. John Foster Dulles, too, tirelessly preached the virtue of "bipartisan" support for the treaties. More than once, Ashida and Dulles tried to prevail on Yoshida to consult the opposition parties. Ashida's former Minseito, previously in coalition with the JSP, even made the JSP's cooperation with Yoshida a condition of its own cooperation with him. In Ashida's judgment, an attempt to carry the rightwing, rather than driving it into the embrace of the Left, was worth a try. Yoshida went through a rather perfunctory motion of negotiating with Katayama and other Socialists, but by late 1950 both sides gave up. In the January 1951 party congress, former Minseito decided to side with Yoshida even in the absence of JSP cooperation. This was the end of the road.

As shown in the remainder of this book, the JSP's opposition to the treaties and Japan's inability to recreate the centrist coalition was to cripple Japan's foreign policy. One can make a plausible case that Yoshida could have prevented those consequences but did not. But why not? Why was he so cool toward "bipartisanship" with the JSP? His handling of former Minseito was also peculiar: Ashida was offering his cooperation over the treaties, but instead of accepting it Yoshida split the Inukai faction away from Ashida. That is not the sort of thing to do when one needs someone else's favor. It is legitimate to ask if Yoshida was acting with a deliberate design.

In the absence of further evidence, we can merely speculate. It is possible that the decisive issue for Yoshida was rearmament, not the treaties. For treaty ratification, he already had an adequate majority of 288, following the Inukai defection in February 1950.[70] He did not need the votes of Ashida or the Socialists. Yoshida did not control the upper house, to be sure. But the constitution stipulates that in treaty ratifications the will of the lower house prevails if the upper house contradicts it. Besides, Ashida would not vote against the two treaties in any case. But being a fervent advocate of rearmament, Ashida could demand it in exchange for voting with Yoshida if Yoshida were to count on his "bipartisan" support. As for the leftwing Socialists, not only did Yoshida not need their votes but he was presumably counting on their objection to rearmament. It was best to leave them alone.

During the April visit, Dulles once again sought a meeting with the JSP leaders to plead for "bipartisan" support, but it was a lost cause. After the unsuccessful meeting broke up, Justin Williams, a GS official and MacArthur loyalist, suggested to the Socialists behind Dulles's back that they might split their votes by supporting the peace treaty but opposing the security treaty (under renegotiation).[71] By July the security treaty was ready for signing, and Dulles wrote to Yoshida asking for his presence in San Francisco—rather than in Tokyo as MacArthur originally planned—in September as head of the Japanese delegation. Apparently Yoshida became reluctant to go. On August 4 SCAP GHQ delivered the final draft of the security treaty to Gaimusho with a request not to divulge its content, so as allegedly not to invite Sino-Soviet denunciation. The peace treaty draft was made public on August 16. So Yoshida had to ask for the oppositions' participation in the delegation without showing the defense treaty draft. The JSP refused. When former Minseito put the question to vote, parliamentary members were split 57 to 26 in favor.

The next scene was September 8, 1951 in San Francisco. At a ceremony that commenced at 10 o'clock in the morning in the Opera House, delegates of 48 nations signed the peace treaty. The Soviet Union, Poland, and Czechoslovakia abstained. The two Chinese governments had not been invited, and the governments of India, Burma, and Yugoslavia had declined invitation. New Delhi was showing its displeasure at American "imperialism" over the retention of Okinawa and the Bonins. To all appearance, it was an occasion marked by an effusion of friendship and conciliation with Yoshida and Dulles basking in applause and attention.

But the opposition members of the Japanese delegation were uncomfortable. Yoshida was asked by Dean Acheson, chairman of the conference, not to mention the security treaty during the proceedings. Furthermore, Yoshida told his fellow delegates that the security treaty signing had been postponed. Following the peace treaty signing, at about eleven o'clock in the evening, however, a State Department official abruptly notified Yoshida that the security treaty would be signed at five o'clock in the afternoon of the following day. At this point, the Minseito delegation had neither seen nor been briefed on the treaty at all. The delegation felt that the whole procedure made a mockery of the pretense that an "independent" Japan was voluntarily entering into the security treaty. It refused to participate.[72] It was the JCS that demanded this procedure out of fear that Japan might renege on the security treaty.

At the appointed hour, the Presidio at the tip of the San Francisco peninsula was shrouded in chilly fog. Yoshida was the sole plenipotentiary to sign for Japan. As he related jocularly later, he expected to be stoned back home for consenting to the stationing of American forces, and he wished Finance Minister Ikeda, a member of the delegation whom he was grooming as his successor, to be spared the blame.

As a result of the Yoshida-Dulles collision, the security treaty of 1951 has had these highly unusual features: It was avowedly provisional. All the obligations were born by Japan and none by the United States. Japan agreed to lease bases, and the U.S. guarantee to protect Japan was de facto, stemming from its right to station troops in Japan. The United States reserved to itself the right to intervene in Japan's domestic disorder as well as the right to veto a third power's military presence in Japan. The Defense Department demanded and received the so-called Far Eastern clause, permitting the United States to use the Japanese bases in defense not only of Japan but of the American interests in the Far East.[73] But there was no clause for "prior consultation" in the face of common danger, an elementary feature of an alliance treaty. The United States was at liberty to project its forces in Japan against the Soviet Union or China without Japan's consent. These provisions were added by Dulles after MacArthur's dismissal.

Furthermore, there was no provision for consultation for movements of U.S.

forces and nuclear arms in and out of Japan. The treaty had no time limits; if the United States refused to consent to a revision or abrogation, it could remain in Japan indefinitely. One may also add that in a supplementary agreement, concluded later and explained below, the United States secured the extraterritorial rights to remove the trials of common crimes committed by its servicemen and their dependents from Japanese courts, rights it did not demand of the Federal Republic of Germany.[74]

Yoshida's critics knew nothing of the fourth intervention or its demise. They reacted to the treaty the way Dulles probably expected them to. To those on Yoshida's right and left, this was a colonial treaty. Even the Gaimusho bureaucracy, wholly under Yoshida's control, contained pockets of discontent. Worst of all, Yoshida's conservative critics were led to believe that he had colluded with MacArthur to write this unequal treaty.

# NOTES

1. For a sample of the view at the Pentagon, see *Foreign Relations of the United States* (Washington, DC: GPO, 1976), 1949, VII, Pt. 2, 884; see also NCS 49 in *FRUS*, VII, Pt. 2, 872.

2. Seigen Miyazato, "Amerika gasshukoku seifu to tai-Nichi kowa" [The United States government and peace with Japan], Akio Watanabe and Seigen Miyazato, eds., *Sanfuranshisuko kowa* [The San Francisco peace] (Tokyo: Tokyo Univ. Press, 1986), p. 122; Takeshi Igarashi, *Tai-Nichi kowa to reisen: sengo Nichi-Bei kankei no keisei* [The peace treaty with Japan and the Cold War: the formation of postwar Japan-U.S. relations] Tokyo: Tokyo Univ. Press, 1986), p. 157; Chihiro Hosoya, *Sanfuranshisuko eno michi* [The road to San Francisco] (Tokyo: Chuo Koronsha, 1984), p. 55. See also Frederick S. Dunn, *Peace-Making and the Settlement with Japan* (Princeton, NJ: Princeton Univ. Press, 1963).

3. *FRUS*, 1949, VII, 907.

4. Miyazato, p. 122.

5. *FRUS*, 1950, VI, 1128, 1134.

6. NSC 44. This was an attempt to revise NSC 13/2 but it was stillborn. Miyazato, pp. 119–20.

7. *FRUS*, 1950, VI, 1134–35; *FRUS*, 1951, VI, Pt. 1, 1286.

8. *FRUS*, 1949, VII, Pt. 2, 978, ff.

9. Miyazato, p. 126.

10. Igarashi, *Tai-Nichi kowa*, p. 183.

11. In February 1950, *FRUS*, 1950, VI, 1134–35.

12. He seemed to discount the chance of isolated Soviet invasion of Japan, which the Pentagon feared. With superior naval and air power, the United States would control the chain of islands from Japan through Okinawa and Taiwan to the Philippines.

13. Martin E. Weinstein, *Japan's Postwar Defense Policy, 1947–1968* (New York: Columbia Univ. Press, 1971), is full of admiration and no grudge.

14. Quotations are form Shigeru Yoshida, *Kaiso junen* [Recollections of ten years] (Tokyo: Shinchosha, 1958), II, 114; see also Weinstein, pp. 23–31; Michael Yoshitsu, *Japan and the San Francisco Peace Settlement* (New York: Columbia Univ. Press, 1983), pp. 15–20. See also Gaimusho, *Kokkai ni okeru kowa rongi* [Deliberations on the peace treaty in the Diet] (Tokyo: Gaimusho, 1951).

15. Kashima Heiwa Kenkyujo, ed., *Nihon gaikoshi* [Japan's diplomatic history], Vol. 27, Kumao Nishimura, *Sanfuranshisuko heiwa joyaku* [The San Francisco peace treaty] (Tokyo: Kashima Heiwa Kenkyujo, 1981), p. 82.

16. *Nihon Shakaito no sanjunen*, I, 26–27.

17. Masatoshi Sakeda, "Kowa to kokunai seiji" [The peace treaty and domestic politics], in Akio Watanabe, *Sanfuranshisuko kowa* [The San Francisco peace conference] (Tokyo: Tokyo University Press, 1986), p. 94.

18. *Nihon Shakaito no sanju-nen*, I, 226–229.

19. For instance, the 1947 peace proposal drafted by the Japanese Foreign Ministry was rejected by SCAP. Michael M. Yoshitsu, *Japan and the San Francisco Peace Settlement* (New York: Columbia Univ. Press, 1983), p. 11. Yoshida was criticized by the *New York Times* in November 1949 for defiance. See Igarashi, *Tai-Nichi kowa*, p. 211.

20. See Sebald's memorandum in *FRUS*, 1949, VII, Pt. 2, p. 862.

21. In the Budget Committee of the House of Councilors on November 28, 1949. The Ministry of Foreign Affairs, *Kokkai ni okeru kowa rongi* [Deliberations on the peace treaty in the Diet] (Tokyo: Gaimusho, 1951), p. 314.

22. Yoshitsu, p. 29.

23. *FRUS*, 1950, VI, 1167.

24. *Sekai*, July 1985, pp. 108–17.

25. Yumi Hiwatari, *Sengo seiji to Nichi-Bei kankei* (Postwar politics and the Japan-U.S. relations] (Tokyo: Univ. of Tokyo Press, 1990), pp. 28–30.

26. Yoshitsu, pp. 32–37.

27. MacArthur himself indicated in April 1950 that his stand on neutrality was designed to entice the Japanese to come forward voluntarily to offer bases. *FRUS*, 1950, VI, 1168. I would not rule out the possibility that the entire script, including MacArthur's censure of Ikeda upon his return, was written by him and Yoshida together. Note that this sort of thing was in Yoshida's repertoire of bureaucratic gamesmanship. See Chapter 3.

28. See Igarashi, *Tai-Nichi kowa*, pp. 171–81, for the best discussion of this topic including SCAP counterintelligence reports on clandestine activities.

29. *Nihon naikaku shiroku*, V, 204. I fail to understand this move to drive the radicals underground, since the purge had to be undone in one year when the occupation ended. It is particularly puzzling since MacArthur refused to recentralize the police apparatus.

30. Koken Oyama, *Sengo Nihon Kyosanto shi* [History of the postwar Japan Communist Party] (Tokyo: Haga Shoten, 1969), pp. 133–40.

31. Michael A. Guhin, *John Foster Dulles: A Statesman And His Times* (New York: Columbia Univ. Press, 1972), p. 1. See also Deane Heller, *John Foster Dulles: Soldier of Peace* (New York: Holt, Rinehart & Winston, 1960); Eleanor Lansing Dulles, *John Foster Dulles, The Last Years* (New York: Harcourt, Brace, 1963).

32. *FRUS*, 1951, VI, 825–26.

33. *FRUS*, 1951, VI, 1115. (Emphasis added.)

34. *FRUS,* 1950, VI, 1213–21; *FRUS,* 1950, VI, 1227–28. See also Sebald's statement to this effect, in William J. Sebald, *With MacArthur in Japan: A Personal History of the Occupation* (New York: W. W. Norton, 1965), p. 256.

35. *FRUS,* 1950, VI, 1120–21.

36. Sebald, pp. 257–58. Emphasis added.

37. *FRUS,* 1951, VI, 832.

38. *FRUS,* 1950, VI, 1166.

39. John W. Dower, *Empire and Aftermath: Yoshida Shigeru and the Japanese Experience, 1878–1945* (Cambridge: Harvard University Press, 1979), p. 316; see also John Lewis Gaddis, *Strategies of Containment: A Critical Appraisal of Postwar American National Security Policy* (New York: Oxford Univ. Press, 1982), Chapter 4.

40. *American Diplomacy, 1900–1950* (Chicago: Univ. of Chicago Press, 1951), p. 52.

41. Hideo Otake, "Yoshida naikaku ni yoru saigunbi," *Hogaku* (October 1986), p. 515; Hideo Otake, *Saigunbi to nashonarizumu* [Rearmament and nationalism] (Tokyo: Chuo Koronsha, 1988), chapter II.

42. Yomiuri Shimbunsha, *"Saigunbi" no kiseki* [The track of "rearmament"] (Tokyo: Yomiuri Shimbunsha, 1981), pp. 174–75.

43. See Diet interpellation on this point, in *Nich-Bei anpo joyaku taisei shi* [A history of the Japan-U.S. security treaty system] (Tokyo: Sanseido, 1970), II, 20–28.

44. For Yoshida's objection to the idea of Japanese volunteers in the Diet, see Shinobu, *Sengo Nihon seijishi,* IV, 1166.

45. See *FRUS,* 1950, VI, 1262–64.

46. Hitoshi Ashida, *Ashida Hitoshi nikki* [The Ashida Hitoshi diary] (Tokyo: Iwanami Shoten, 1981), III, 328.

47. Cited in Igarashi, *Tai-Nichi kowa,* p, 242.

48. Ashida, III, 328; IV, 155, 167; Hideo Otake, *Saigunbi to nashonarizumu,* pp. 127–45.

49. NCS 60/1 of September 8. See Miyazato, pp. 128–29.

50. The waiver was later amended because of a strong objection from Manila.

51. It may be borne in mind, however, that had the Soviet Union chosen to be a signatory to the San Francisco peace treaty, the American officials were inclined to cede the Kuriles and Sakhalin to it. *FRUS,* 1951, VI, 795.

52. NSC, 48/4, cited in *FRUS,* 1951, VI, 38. British intelligence anticipated a Soviet military move toward Hokkaido in January, and it was feared in Washington that Dulles's trip to Japan might provoke an invasion.

53. Takeshi Igarashi, "Peace Making and Party Politics: The Formation of the Domestic Foreign-Policy System in Postwar Japan," *Journal of Japanese Studies,* Summer 1985, p. 350. Yoshida tried to prevent Dulles from meeting the opposition leaders. *FRUS,* 1951, VI, 810.

54. I discount Weinstein's argument that Yoshida's pacifism stemmed from his fear of antagonizing the Soviet Union. Even in extreme circumstances, such as in January 1951, he did not neglect domestic politics. See Weinstein, pp. 2–3.

55. *FRUS,* 1951, VI, Pt. 1., p. 829.

56. Ichiro Hatoyama, *Hatoyama Ichiro kaiko roku* [Memoir of Hatoyama Ichiro] (Tokyo: Bungei Shunjusha, 1957), pp. 85–92.

57. Kiyotada Tsutsui, *Ishibashi Tanzan: ichi jiyu shugi seijika no kiseki* [Ishibashi

Tanzan: the record of one liberalist politician] (Tokyo: Chuo Koronsha, 1986), chapter 1. This is the best source on this episode.

58. Nishimura, p. 88.

59. *FRUS*, 1951, VI, 811–12. Emphasis added.

60. Ibid. See also ibid., p. 818.

61. *FRUS*, 1951, VI, 822–23.

62. The peace treaty, he said, during the June 1950 visit, should "take note of, but not embody contractually, the military renunciation of the Japanese Constitution." *FRUS*, 1950, VI, 1210.

63. *FRUS*, 1951, VI, 829.

64. Igarashi, *Tai-Nichi kowa*, pp. 199–200; Yoshitsu, pp. 56–62; Hideo Otake, "Yoshida naikaku ni yoru 'saigunbi' " ["Rearmament" by the Yoshida cabinet], *Ho-gaku*, 50, No. 4, 524.

65. *FRUS*, 1951, VI, 857.

66. Nishimura, p. 93.

67. *FRUS*, 1951, VI, 968.

68. *Asahi Shimbun*, April 15, p. 1.

69. Igarashi, *Tai-Nichi kowa*, pp. 205–6.

70. Ibid., p. 210.

71. Ibid., p. 254.

72. Nishimura, pp. 178–80, 304–05.

73. Miyazato, p. 133.

74. Article VXII, Paragraph 2 of the Administrative Agreement, in Nishimura, p. 435. See Appendix II of this volume for the text of the treaty.

# Chapter 5

# Postoccupation Tutelage

With all due regard for exceptional circumstances, six years (by then) of military occupation was too long. Eagerly the Japanese waited for its end, as the news coverage of the San Francisco conference kept building their anticipation with upbeat messages about peace, independence, equality, etc. The Japanese would be able to sing the national anthem, play judo, and see uncensored Kabuki theater, or take out a family heirloom sword once again. Contrary to his fear of being stoned for having signed the security treaty, Yoshida's popularity as prime minister shot up to 58 percent in the polls.[1] But it did not stay there long. A nagging sense of malaise, discontent, and listlessness soon seeped into the body politic.

The reason was the unresolved difference between the United States and the Yoshida government over the latter's defense policy. Washington was not happy with Yoshida's continued foot-dragging on rearmament. Using his promise to rearm, inserted into the security treaty at Dulles's insistence, as leverage, Washington renewed its demand for rearmament. With MacArthur gone, the U.S. government was at liberty to ask for constitutional revision. In the remainder of the Truman administration, it fell to General Mathew B. Ridgway, MacArthur's successor as SCAP, and U.S. Ambassador Robert Murphy to prod Yoshida. Then Dulles returned to the scene in 1953 as President Eisenhower's secretary of state. He resumed his push for the Adenauer model and collided with Yoshida defending the MacArthur legacy. The conflict was between earlier and later occupation policies, whose resolution was delayed by MacArthur.

Under continued external pressure, the realignment in domestic politics proceeded. The purged politicians were coming back en masse. They were critical of the excesses of occupation reforms, the rapid expansion of revolutionary political forces, and the continuation of occupation de facto. Most of them belonged to the conservative parties. At the same time, the radical-liberals continued their leftward move that began in reaction to NSC 13/2 in 1948, and a chasm yawned between them and the conservatives. I attribute the intensification of the Left-Right division at this time to the U.S.-Yoshida conflict primarily. At this stage, the JCP's influence had peaked and the Soviet Union stayed clear of U.S.-Japan conflict.[2] That conflict in turn drove home to the Japanese consciousness the nature of the bargain Yoshida accepted in San Francisco, the "unequal treaty."

Dulles found an ally among the revisionist politicians led by Hatoyama. Yoshida fought them back with a strenuous rear-guard action, producing a standoff until late 1954, when he finally succumbed and resigned. The standoff prevented the Japanese government from acting with dispatch, energy, and coherence at what could well have been a time for change. Instead, the combination of external pressure and domestic impasse created an oppressive atmosphere in Tokyo and amplified xenophobic reaction.

Because Yoshida refused to take the lead in national defense, Japan's defense efforts—including the maintenance of the U.S. bases—had to be justified as an accommodation to American pressure. To quote U.S. Ambassador John M. Allison, Murphy's successor, this was "the same attitude as was prevalent during the Occupation, when unpopular measures were . . . explained as being the result of United States pressure."[3] Patriotism, the only ingredient that would have satisfied Japan's amour propre, was suppressed. There was no heroic call to stand shoulder to shoulder with the American ally. Publicly Yoshida treated the new Japanese armed forces as if they were a favor to the Americans. Under pressure he grudgingly upgraded their status from Police Reserve to Security Forces (Hoantai) to Self-Defense Forces (Jieitai)—always insisting that they were not an "army." He might as well have invited the radicals to despise them. At the same time, however, there was no room for doubt that he was fighting off the American colossus with the constitution. He was the enemy of the Socialists' enemy, hence a friend—at least on the rearmament issue. In resisting rearmament and Dulles's arm-twisting, Yoshida was channeling nationalism to the neutralist track.

It should not be thought, however, that the Americans were single-minded in demanding Japan to rearm. On the contrary, judging from those who wrote on the subject, Americans remained deeply suspicious of it. Indeed, now that Japan was thought to be going independent, the suspicion intensified. They felt the purged politicians, now coming back, resented the United States. They conceded that some sort of reaction to the occupation and its intense reforms was almost inevitable, and they held their breath as if they were releasing a wound-up toy.[4] Their suspicion of Japan was a passion that remained the major unstated premise of U.S. policy toward Japan to this day. It consisted of a simple powerful formula that was thought to be self-evident: a race of samurai warriors, Japan rearmed would revive militarism. Professor Edwin O.

Reischauer, dean of Japanology in America and soon to be enlisted in the U.S. government's efforts to give an ideology to the Japanese, voiced this fear.

If I may speculate on Reischauer's motive, it probably could not have been more generous. He was thoroughly familiar with the origin of Japan's constitution and the history of occupation. He was undoubtedly in agreement with MacArthur that the security treaty's provisions were "imperialistic." And he was counseling Washington to moderate its demands for rearmament by echoing Yoshida's argument that that would arouse the "underground militarists." Whatever the case, he was to carry the torch of MacArthur among the American liberals, of whom he was en esteemed member.[5]

The lifting of the purge began in the fall of 1950, but there were irregularities. Hatoyama and a few of his friends were told that their depurge would be delayed, and both he and contemporary observers attributed this to the Yoshida-SCAP collusion. Unless the Government Section was willing to look the other way, Yoshida could not have abused the power of purge in so repugnant a fashion. But if the GS was prepared to use military police to forestall Dulles's meeting with Hatoyama and other "underground militarists," delaying a few cases of depurge mattered little.[6]

Unfortunately, this was not about a bruised ego or bureaucratic red tape. It was about the birth of a bogeyman called "Japanese militarists." Undoubtedly there were some militarists among those who were purged, as Yoshida alleged, although their restorationist scheme, if ever they entertained one, had to contend with nearly half a million American soldiers in or about Japan, the 1,300 military installations, and the Pentagon and MAAG (Military Assistance and Advisory Group) breathing down the neck of the Japanese armed forces. But that was not the point. The "Japanese militarists" were defined by MacArthur and Yoshida as those who talked of mutuality in the U.S.-Japan relations, as those who sought to revise the constitution, as those who opposed Yoshida, and as those who were purged. This was perverse. Quite a few Americans in Tokyo who had the firsthand knowledge of the purge administration felt that many purgees were wronged.[7] The pang of their conscience gave rise to misgivings— about the motives of the purgees now returning en masse. After all, did not the supreme commander and the prime minister vouch for their rightwing leaning? In this way, the initial purge of 1946, biased against politicians and favoring bureaucrats, was snowballing into a self-fulfilling prophecy. The bogeyman began to exercise tyranny over the U.S.-Japan relations. America was among its victims.

If the maladministration of the purge was on the conscience of upright Americans, it was envenoming and inflaming the purged politicians and inviting the rapt attention of Nagata-cho (the Diet area), Kasumigaseki (the ministries), and

Marunouchi (big business) in Tokyo. The purge produced a celebrated court trial and a martyr in 1949. Earlier, SCAP's Government Section became interested in investigating irregularities in campaign fundraising. Somehow Hatoyama and Kono Ichiro were caught in the dragnet and were charged with violations of purge regulations. The case against Hatoyama was dropped. But Kono was found guilty and appealed the verdict all the way to the supreme court. There is little reason to believe that he was not guilty because he thought of the purge itself as extra-legal. Nothing, not even the occupation army, could force this fireball of a politician to live like a monk. Predictably Kono lost and was given a four-month jail sentence.[8] He and his purged friends could hardly wait for the end of occupation and a chance to settle accounts with Yoshida.

And the prime minister was vulnerable once MacArthur was gone. His enemies professed to be disturbed and puzzled by his fork-tongued approach to rearmament. "Mr. Yoshida's thesis," Hatoyama declared, "is that a white horse is not a horse," quoting an ancient Chinese riddle.[9] That Washington had a serious policy difference with Yoshida did not escape their notice. They wondered why Yoshida needed an American prodding to assert Japan's equality. To make matters worse, Yoshida "could not spill his guts" and explain the rationale for postoccupation tutelage.[10] So he hemmed and hawed. He was evasive and equivocal, arrogant and curt, devious and disingenuous. That, too, was a grist for the opposition mill. In short order, the Socialists and the depurged politicians, the natural enemies of each other, discovered that they shared the same revulsion against the "Potsdam establishment faction" and its "subservience" to Washington.

Public attention was glued on Hatoyama Ichiro, Miki Bukichi, and Kono Ichiro, who had relinquished former Seiyukai to Yoshida's control upon purge and who wanted the party apparatus back in keeping with their agreement with Yoshida. The three were sworn to comradeship through their long careers of fighting the imperial bureaucracy before the war, the militarists who had banished them to exile during the war, and now Yoshida. Hatoyama's hands were strengthened when Dulles sought him and his compatriots out in February 1951. But it remained to be seen whether Hatoyama was anything more than a card for Washington to play against Yoshida, for American officials were afraid of the revisionists. The U.S. embassy in Tokyo watched Hatoyama and his friends with apprehension and reported that the "future importance of the purgees and the extent of their anti-Americanism are not presently foreseeable." The natural inclination of the Tokyo Embassy was to side with tried-and-true Yoshida.[11]

As expected, Yoshida refused to keep his promise of relinquishing the presidency of former Seiyukai. Hatoyama, Miki, and Kono thought of organizing a separate party. But the attempt was abandoned because Hatoyama was stricken with paralysis, and they returned to former Seiyukai. Thus one and the same party hosted two leaders representing, respectively, the MacArthur legacy and the policy opposed to it. Former Minseito in the opposition had been feeling the same divisive pull since 1950, when one faction was coopted by Yoshida and the remnants rallied around Ashida, advocating rearmament. A new cleavage defined by the Yoshida-Hatoyama conflict was crosscutting the two existing conservative parties—to produce a four-way split. Subsequent history might have been different had the Yoshida-Hatoyama cleavage overlapped the Seiyukai-Minseito cleavage.

The wartime Minseito was in effect the agit-prop department of the war efforts. Only Seiyukai, defending the tradition of Hara Kei (father of prewar democracy), sought to preserve the independence of the Diet and paid a price for it. On two counts—of having been politicians and nationalistic, to boot—the members of Minseito were devastated by the purge. Exactly what went on among them between the surrender and the purge is very murky and, to all intents and purposes, did not seem to matter.[12] For by the time the survivors of the purge and the new recruits regrouped, former Minseito acquired a new leader and a new face. Ashida Hitoshi, former diplomat and former editor of the *Japan Times and Mail,* left Yoshida's party to become former Minseito's leader in the wake of the initial purge. SCAP's Government Section spared him from the purge for fear that without him former Minseito may disintegrate.[13] In 1947–48, the GS showered favors on it to make a go of the coalition with the JSP, and Ashida kept trying to resurrect that coalition through 1949. In this effort, he was hobbled by the prolonged trial of the Showa Denko bribery case. When Yoshida weaned away the Inukai faction from it in February 1950, former Minseito was decimated. What was left of it merged with its former coalition partern, the Cooperative party under Miki Takeo. The Korean War converted Ashida into an advocate of rearmament, the first of its kind in post-war Japan. By 1952 he espoused the cause of constitutional revision as well. By then the depurged politicians came back.

The coexistence of Ashida, Miki, Kitamura (Nakasone Yasushiro's mentor), along with the returning Minseito politicians gave the party a strange, schizo-phrenic outlook. The common denominator that held the party together was what the Japanese called "revisionist capitalism," or a combination of government planning and private property, a program that was triggered by Japan's defeat and the purge. Former Minseito's leadership passed in June 1952 from Ashida to Shigemitsu, the former foreign minister who had been dismissed by MacArthur in October 1946, subsequently tried and convicted as a class A war criminal and released after independence. He was a hardliner against the Soviet Union.

The return of the purgees—including some to the rightwing JSP—affected politics immediately, though they were still outside the Diet. Yoshida's commanding majority of 288 seats cracked as 119 members leaned to Hatoyama, giving Yoshida only 140.[14] With the ratification of the two treaties coming up in the fall, Yoshida ran into his first snag in May 1951. He could not appoint Hirokawa Kozen secretary general of his own party. A Hatoyama follower was chosen instead.

Yoshida did the obvious things. He surrounded himself even more with bureaucratic followers or the "inner court," of which Ikeda Hayato was the most trusted. Because his own party was split with the return of the purgees, he continued his attempt to split former Minseito and enlist a breakaway faction. This move—confined solely to the Yoshida faction for the moment—was called "conservative merger" (*hoshu godo*), but it would turn into a much broader movement. Then Yoshida tried to "fish" for individual members of the Hatoyama camp as well with the lure of appointments.

But then there were occasions for Yoshida to collaborate with the revisionists in 1951, as the government undertook a review and revision of the occupation reforms. Earlier, in 1948, Kennan's NSC 13/2 sought to accomplish that, but, frustrated by MacArthur's foot dragging, the "reverse course" was confined to economic rehabilitation. Yoshida's repeated pleas with MacArthur to recentalize the police apparatus, for instance, had been rebuffed. Now it was time for General Ridgway to complete the unfinished "reverse course" whose overall aim was to restore the state to a minimum level of internal viability. In May, one month after Ridgway's arrival, Yoshida commissioned an informal committee called the Legislative Consultative Council to review legislative proposals to correct the defects of occupation reforms on a broad range of subjects such as the purge, education, police, labor, and the economy.[15]

It may sound puzzling, but following the peace treaty, Yoshida showed an acute interest in reintroducing the theme of patriotism in public education and in restoring the Yasukuni Shrine as the place to honor the war dead. It turns out that Yoshida was a selective revisionist, as eager to move forward on domestic revision as he was opposed to foreign policy revision. He clearly implied that his objection to rearmament was a temporary one, a mere postponement, and a matter of policy. But his selective revisionism was self-defeating in the end. Although the returning depurgees supported Yoshida, the JSP—no longer in power—threw down the gauntlet.

It is a testimony to the Socialist party's peculiar traits that the rightwing reacted more violently to domestic revision that began in 1951 than to rearmament. This puzzling reaction can be explained in part as an accidental consequence of the purge. The rightwing Socialists who dominated the JSP until the

San Francisco peace conference consisted of the pragmatic union-steward type (of the Shamin faction such as Nishio Suehiro) and the socialist-intellectual type (the Nichiro faction). Ideologues to the core, many in the Nichiro faction were swept off their feet by the fatherland's call to arms during the war and acted on their belief in public. After the war, they were purged and singled out for vicious denunciation by the Communists, the only ones with clear conscience. Guilt-stricken, the Nichiro leaders felt compelled to overcompensate for their "sin," but the purge kept them out of public life. Hence they could not react to the first wave of reverse course in 1948. When at last the purge was lifted, they began to compete with the Communists in swearing their fidelity to the philosophy represented by E. H. Norman and the early occupation reforms.[16]

That philosophy was materialist or reductionist, seeing foreign policy as an emanation of social structure. Foreign policy was secondary, and social structure was primary. Hence the Socialist liberals professed to see a conspiracy of "emperor fascism" and "American imperialism" behind any attempt to revise the social structure left behind by the early occupation reform. As the depurged rightwing leaders returned to active party life in 1951, the JSP rightwing collapsed of its own accord.[17]

Among the intellectuals at large, the Peace Problem Symposium was the weather vane, and Maruyama Masao, Tokyo University political scientist, was its chief theoretician. Whether Maruyama was a Marxist may be disputed. But in order to switch—with a measure of respectability—from supporting American universalism to denouncing it, one almost had to resort to Marxism, for only Marxism provided a common framework for viewing Japanese militarism and "American imperialism" as parallels. From the vantagepoint of class analysis, one form of "monopoly capital" was no better or worse than another. Marxism taught this dictum matter-of-factly and with refreshing candor.[18]

Feeling jilted and betrayed, the liberal intellectuals saw only blemishes and faults in America from here on. That was not difficult because the United States was now calling for constitutional revision, rearmament, and weeding out of early occupation reforms, in an ambience defined by Senator Joseph McCarthy. The end of occupation censorship opened the floodgate of photo exhibits on the horrors of Hiroshima and Nagasaki, of which the Japanese had been ignorant till then. The liberal intellectuals chose to believe that the United States had started the war in Korea or had used bacteriological weapons. Japan had sinned in war, they admitted. Hence the only absolution for them would be to defend the radically utopian constitution and damn the consequences. Nakano Yoshio, a well-known literary critic, maintained that he would rather live under the occupation and keep the constitution than be forced to live in the world of power politics on the outside.[19] The constitution made them something special and holier. Somehow it seemed fitting that on the morrow of their independence, they should be casting stones at "American imperialism" and joining the Chinese and other "oppressed" peoples of the world in their wars of "national liberation."[20]

As the days of their rule were numbered, SCAP officials busied themselves completing the reverse course. They raced against time to clear a firebreak between the JCP and the "centrist" forces, that is, to split the people's front. But with their authority rapidly dwindling, their efforts were often counterproductive. In July 1950 the Labor Section played midwife to the birth of Sohyo (General Council of Trade Unions), and gave it an anticommunist mandate. It was to supplant the Communist-controlled federation, Sanbetsu.[21] Like several other organizations created by SCAP, however, Sohyo became overtly anti-American, under the first secretary general, Takano Minoru, a subrosa Communist party member. "The chicken turned into a duckling," to quote the *Pacific Stars and Stripes,* the newspaper of the U.S. armed forces, commenting on Sohyo's second general meeting, just before the San Francisco peace conference.

From here on, the JSP leftwing became entirely dependent on Sohyo for votes, funds, membership, and parliamentary candidates. The dependence was dictated by the JSP's truncated organizational structure. Although it had polled close to a third of the national vote since 1947, its partly membership had stagnated around a minuscule 50,000 (of which 15,000 came from Sohyo). But Sohyo boasted a membership of 4 million at the time.[22] As the popular saying had it, "Sohyo is to today what the imperial army was to yesterday." At a party congress in January 1951, the JSP added constitutional defense to the Three Principles of Peace laid down in December 1949, to make the Four Principles of Peace. This became the joint battle cry of the JSP and Sohyo.

Sohyo's impact on the JSP became evident three months later when the two treaties were put to a vote of ratification. SCAP officials summoned the secretaries general of both the JSP and Sohyo daily before the vote and pressed them to endorse the treaties.[23] But the voting revived the JSP's ongoing internal disputes. The rightwing pushed a resolution that singled out the peace treaty for acceptance, and it collided with the leftwing, which opposed both treaties. After an all-night session, the delegates split right down the middle: 161 sided with the rightwing and 193 the leftwing. Sohyo—calling on the Socialists to be "principled"—stiffened the back of the leftwing.[24] Two Socialist parties were born.

Former Minseito, whose representatives refused to sign the security treaty in San Francisco, came around to endorsing both treaties with this proviso: the security treaty would be rewritten once national defense forces and a collective security measure were established. But Sonoda Sunao (later foreign minister in the Suzuki cabinet) and two others resigned from the party in order to vote against both treaties; two others (including Kitamura) absented themselves; and Nakasone and two other Dietmen counseled a vote against the security treaty on the ground that the government had failed to give an adequate explanation, but they were overruled.[25]

The October 1951 tally in the lower house was 307 to 47 in favor of the peace treaty and 289 to 71 in favor of the security treaty; the November vote in the upper house was 174 to 45 in favor of the peace treaty and 147 to 76 in favor of the security treaty. The Communists—decimated by the red purge and expulsion from the Diet—voted against both. (The Socialists of both wings numbered only 48 in the lower house.)

To summarize developments up to this point, a major realignment was taking place in Japanese politics because of the incomplete reverse course. Yoshida's rear-guard action had created the Yoshida-Hatoyama rift in his own party. That deprived him of a stable majority in the Diet. The incomplete reverse course at once provoked and encouraged the radical-liberals: provoked because it was after all the reverse course, and encouraged because it was incomplete (i.e., left the constitution intact). Thus underlying the conventional division (Seiyukai, Minseito, the radical-liberals), there were three major forces at work: Yoshida, Hatoyama, and the radical-liberals. The Hatoyama faction vetoed Yoshida's candidate for secretary general in May 1951 (Hirokawa) and once again in March 1952 (Fukunaga Kenji). The next development was all too natural. As Yoshida lost his majority, he became vulnerable to the combination of the revisionists and the radical-liberals in the opposition. The Socialists began to intervene between Yoshida and Hatoyama—with opportunism and willfulness of the balancer of power.

The combination of the revisionists and the radical-liberals materialized in the fall of 1951, when the Yoshida government ran into its firs postindependence snag in the Diet. The combination was full-blown in the spring of 1952, over two major foreign-policy issues: in January, Yoshida disclosed that because of pressure from the U.S. Senate, Japan would have to conclude a peace treaty with the Chinese Nationalist government in Taiwan rather than with Peking; then the Diet debated the Administrative Agreement just concluded. They were both potentially explosive issues that called Japan's independence into question.

The Administrative Agreement defined the status and rights of the U.S. garrison forces in Japan. Originally, the United States government wanted to include such an agreement in the security treaty itself. But the Japanese government feared the provision would jeopardize the treaty's ratification, so the status-of-forces problem was shunted to an executive agreement, free of Diet ratification. Therefore, some of the rather sensitive demands of the Pentagon were in the Administrative Agreement. Negotiations started between Okazki Katsuo, Yoshida's disciple and foreign minister, and Dean Rusk in January 1952. The American side seemed to regard the U.S.-Philippine agreement rather than the NATO agreement as the model.[26]

There were three major problems. All installations and bases were to revert to Japanese control within 90 days of the effective date of the security treaty, and new U.S. leases had to be negotiated prior to that date. The U.S. team could not trust the assurance of Okazaki that Japan would negotiate leases in good faith before the deadline. Rusk, obviously under Pentagon pressure, demanded the automatic extension of leases for installations for which negotiations might not be completed. Okazaki found the demand "repulsive,"[27] but gave in after President Truman intervened with a telegram. The escape clause was agreed to in separate letters exchanged between the parties.

Mindful of the precedent of NATO, the United States demanded joint command over the Japanese forces in the event of war. For political reasons, Yoshida objected to its formal stipulation. The two sides instead arrived at an inoffensive phrase, "agree to consult" (in event of war), a phrase that should have been included in the security treaty but was excluded from it because the treaty was not mutual. On the other hand, Yoshida knew that joint command would be inevitable if Japan was invaded, so he agreed to it orally.[28]

Last but not least in it sensitivity was criminal jurisdiction over U.S. military personnel and their dependent. The Japanese government was aware of the status-of-forces agreement among the NATO nations and wanted a parallel arrangement. But Rusk demurred and insisted on extraterritorial privileges. He was under enormous pressure from the JCS to preserve as many of the occupation privileges as he could salvage. The JCS feared the Japanese might "trump up charges" to retaliate for war crimes trials.[29] It said, "the position of Japan, as a conquered nation and as an oriental nation, is not analogous to that of the North Atlantic Treaty Organization nations."[30] Rusk had to tell Okazaki that there just was not enough trust in the United States toward Japan, and he won the concession pending future renegotiation. The JCS maneuvered in the U.S. Senate to withhold ratification of the treaty until Japan concluded the Administrative Agreement on February 28, 1952. SCAP was disbanded on April 28, 1952, and General Matthew Ridgway, remained as simply Commander in Chief, Far East (CINCFE).

Since the red purge was lifted on the same day, it was a foregone conclusion that the first postoccupation May Day, slated three days later, would be chosen by the JCP to make some sort of statement. A march by half a million workers in downtown Tokyo turned violent in front of the GHQ building. American servicemen were assaulted, military vehicles overturned and set afire, two men killed, and nearly a thousand injured in the melee.[31]

The proposed peace treaty with Taiwan and the Administrative Agreement were denounced by former Minseito, the JSP, and the JCP. As Nakasone Yasuhiro, a nationalist young Turk of former Minseito, said later, "The security treaty was concealed behind the peace treaty, and the Administrative Agreement was concealed behind the security treaty." The Japanese were beginning to discover that the occupation was continuing de facto. A new, broadly supported political agenda, treaty revision, was in the offing.[32] But on the two votes at hand, Hatoyama sided with Yoshida. In addition, they cooperated in passing the bill establishing the Security Agency, in the prime minister's office rather than as a regular government department, in July. The Security Agency was in charge of the Police Reserve, now renamed the Security Forces (*Hoan-tai*), and the coast guard.[33]

Yoshida's approval rating of 58 percent immediately after San Francisco fell to 33 percent in March 1952.[34] Yoshida hung tough. His hope for survival came to rest on American aid. Both he and the business leaders, who favored him by a large margin at this time, assumed that Japan's future depended critically on close economic integration with the United States and that an economic tie would overlap the military tie. Their expectation was more than met when vast sums of military procurement fund for the U.S. forces fighting in Korea were released in Japan, thereby pushing Japan's gross national product to past the prewar level. Japan's "pacifism" was as yet a thing of the future because the conservatives had not sanctioned it, and there was no objection to arms export. At the same time, Dulles's decision to cut Japan off from the China market created a moral obligation for the United States to find a substitute. Both Yoshida and the business community anticipated large-scale U.S. aid as a bootstrap with which Japan could put itself back on its feet.

In June 1952 Yoshida and his protege and finance minister, Ikeda, invited U.S. ambassador Robert Murphy to dinner and resumed their aid-requesting routine. Speaking on Yoshida's behalf in a conversation with Murphy before dinner, Ikeda asked for a line of credit in the neighborhood of $100–$200 million, "in view of the elections."[35] One month later a dispatch from the Tokyo embassy discussed Yoshida's request for $1.5 billion, "motivated chiefly by political considerations, particularly a desire to demonstrate that the United States is willing to continue its support of the Japanese economy."[36] The dispatch commented, "Should the Liberal Party [former Seiyukai] lose the next election, or should the Yoshida faction lose control of the Liberal Party, it is by no means certain the resulting government would be so cordially disposed," and asked for a favorable action. The Tokyo embassy seemed to regard Hatoyama as a threat.[37]

As the Yoshida government kept up its routine of requesting aid in 1952, so did the American side its routine of pressing Japan to rearm. An exchange relationship—economic aid in return for defense—was taking shape. It presupposed MacArthur's thesis that Japan had to be well off before taking care of is defense. The prime minister had three obligations involving defense arising out of the peace negotiations. He agreed to the statement in the preamble of the security treaty: "Japan will itself increasingly assume responsibility for is own defense against direct and indirect aggression." In addition, he promised a "general staff" and a "defense department." Yoshida proceeded with incrementalism.[38]

General Mathew Ridgway took a crack at the constitution in early 1952, just before the end of the occupation. Yoshida seemed enthusiastic and told of his plan to start a national education campaign. "Rather than me urging rearmament," said Yoshida, "I want the demand for it and for revision of the Constitution . . . to come from the people."[39] Ridgway was acting as a middleman for the JCS, which was demanding a 325,000-men force in 10 divisions with corresponding increases in defense budget.[40]

Yoshida dissolved the Diet by surprise—without the countersignature of his cabinet ministers—in August 1952, hoping to catch the Hatoyama faction, which was starved for money, unprepared for an election. In the ensuing campaign, 121 prewar politicians, mostly depurgees, were returned. Of this number, about 100 were conservatives and the remainder rightwing Socialists. Now the Hatoyama faction was in the Diet, though its following decreased in this election to about 80.[41] The results of the October poll were: former Seiyukai 240 (down from 282); former Minseito 85 (up from 84—this figure is the sum of former Minseito and the Cooperative party in the last election); the JSP leftwing 54 (up from 16);[42] the JSP rightwing 57 (up from 32); and the JCP 0 (down from 35). The most startling thing about these results was the damage done to the Communists by their violent tactics, and the obvious transfer of previous Communist votes to the Socialist Left.[43] Yoshida's plurality in the Diet was reduced to 6, and Hatoyama could deny it to him.

In this election Ogata Taketora, a former *Asahi* newspaperman and depurgee, was elected to Yoshida's party and was immediately promoted to be his chief adviser and heir apparent. Ogata eclipsed Hirokawa, Yoshida's righthand man and party secretary general, whereupon Miki Bukichi—Hatoyama's friend—began trying to seduce Hirokawa into revolting against Yoshida. At the same time, Hatoyama organized the Democratization League, an anti-Yoshida faction with 50 members, to make life miserable for Yoshida in the party. In

November, Ikeda, minister of International Trade and Industry, committed a faux pas with his Diet statement that the government could not help suicides among small businessmen going bankrupt. The entire opposition called for a vote of censure, which passed when the Hatoyama faction absented itself from roll call. This was the first occasion on which Hatoyama split the party to vote with the radical-liberals.

But there was much more to the fracas than met the eye. Behind the scenes, U.S. Ambassador Robert Murphy was choreographing it. Side by side with the vote of censure against Ikeda, the Socialists were pushing for a vote of noconfidence against Foreign Minister Okazaki Katsuo with the help of the Democratization League. Summoning the Hatoyama faction, Murphy concurred with the vote against Ikeda but not against Okazaki, on the ground that the latter was a foreign policy matter.[44] Apparently the State Department just could not rid itself of the habit of micromanaging Japan, down to key appointments. Murphy could not have been obtuse to the fact that he was fanning anti-American sentiments with his intervention, especially because it was Dulles's own policy that egged Hatoyama against Yoshida. If there was an extenuating circumstance to Murphy's act, it was the fact that some American officials at the time gave Japan only a few more years before it turned to neutralism.[45] America appeared to be seized with morbid fear of communism, a passion that the Japanese would in time learn to use.

These are unpleasant tales, but we must continue with a bare outline in order to make subsequent events intelligible. Hatoyama now had the crucial votes for frustrating Yoshida. The Democratization League went on the offensive in the party's Executive Committee, an organ of ultimate decision making, and the Political Affairs Research Committee, a legislative clearinghouse. In December 1952 Miki Bukichi held the government budget hostage to extract concessions from Yoshida.[46] Yoshida was being cornered, and to make matters worse Washington would step up its pressure.

In November 1952, Dwight D. Eisenhower easily defeated Adlai Stevenson to become the first Republican president since Herbert Hoover. Eisenhower's mandate was to bring an end to the war in Korea and fiscal conservatism to the management of runaway defense budget. This was to be the first in the postwar cycles of defense retrenchment, which was to repeat itself under Nixon and Bush. Fiscal retrenchment translated into a greater reliance on nuclear weapons and allied contributions for local and regional defense, and a large displacement of economic aid with military. But NSC 68 remained the major U.S. policy.[47]

Another problem on U.S. agenda was the future of the Japanese economy. Whereas it was almost punch-drunk for the time being with the sudden, massive windfall of Korean War procurement, the situation would not last since

Eisenhower was determined to terminate the war. Japan's artificial detachment from the China market was still staring it in the face. As ceasefire negotiations got underway in the spring of 1953 (concluded in July), Japan's dollar earnings began to plummet. Japan's anemic economy was a problem in its own right. But more important, the money wasted by the Tokyo government was the money not spent on rearmament, as far as Washington was concerned. It was primarily for this reason that the Truman administration kept hectoring Finance Minister Ikeda to observe a sort of revised Dodge Line. The policy would be continued under Eisenhower.[48]

For the Japanese, the new Republican president was magnanimous, above board, full of common sense, and a refreshing contrast with his predecessor in the White House. In addition, some Japanese felt Ike might give them a relief from the heavy-handed legacy of MacArthur, Ike's rival. Eisenhower chose Dulles as his secretary of state, and Dulles resolved to complete Japan's rearmament, which he had left in a compromise with MacArthur. For his first ambassador in Tokyo, Dulles chose John M. Allison, an experienced Japan expert and former deputy director, Office of Far Eastern Affairs. But Allison, a career diplomat, appeared to be more comfortable with the MacArthur legacy than with Dulles's attempt to overturn it, or with Yoshida than with Hatoyama.[49]

Early in the first term, the new administration's debate on Japan focused more on its strategic predicament than on economic problem per se. At a National Security Council meeting, for instance, Secretary of the Treasury George Humphrey asked, "Was it even thinkable that Japan can have a viable economy if . . . it was confined to the home islands?" President Eisenhower said, "there was no future for Japan unless access was provided for it to the markets . . . of Manchuria and North China."[50] Upon making an identical point at another NSC meeting, Eisenhower was to say with a smile, "This was what the [Japanese] warlords of the thirties had said."[51] Secretary Dulles was in the habit of repeating at this time that there was no market in America for shoddy Japanese merchandise.[52] "In some respects," it seemed to Humphrey, "we had licked the two wrong nations in the last war." The president said, "You don't mean that; you mean we licked these two nations too thoroughly." At the end, Lloyd Cutler of NSC asked if anyone would like to propose that Japan should be restored to its colonial empire![53] Soon thereafter, the Eisenhower administration opted for the policy of opening Southeast Asian markets to Japan and underwriting that link with U.S. influence. But the Vietminh War made the prospect at best bleak.

Yoshida kept stonewalling about rearmament, blackmailing Dulles with an "upheaval" if he were displaced from office.[54] Shorn of his majority, "One Man" Yoshida often flew off the handle. The fight between him and Hatoyama was degenerating into ugly feud, and the government was drifting without any legislative accomplishments. In the Diet session that opened in late January 1953, Yoshida submitted five major bills that were designed to correct the "excesses" of occupation reforms. It seemed that he hoped to make amends with the revisionists by playing to their legislative preferences. During the Budget Committee interpellation on February 28, a Socialist Dietman—up in arms over the "reverse course" bills—chatised Yoshida for his studied equivocation. "Damned fool," Yoshida's reply, threw the session into turmoil. He immediately retracted his remark, but the opposition wanted his scalp.

The motion to censure the prime minister came up for vote on March 2, and it carried 191 to 162 because Hatoyama's Democratization League, 22 strong, and the 30-member Hirokawa group, smitten by Yoshida's favoring Ogata over Hirokawa, absented themselves. The opposition proceeded to a vote of noconfidence. To strengthen their bargaining position and internal unity, the rebel groups organized themselves into a splinter party. When the vote carried, 229–216, Yoshida dissolved the Diet—the "Name-Calling Dissolution"—to fight a second election campaign in six months.

Against the backdrop of the Korean ceasefire negotiation, the campaign issue was formally rearmament but in fact Yoshida himself. The results were as follows: Yoshida 199 (down from 242), former Minseito 76 (down from 89), Hatoyama 35, leftwing JSP 72 (up from 56), the rightwing JSP 66 (up from 60), and the JCP 1 (up from 0). The revisionists were shocked to learn that the radical-liberals had captured the one-third of the lower house needed to frustrate constitutional revision. Yoshida lost his majority, and the opposition parties took the speakership and vice speakership from him. Two successive defeats at the polls did not faze Yoshida, however, and he hung on. The leftwing JSP was emboldened by the consecutive victories and by its having leapt ahead of the rightwing. In the ensuing election for prime minister, Sohyo tried to talk the two wings of JSP into voting for Shigemitsu of former Minseito but was refused on the ground that he stood for rearmament.[55] Yoshida defeated Shigemitsu to form a minority government (the fifth Yoshida cabinet) in May 1953.

The Shigemitsu candidacay was a bad augury. Having expanded from 111 to 138 in the 466-member house in six months, the Socialists acquired the power to intervene decisively in the conservative feud and name a prime minister. Desperately Yoshida tried to expand his party strength by coopting the conservative opposition under Hatoyama and Shigemitsu. He wanted a stable majority in order to qualify for Washington's trust and large-scale aid. In turn, an aid package would buttress his domestic position.[56] But it so happened that both Shigemitsu and Hatoyama favored a national defense force. Former Minseito had already adopted the policy of formal rearmament at its party congress in February.[57]

The Diet session that opened in May after the election had many important bills and issues on its agenda. There were soul-searching debates on rearmament and constitutional revision because the Diet was looking at U.S. military assistance under the Mutual Security Act (MSA). With the Vietminh War in French Indochina escalating in 1953, the U.S. Congress passed the MSA bill to provide military aid to the allies willing to undertake self-help. In Asia Eisenhower's preference was for "Asiatics to fight Asiatics." It was understood in Tokyo that vis-a-vis Japan MSA would be used as a carrot to reopen the rearmament issue. Yoshida was ambivalent: he wanted an aid but no strings. In the wake of two successive elections that weakened the squabbling conservatives, a conservative merger movement was underway. It was endorsed by a surprisingly broad coalition of conservative leaders from both parties such as Miki, Ashida, Ogata, Kishi, and Ishibashi. The political situation was in flux—"as if on the eve of a revolution."[58]

A consensus was emerging among the conservatives that the nation had to be protected from the expanding radicals, that Yoshida was standing against the current, both internal and external, creating an impasse and the sense of rudderlessness, and that he or anyone who stood in the way of a resolution had to be thrown out. Soon, the conservative merger movement would take up constitutional revision and rearmament as its agenda. A note of urgency was added by another victory by the two wings of the JSP in the regularly scheduled upper house election in April 1953.

Just prior to the lower house election, four business organizations led by Keidanren (the Federation of Management Organizations) and representing the entire business community of Japan issued a statement calling for a strong conservative government. To begin with, business was intimidated by the radicalization of labor under the influence of the leftwing JSP and Sohyo, whose forte was "political struggle" of the anarcho-Syndicalist variety based on huge industrial unions.[59] Second, as the Korean War wound down, the Japanese economy slid into a recession in 1953, and business leaders were looking for new economic opportunities through closer U.S.-Japanese ties. Keidanren, the powerful spokesman of elite corporations, concluded that Japan's future lay mainly in arms production for the United States in the Cold War, a conclusion that has since been confounded by history.

Already in 1952, Keidanren had organized the Economic Cooperation Forum and the Defense Production Subcommittee, and made public a six-year rearmament plan the year after.[60] Keidanren jumped at the opportunity offered by MSA assistance as a substitute for Korean War procurement. The price, Keidanren knew, was Japan's rearmament and the means a stable conservative government.[61] In early 1953 Keidanren rapidly lost interest in Yoshida.

In the summer of 1953 Yoshida, Hatoyama, and Shigemitsu temporarily buried their hatchets to pass a series of domestic and international measures designed to correct the excesses of occupation reforms and "restore autonomy" (*jishu-sei kaifuku*). They were: (1) a bill restricting strikes in key industries, (2) a bill recentralizing the police, (3) a bill restoring pension payments to former servicemen, (4) a bill relaxing anti-monopoly controls, and (5) two education bills designed to check the activities of the radical Japan Teachers' Union, an affiliate of Sohyo.[62] In addition, two bills establishing the Defense Agency (upgrading the Security Agency) and the Self-Defense Forces (upgrading the Police Reserve), the MSA agreement, and a bill protecting military secrets called for by the MSA agreement were passed (Japan had no antiespionage law).

But what was "restoration of autonomy" to the conservatives was "reverse course" and "rearmament by installment" (*nashikuzushi saigunbi*) to the radical-liberals. The police bill in particular was resisted to the bitter end by the Socialists, who resorted to physical violence and obstruction in June. The speaker had to summon the police to the chamber floor to cope with them. This was an ominous precedent for subsequent developments. What was noteworthy here, however, was that when the conservatives were united, the JSP was powerless.

In 1953 Miki struck the keynote of conservative realignment in his sharp interpellation of Yoshida's "rearmament by installment."[63] Miki seized on the government's contention that constitutional revision was unnecessary because Japan's defense capability had yet to reach the level of "war potential," forbidden by Article IX. "War potential" meant an ability to carry out an aggressive war, according to Yoshida's sophistry. Put differently, Yoshida would consent to constitutional revision if and when Japan acquired a capability for "aggression"! Such logic would tempt Japan's neighbors to oppose any change in the constitution, Miki pointed out, and to turn it into an international disarmament treaty against Japan.[64] Miki was proven correct by subsequent history. But once again Yoshida evaded Miki.

The knowledge that Washington was seeking Japan's participation in the MSA program set off an alarm and protest among the pacifists. The public demanded to know what strings would be attached to MSA aid. Under heated questioning in the Diet, Yoshida said that Japan's promise in the security treaty to assume greater responsibility for defense was "not an obligation but only an expectation by the United States," and that the MSA program would not affect Japan's abstention from rearmament.[65] However, a United Press International bulletin of July 10 from Washington published in Japanese newspapers quoted Secretary Dulles's testimony before the Senate Appropriations Committee to the effect that the new Japanese defense budget envisaged ten divisions.[66] That caused a small tempest. The new American ambassador, John Allison, wired back to Dulles and asked for a clarification. Instead, Dulles issued a statement that made matters worse by affirming "our tentative thinking" that a 350,000-man force was needed in Japan.[67]

As recalled by Miyazawa Kiichi, a young Finance Ministry official and a secretary of Ikeda's, Yoshida's views on defense at this juncture were as follows:

> We can never pull off the so-called rearmament for the time being, nor is there any interest in it among the people. On the other hand, it is not something that justifies the government's initiative to impose on them. The day [we rearm] will come naturally if our livelihood recovers. It may sound selfish, but let the Americans handle [our security] until then. It is indeed our god-given luck that the constitution bans arms. If the Americans complain, the constitution gives us adequate cover. The politicians who want to amend it are oafs.[68]

In November, Ikeda and Miyazawa were slated to go to Washington for MSA negotiation. This provided the occasion for Yoshida to make his final leap on rearmament, from internal security forces to regular armed forces (agreed to in 1951). To negotiate in Washington from a position of strength, he had to close ranks with the opposition. Yoshida met Shigemitsu privately in September and agreed in writing to (1) drafting of a long-term defense plan, (2) establishment of the Self-Defense Forces, (3) upgrading the SDFs' capability to coping with direct aggression, but (4) leaving the constitution intact. Shigemitsu agreed to the last point because former Minseito was divided on the issue at the time.[69] Yoshida was hoping to visit Washington himself, take credit for a major economic concession, and dominate the coalition with Shigemitsu. Ikeda and Miyazawa were to arrange that concession.

The American side, headed by Assistant Secretary of State Walter S. Robertson, was determined to rearm Japan once and for all. However, he was instructed by Dulles not to corner the Japanese on the constitution.[70] He presented a grand arms buildup plan with a tight timetable, leading up to 10 divisions and 350,000 men.[71] A doubling of the Japanese defense budget to reach a little under 4 percent of GNP was presupposed.[72] The American government was to provide the hardware in grants. The requirements above were based on the estimate that the Soviet-Chinese alliance posed a double-pronged threat to Japan—from the north against Hokkaido and down the Korean peninsula against Kyushu. Soviet strength was estimated to be 500,000 men and 6,000 aircraft. The United States was anticipating a direct Soviet invasion of Japan.

The United States proposed to eliminate all its forces except air and naval arms from the bases in Japan proper (that is, excepting Okinawa and the Bonins) by 1958, in tandem with the Japanese buildup. Japan's fiscal contribution to the U.S. military presence would also decrease. The U.S. government in addition asked for repayment of postwar relief assistance, titled GARIOA, which came to $750 million.

To blunt the U.S. demands and scale them down, Ikeda expanded his agenda and offered lengthy and repeated briefings on the political and economic difficulties that faced Japan. He said that although Yoshida's coalition talk with Shigemitsu had touched on arms expansion, constitutional revision was impossible for the foreseeable future. Asked by Robertson how he proposed to proceed, Ikeda said, "I think there is no way except to proceed with an incremental plan, the minimum necessary."[73]

Asked by the American press how arms expansion without constitutional revision was possible, he lectured on a line of legal interpretation that the Yoshida government had devised in the course of Diet interpellations. It went this way: that "the Japanese people forever renounce war as a sovereign right of the nation and the threat or use of force as means of settling international disputes"; that in order to accomplish *this aim,* "land, sea, and air forces, as well as other war potential, will never be maintained" (as Article IX states), but that maintaining the means of self-defense not aimed at settling international disputes was legitimate. In short, Japan could possess the means of self-defense so long at it was not a "war potential."[74]

We must pause here to ask whether Yoshida was saying one thing to domestic opposition and another to Robertson. Yoshida promised to upgrade the SDF's capability to cope with direct aggression but denied that such a capability was a "war potential." Was this slicing the salami very thin, or was it really a sleight of hand? The answer is the former: Yoshida's point was to comply with Dulles's demand for regular armed forces (to cope with direct aggression) without consenting to sending them abroad (regional collective security). To fit this straightjacket, government bureaucracy would invent the concept of "passive defense" (*senshu boei*) later. Under this rubric, the SDFs became modern armed forces, but they were forbidden to initiate hostilities even in self-defense. They would engage an enemy only when attacked, using the minimum of means. In terms of weapons, for instance, bombers were "war potential" but fighter aircraft were for self-defense. In practice, this came to mean that the SDFs would confine their activities to Japan's territorial spaces, although Japan would accept allied military assistance beyond its borders. Hence, "collective security" became a one-way benefit to Japan. The SDFs would refuse to go to the aid of the U.S. forces fighting beyond Japan's borders even if the operation was in direct defense of Japan.[75] Yoshida probably did not know what far reaching consequences his bureaucratic mincing of words would have on the future conduct of Japan.

Ikeda was disappointed to find that MSA assistance consisted only of end-item weapons and no economic aid.[76] He agreed in principle that GARIOA was a debt, but the final joint communique put off its settlement until further negotiation. He apparently concluded that it was political suicide for him to return home with only huge obligations and no gift. So he dug in his heels and bargained hard for the whole month of October.

On October 13 Ikeda handed Robertson a memorandum outlining a five-year defense plan, with a proviso that it was unofficial: In the three years between 1954 and 1957, ground forces would be increased to 180,000 men in 10 divisions. Ikeda argued that the division size in the Pentagon proposal, modeled after that of the U.S. Army, was too large because it included a large support element, which was unnecessary in Japan.[77]

On October 21, Robertson returned with the American reply. He said he recognized the political and economic difficulties facing Japan in arms buildup. But he persisted with his demand for an ultimate ground force level of 325,000–350,000. For the immediate future, he demanded a 180,000-man ground force. Robertson made it clear that Congress would not countenance any aid unless Japan delivered the 180,000-man buildup at the minimum. He was vague about any economic aid, except for an offer of $50 million in agricultural-surplus products. The Japanese delegation felt that it could bury the figures of 325,000 or 350,000 if it agreed to a 180,000-man force.[78] But in the end, Ikeda decided that he could not afford to go home with two obligations, the defense plan and GARIOA repayment. The only specific in the final statement was the promise of $50 million in U.S. aid.[79]

Upon returning home, Ikeda told Ambassador Allison his government would deliver a defense program substantially along the lines of his personal memorandum.[80] Immediately, Secretary Dulles decided to clinch an agreement on that basis.[81] In March 1954 the MSA agreement (the Mutual Defense Assistance Agreement) was formally concluded. Amid great confusion and a melee—caused by the JSP's physical obstruction—the Diet passed two bills, authorizing the supersession of the Secretary Agency by the Defense Agency, and the establishment of Ground, Air, and Maritime Self-Defense Forces.[82] The force level of Japan's Self-Defense Forces has remained unchanged to this day.

While Ikeda was in Washington, Vice-President Richard Nixon visited Tokyo at Dulles's request to press Yoshida to move on the constitution. In a speech before the America-Japan Society in Tokyo, Nixon said, ''Now if disarmament was right in 1946, why is it wrong in 1953? And if it was right in 1946 and wrong in 1953, why doesn't the United States admit for once that it made a mistake? And I am going to do something that I think perhaps ought to be done by people in public life. I'm going to admit right here that the United States did make a mistake in 1946."[83] Evidently the Eisenhower administration was taking the two-track approach to the constitution and rearmament.

Nixon did more than make a speech, the Japanese speculated, in his meeting with Yoshida. For one thing, Yoshida's nose bled profusely during the meeting, owing to high blood pressure, it was said with tongue in cheek, caused by Nixon.[84] For another, Yoshida swallowed Hatoyama's condition for returning to former Seiyukai: to establish the Constitution Investigation Commission in the party. A rumor had it that Nixon had something to do with this development. Yoshida appointed Kishi Nobusuke the commission chairman.[85]

The Yoshida cabinet was in its death throes in the spring of 1954, when a bribery scandal implicating Ikeda and other high officials was exposed. By June conservative politicians of all parties were joined by the business community in the search for a stable government. In the midst of a general listlessness, the Finance Ministry began working on a plan to cut back the following year's budget by 10 percent as part of a general fiscal retrenchment.[86]

In the meantime, Ikeda doggedly kept up the salvage operation for Yoshida, still refusing to stand down. Ikeda kept pleading with Allison for "real presents from [the] US."[87] He was to be the first disciple of Yoshida to become prime minister and to deliver his mentor's dream of building an economic superpower. A man of unusually strong character, he often landed himself in trouble for talking straight. Out of his loyalty to Yoshida, he tried everything with Allison, from bluff to begging. Following a stiff, tutelary admonition by Allison at a meeting, Ikeda smiled and said, "Perhaps the United States was making a mistake to treat Japan as a sovereign nation equal in strength and importance to itself. Perhaps . . . it would be better if the relationship were that of a teacher to his student." Japan was asking for the return of the occupation "Shogun," noted Allison.[88]

The climax came in September. Yoshida had to go through with the 10 percent budget cut, and the MSA accord of the spring was a dead letter. The United States faced "the most important decision" in Japan, Allison advised Washington, and went on:

> It is possible that, by a major effort which would shake US-Japan cooperation to its foundations, we could . . . obtain the same, or a slightly higher, level of military expenditure by Japan—for another year at least. This would involve the exertion of great persuasion and unquestionably a substantial increase in economic aid. And the amount of persuasion and the *close link between a military*

*buildup and economic aid* would largely nullify the friendly benefits we should expect from expanded assistance.[89]

When implicit linkage became explicit, Allison backed off. However, given the rules of the game—swapping self-defense for aid—it is difficult to say that Washington was shortchanged. It was offering only $50 million in economic aid and refused to raise the ante. (Its offer of $800 million in surplus military hardware did not interest Yoshida.) Allison's tirade—"Japanese have no abstract sense of right or wrong"—is understandable but seems misplaced. He should have criticized the rules of the game, determined by MacArthur's dicta that Japan should get rich before rearming or that rearmament will revive militarism. There were Americans who denounced these rules themselves. Lieutenant General Carter B. Magruder, chief of staff, Far East Command, bitterly complained:

> The conception of making Japan rich before we make her militarily strong would only weaken the moral fibre of her people and delay indefinitely Japan's achieving the ability to defend her own interests. [It would also] make her a more desirable prize to the Russians. . . . If we cannot inculcate in Japan a spirit, such as now motivates Germany to rise from defeat . . . it would be a waste of money to invest in Japan. . . . Before we accept a defeatist approach, I feel we should endeavor in every way to kindle in Japan a more aggressive spirit such as, for example: by urging the Japanese Government to establish itself more strongly with respect to Japan itself, by actively seeking the replacement of the present Japanese Government if it is unable to take a stronger grasp on Japan's affairs; by discontinuing economic aid so that Japan has to struggle for her livelihood and therefore feel the need of military power in supporting her commercial ventures such as fishing in the waters off the Kurile Islands and Korea; by urging Japan again to seek a position of leadership in Northeast Asia; by seeking to arrange a Northeast Asia pact in which Japan would be the leader and even by indicating that the United States would view favorably the re-establishment of the Japanese Empire under a moderate Japanese Government."[90]

These were straightforward alternatives. The State Department and the Tokyo embassy, too, entertained open intervention in passing, but desisted.[91] As the architect of the security treaty, Dulles was, according to a State Department memorandum, "grievously disappointed" that there had been "no revival in Japan of the spirit of sacrifice and discipline" or "great national spirit."[92] When all was said and done, Washington was hostage to Yoshida. His "deficiencies" were thought to be "outweighed by achievements" at the State Department.[93] His visit to the United States was resurrected after an earlier cancellation. But then Yoshida never established a meeting of the minds with American officials.

Since "Japan has no basic convictions for or against the free world," said Allison, the "Japanese must be convinced that ours is [the] winning side."[94] At an NSC meeting in September, "Secretary Dulles expressed the belief that we may have to lower our sights on Japanese rearmament."[95]

A new development in American strategic thinking also favored Japan's remaining in the MacArthur legacy. The testing of hydrogen bombs and thermonuclear weapons that had started under the Truman administration convinced the strategists in Washington that they had found a means of deterring all wars, large and small. At Dulles's initiative, the Eisenhower administration had decided to place its reliance on "massive retaliation" directed at Moscow, a technological substitute for conventional defense and allied "burden sharing." This so-called New Look would suffice until the Soviet retaliatory capability in nuclear arsenal would be built up.[96] In December 1954 Secretary of Defense Charles Wilson pulled out a division of U.S. forces from Japan without prior consultation that would have been called for in a normal alliance.[97] But no one protested.

# NOTES

1. Shigeru Hayashi and Kiyoaki Tsuji, eds., *Nihon naikaku shiroku* [History of Japan's cabinets] (Tokyo: Daiichihoki, 1981), V, 224.

2. Many Japanese were puzzled by the sudden expansion of the JSP immediately after the peace conference because they do not see Yoshida's influence on the Left. See Junnosuke Masumi, in Yoshitake Oka, ed., *Gendai Nihon no seiji katei* [The political process of contemporary Japan] (Tokyo: Iwanami, 1958), p. 383.

3. *Ambassador from the Prairie or Allison in Wonderland* (Boston: Houghton Mifflin, 1972), p. 244.

4. On the disposition of occupation reforms in posttreaty Japan, Sebald said, "A delicate balance will have to be drawn in United States relations with the Japanese Government between what the United States considers basic and what it considers expendable. In some instances we may need to bend over backwards in limiting for psychological reasons overt evidence of United States control. On the other hand we may have to exert what pressures we possess to fortify those reforms we consider basic." *Foreign Relations of the United States* (Washington, DC: GPO, 1977), 1951, VI, 1364–65.

5. *The United States and Japan* (Cambridge: Harvard Univ. Press, 1957), xx. See the full quotation in Chapter 1.

6. Ichiro Hatoyama, *Hatoyama Ichiro kaikoroku* [Memoir of Hatoyama Ichiro] (Tokyo: Bungei Shunjusha, 1957), pp. 93–97. See also Ichiro Kono, *Kono Ichiro jiden* [Kono Ichiro: an autobiography] (Tokyo: Tokuma Shoten, 1964), pp. 201–18, for Kono's own story. Note that Kono cites Yoshida's letter to General Whitney asking for a permission to purge Matsumoto Jiichiro. Ibid., p. 121.

7. *Newsweek*'s editorial staff were among them. But there were others.

8. *Kono Ichiro jiden*, pp. 201–18.

9. *Nihon naikaku shiroku,* V, 220.

10. Ikeda, quoted in Shigeru Yoshida, *Kaiso sanju-nen* [Memoir of thirty years] (Tokyo: Shinchosha, 1957), pp. 145–46.

11. Richard Finn, in *FRUS,* 1952–54, XIV, 1250.

12. See articles by Hideo Otake, Kiyotada Tsutsui, Takashi Ito in Tetsuya Kataoka, ed., *The 1955 System of Japan's Politics: Its Origin and Consequences* (forthcoming); Seizaburo Shinobu, *Sengo Nihon seijishi* [Postwar politics of Japan] (Tokyo: Kenso Shobo, 1967), IV, 1356–57.

13. Has H. Baerwald, *The Purge of Japanese Leaders under the Occupation* (Berkeley: Univ. of California Press, 1959), pp. 95–96. It seems that the GS reconstituted this party, but the extent of GS involvement remains unknown.

14. Junnosuke Masumi, *Sengo seiji* [Postwar politics] (Tokyo: Tokyo Univ. Press, 1984), pp. 407–8.

15. *Nihon naikaku shiroku,* V, 211–12; Shinobu, *Sengo Nihon seijishi,* IV, 1269–71, 1366–68.

16. Hideo Otake, *Saigunbi to nashonarizumu: hoshu, riberaru, shakai minshushugisha no boeikan* [Rearmament and nationalism: the defense philosophy of the conservatives, liberals, and social-democrats] (Tokyo: Chuo Koronsha, 1988), pp. 185–214.

17. For a good psycho-political analysis of this point, see Sekai Mondai Kenkyu-kai, "Nihon no unmei" [Japan's fate], *Chuo Koron,* (January 1952), pp. 15–31.

18. Shumpei Ueyama made this point eloquently, in *Dai-Toa senso no imi* [The meaning of the Greater East Asian War] (Tokyo: Chuo Koron-sha, 1964).

19. See "Mushiro senryo no keizoku o erabu" [I would rather choose the continuation of occupation], *Chuo Koron,* (April 1952), pp. 40–45.

20. For a good representative sample of these views, see Hitoshi Yamakawa, "Nihon o yugameru mono: tenno no shinkakuka" [What distorts Japan: deification of the emperor], *Chuo Koron,* (December 1951), pp. 23–27.

21. SCAP Labor Section's mandate to Sohyo was: (1) anticommunist unionism, (2) a congress of industrial unions based on the CIO model, (3) boycott of the left-leaning WLO and choice of affiliation with IFLO, and (4) stress on economism rather than on politics. Shoichi Okamoto, *Sohyo o kokuhatsu suru* [Indicting Sohyo] (Tokyo: Eru Shuppan, 1971), pp. 109–28; Shinobu, *Sengo Nihon seijishi,* IV, 1091–97.

22. Ibid., p. 1157.

23. *Nihon Shakaito no sanjunen,* I, 295–96.

24. Koken Oyama, *Nihon Shakaito shi* [History of the Japan Socialist Party] (Tokyo: Haga Shoen, 1965), p. 103; *Nihon Shakaito no sanjunen,* I, 288.

25. *Nihon naikaku shiroku,* V, 218; Shinobu, *Sengo Nihon seijishi* IV, 1365–66.

26. Shinobu, *Sengo Nihon seijishi,* IV, 1399.

27. Yoshitsu, p. 93.

28. *FRUS,* 1952–54, XIV, 1275.

29. *FRUS,* 1952–54, XIV, 1099–1100.

30. *FRUS,* 1951, VI, 1286.

31. Koken Oyama, *Sengo Nihon Kyosanto-shi* [History of postwar Japan Communist Party] (Tokyo: Haga Shoten, 1969), pp. 133–40; Shinobu, *Sengo Nihon seijishi,* IV, 1431–33. To make a point with the Americans, I infer, the Yoshida government did

nothing. The metropolitan police had been reorganized by SCAP as a local police force and divorced from government supervision.

32. *Chuo Koron* commented on the Administrative Agreement and said, "how hopeless Japan's future is," in an editorial, *Chuo Koron,* (April 1952), pp. 1–3.

33. In addition, a major domestic bill, the Subversive Activities Prevention Law (*Haboho*), was passed.

34. *Nihon naikaku shiroku,* V, 224.

35. *FRUS,* 1952–54, XIV, 1268.

36. *FRUS,* 1952–54, XIV, 1284.

37. *FRUS,* 1952–54, XIV, 1743–44.

38. See Otake, *Saigunbi to nashonarizumu,* pp. 89–121.

39. *FRUS,* 1952–54, XIV, p. 1218.

40. These figures materialized in the NSC 125 series. See NSC 125/2, "United States Objectives and Courses of Action With Respect to Japan," August 7, 1952, ibid., pp. 1300–1308. See also Eiichi Tatsumi, "Saigunbi ni hantai shita Yoshida Shigeru" [Yoshida Shigeru against rearmament], *Toki no Kadai,* March 1973, p. 116.

41. Tatsuo Mitearai, *Miki Bukichi den* [Biography of Miki Bukichi] (Tokyo: Shikisha, 1958), p. 350.

42. Masumi, II, 410.

43. Mitearai, p. 350.

44. Yumi Hiwatari, *Sengo seiji to Nichi-Bei kankei,* [Postwar politics and the Japan-US relations] (Tokyo: Tokyo Univ. Press, 1990), pp. 68–69.

45. Ibid., p. 67.

46. Mitearai, pp. 360–62. Yoshida had earlier expelled Ishibashi and Kono from the party, but he agreed to their return. In addition, he gave up key party appointments to Miki.

47. Fred Dickinson, "Nichi-Bei anpo taisei no henyo" [The transformation in the Japan-U.S. security system], *Hogaku Ronshu* (Kyoto: Univ. of Kyoto), Vol. 121, No. 4, Vol. 122, No. 3.

48. Yumi Hiwatari, *Sengo seiji to Nichi-Bei Kankei,* pp. 62–67, 90–102.

49. See John M. Allison, *Ambassador from the Prairie* (Boston: Houghton Mifflin, 1973). He is mum on the Hatoyama administration.

50. *FRUS,* 1952–54, XIV, 1406–07. See NSC 125/2 of April and NSC 125/6 of June 1953, in ibid., pp. 1305, 1413.

51. Ibid., p. 1799.

52. Ibid., p. 1693.

53. Ibid., p. 1407.

54. Ibid., p. 1364.

55. *Nihon Shakaito no sanjunen,* I, 385–89.

56. Mitearai, p. 375.

57. *Nihon naikaku shiroku,* V, 258; Hitoshi Ashida, *Ashida Hitoshi nikki* [The Ashida Hitoshi diary] (Tokyo: Iwanami Shoten, 1986), IV, 3–14.

58. Quoted in Ashida, V, 245.

59. For the best available account, see Seizaburo Shinobu et al., "Shihai kenryoku no kabu-kozo" [The infrastructure of the ruling power], in Yoshitake Oka, ed., *Gendai Nihon no seiji katei* [The political process in contemporary Japan] (Tokyo: Iwanami Shoten, 1958), pp. 167–314.

60. Teiso Horikoshi, ed., *Keizai Dentai Rengokai junen-shi* [Ten-year history of Keidanren] (Tokyo: Keidanren, 1963), II, 566–647.

61. Oka, pp. 222–23.

62. These bills had been submitted at the previous session but shelved because of Yoshida's "Name-Calling Dissolution." *Nihon naikaku shiroku,* V, 243–44, 264–68.

63. Mitearai, p. 381. Miki's secondary goal was to find a face-saving device to enable Hatoyama to return to Yoshida's fold. Hatoyama was caving in to Yoshida's entreaties and wanted a government concession to his demand for rearmament.

64. Bukichi Miki, *Saigunbit to kempo mondai* [On rearmament and the constitutional problem] (Tokyo: Nihon Jiyuto, 1953), pp. 10–11.

65. *FRUS, 1952–54,* XIV, 1455–56.

66. Ibid., p. 1459.

67. Ibid., p. 1460. Allison wired Dulles again and lectured him: don't give newspapers like *Asahi* any ammunition; don't rock the boat. Ibid., p. 1485. The idea of a 325,000-man force was first mentioned by Ridgeway in 1952.

68. Kiichi Miyazawa, *Tokyo-Washington no mitsudan* [Secret talks between Tokyo and Washington] (Tokyo: Jitsugyo no Nihonsha, 1956), p. 160. The subject of MSA aid came up for discussion in August, when Dulles visited Yoshida in Tokyo to renew the pressure for rearmament.

69. Miyazawa, pp. 194–201; Ashida, IV, 366–76.

70. Ichiya Sakamoto, "Aizenhaua no gaiko senryaku to Nihon" [Eisenhower's diplomatic strategy and Japan], *Hogaku Ronshu,* 122, No. 3, 71.

71. The ground forces would be increased to six divisions by 1954, eight by 1955, and ultimately to 10 divisions with 325,000 men by 1956. A total ground-force manpower of 350,000 was also mentioned by the American side and puzzled the Japanese. The air arm was to have 800 aircraft and 30,000 personnel. The navy was to have 18 frigates and 50 landing craft immediately and unspecified future additions, with 13,500 personnel. *FRUS, 1952–54,* XIV, Pt. 2, 1527–28. Hisao Nagasawa, "Ikeda-Robatoson kaidan" [The Ikida-Robertson negotiation], *Kokubo,* March 1978, pp. 21–33.

72. *FRUS, 1952–54,* XIV, Pt. 2, 1524–28.

73. Miyazawa, p. 127.

74. Ibid., pp. 215–16. This line of interpretation was first proposed by Ashida. There is some dispute as to when Ashida hit upon the idea. See Osamu Watanabe, *Nihon kempo 'kaisei' shi* [History of Japan's constitutional 'revision'] (Tokyo: Nihon Hyoronsha, 1987), p. 134.

75. See Defense Agency, *Defense of Japan* (Tokyo: Defense Agency, 1986), p. 83.

76. Before Ikeda left Tokyo, Yoshida said to him on GARIOA loan, "I promised Dulles time and again that we'll pay it back. Japan is a samurai nation. But we need new money to pay it back with. I asked for that, too." Miyazawa, pp. 211–12.

77. In addition, the following was promised: (1) in five years, the navy would have 210 ships of 156,550 tons, of which 74 would be escort ships and 31 minesweepers, and personnel would be 31,300; (2) in five years the air force would have 518 aircraft, consisting of two wings of jet fighter-bombers (150 F-84Gs), one wing of all-weather jet fighters (36 F-94CS), 300 trainers, and others, and personnel would be 7,600; (3) an air-control-and-warning unit would have 13,100 men; (4) the cost would be ¥900 billion, of which Japan would bear ¥620 billion and the United States ¥280 billion, or $800 million. Miyazawa, pp. 234–35. Note that the Security Agency had published a so-

called five-year plan in September 1953, which envisioned 210,000 ground troops, ship tonnage of 145,000, and 1,400 planes by 1957, based on $1.5 billion in MSA aid in five years (*FRUS,* 1952–54, XIV, 1511–12). Ikeda regarded this plan as a "leak" to embarrass him in Washington. Miyazawa states that Japan's defense bureaucracy—in the habit of scheming with the Pentagon—had to be kept out and that Ikeda's plan was put together by the Japanese delegation in Washington. But it seems more proper to assume that it had Yoshida's approval.

78. Miyazawa, pp. 186–89, 233–34.

79. Ibid., p. 268; see also *FRUS,* 1952–54, XIV, 1549–50.

80. Ibid., p. 1556.

81. Ibid., p. 1566.

82. *Nichibei ampo joyaku taisei-shi* [History of the Japan-U.S. security system] (Tokyo: Sanseido, 1970), II, 486. The force level at this point was 130,000 for Ground SDF, 15,800 for Maritime SDF, 6,280 for Air SDF, and 10,000 civilian employees.

83. *The Memoirs of Richard Nixon* (New York: Grosset and Dunlap, 1978), pp. 129–30. See the *Ashai Shimbun* report that Washington expected a revision in 1955, November 29, 1953, p. 1. Nakasone Yasuhiro takes credit for the Nixon visit. See Nakasone et al., "Beikoku no atsuryoku to Nihon no teiko" [U.S. pressure and Japanese resistance], *Bungei Shunju,* (January 1954), p. 70.

84. *Asahi Shimbun,* November 16, 1953, p. 1.

85. *Nihon naikaku shiroku,* V, 260. Kishi, a revisionist, was surprised that Yoshida picked him, giving him to understand that constitutional revision was not too far off.

86. See Defense Agency vice minister Masuhara's explanation to Allison in July in *FRUS,* 1952–54, XIV, 1690.

87. Ibid., p. 1705.

88. Ibid., pp. 1658–59.

89. Ibid., p. 1718. Emphasis added. This and another report, Allison's agonizing reappraisal as it were (ibid., pp. 1714–15), are highly revealing documents.

90. Ibid., pp. 1731–32.

91. State and the Pentagon had staked out opposing positions earlier, in June 1952. "While State took the position that the United States should not interfere in Japanese domestic affairs unless internal developments gravely threaten United States security interests, Defense proposes United States intervention 'to prevent internal developments from gravely threatening United States security interests.' " Ibid., 1271–72.

92. Ibid., pp. 1482, 1703.

93. Ibid., p. 1744.

94. Ibid., p. 1714.

95. Ibid., p. 1725. See Eisenhower, ibid., p. 1662; and Truman, ibid., p. 1161. "There is a growing assurance among Japanese officials that our renewed emphasis on Japan greatly enhances their bargaining position," observed a report. Ibid., pp. 1685–86.

96. See how the military adjusted to the "New Look" in Japan; ibid., p. 1768.

97. Ibid., p. 1811.

# Chapter 6

# The Revisionists and Their Vision

Miyazawi Kiichi, the last remaining disciple of the Yoshida School, once wondered aloud what might have happened to Japan had Yoshida retired from politics upon concluding the peace treaty. He thought Japan would have been different, though he did not spell out what the alternative might have been. Indeed the first few years of independence—coinciding with Yoshida's last years of rule—were formative years in which large alternatives and choices were still debated. The revisionists talked of autonomy. Interestingly, Yoshida had no shorthand for his alternative, which we have called postoccupation tutelage.[1]

Yoshida's students maintain that, either way, Japan's status and external conduct would not have been much different. In the nuclear age, they say, only the two superpowers are fully sovereign, all the other nations having to curb their autonomy more or less.[2] But this argument is specious. Accession to the nuclear power status may be externally constrained. But it is one thing to accept a nonnuclear status and quite another to argue for the protectorate status that the security treaty represented. At least John Foster Dulles and the State Department invited Japan to explore avenues toward greater equality in spite of the JCS's objections. But it was Japan itself that imposed limits on its status and conduct on the grounds of constitutionality. Because of the constitution, Japan had to decline participation in all collective security arrangements, regional or UN-sponsored.

Because the constitution was kept when it was no longer externally necessary, Japan's domestic politics was also negatively affected. Yoshida's implied position that domestic order could be divorced from foreign policy was not valid, for Yoshida's foreign policy was predicated on the leftwing Socialists' defense of the constitution. They and the constitution reinforced each other to give rise to many of the maladies of the body politik, the chief among which were the LDP's one-party dominance and factionalism. Had the constitution been revised, the Socialists' neutrality rhetoric would have been deprived of institutional underpinnings. Nationalism on the Left, where it was perversely combined with neutralism, would have been drained off and channeled into a more constructive direction. The rightwing Socialists could have dominated and absorbed the leftwing. Together they might have taken the path parallel to that taken by the German DSP after the Bad Gordesburg Conference of 1959. The JSP could have produced a Helmut Schmidt of Japan.[3]

The revisionists—whose core consisted of Seiyukai's professional politicians plus Kishi, a bureaucratic statesman—envisioned a very different Japan. There were four major components to their goal: constitutional revision, the sine qua none of collective security; greater and mutual equality in Japan's relations with the United States, based on rearmament; restoration of alternating two-party system at home; and a curb on the excessive power of the central ministry bureaucracies. It is the burden of this and the following chapters to show what the revisionists dreamed of and how they failed.

Let us now turn to April 1953, the aftermath of the Name-Calling Dissolution, to understand the political predicament of the conservative leaders as they debated large choices for the country. Table III shows the election results for the lower house of the Diet between 1946 and 1958. Our main interest is in the rise of the JSP's electoral fortunes. On the strength of the 1947 election results, a Socialist prime minister was born. But the Socialist-conservative government went down to defeat in the anti-American 1949 election. A good number of Socialist votes went to the JCP and a lesser number to Yoshida. The "reverse course" was already in motion. The JCP resorted to clandestine war, and the JSP received an injection of new blood from Sohyo.

In 1951 the JSP adopted the neutralist Four Principles and split over the peace and security treaties. Following the Surprise Dissolution of the Diet by

**Table III**
Lower House Election Results
(By number of seats)

|      | Conservative parties | JSP Left | JSP Right | JCP | Others |
|------|----------------------|----------|-----------|-----|--------|
| 1946 | 272                  |          | 94        | 5   | 129    |
| 1947 | 291                  |          | 143       | 4   | 34     |
| 1948 | 333                  |          | 48        | 35  | 50     |
| 1952 | 325                  | 54       | 57        | 0   | 30     |
| 1953 | 310                  | 72       | 66        | 1   | 17     |
| 1955 | 297                  | 89       | 67        | 2   | 12     |
| 1958 | 287                  |          | 166       | 1   | 13     |

Yoshida, the two wings of the JSP fought separate campaigns, and the leftwing expanded. After the election of 1953, the leftwing emerged as the unquestioned leader of the neutralist camp. The two wings campaigned on the issue of rearmament, and captured one-third of the lower house. Constitutional revision became more difficult.

This is where we stand. None of the conservative leaders—absolutely no one—could trust the leftwing Socialists because of their revolutionary commitment, genealogy, and outlook. Yoshida, Hatoyama, Ikeda, Kishi, Kono, Miki Bukichi, Miki Takeo, Ashida, Shigemitsu, Matsumura, Ogata[4]—all mistrusted the leftwing Socialists. Particularly noteworthy was the case of Miki Takeo and Matsumura, since they were on the far left of the conservatives and quite tolerant of the Socialists.[5] LDP leaders took a dim view of the fact that a sizable portion of the electorate was shifting between the JSP and the JCP. At a time when the JCP was in a full-scale war with the government, the Socialist leftwing appeared to them a Communist surrogate. Last but not least, there was no way of knowing that the JSP would not go on growing to capture power in a few more elections, as the JSP itself boasted.

The conservative leaders, especially those in former Seiyukai, which held the initiative because of its superior position, had been debating what to do long before 1953. A natural solution was to tame the Socialists, invite them to revive a conservative-Socialist coalition, and return to the prewar two-party system. Ashida, Ogata and Kishi felt this was the thing to do.[6] Kishi, the "radical bureaucrat" of the militarist era, shared that "revisionist capitalist" inclination of former Minseito, and immediately after the purge was lifted, he tried to organize a new political party by recruiting the rightwing Socialists.[7]

Like his colleagues, Kishi was troubled by conservative factionalism—so much so that when he became prime minister in 1956 he initiated the ritual, repeated ever since by LDP leaders, of declaring factions abolished. The same concern was behind his sponsorship of the conservative merger. But he knew that it would be meaningless unless the JSP grew into a responsible opposition. Partly as a stimulus to induce the quarreling conservatives to merge, he first persuaded the Socialists to merge.[8]

Then there were those such as Miki Takeo and Matsumura, who insisted on a two-conservative-parties system, never mind the radicals.[9] That is to say, they would simply ignore the presence of the JSP and go about business as usual. But this was burying one's head in the sand. On critical votes the minority conservative party was bound to enlist the JSP to outvote the majority party. This was the trouble with the system—a radical party held the balance of power.

Up to this point, the more notable instances of conservative-JSP cooperation against another conservative group were (1) the vote of censure against Finance

Minister Ikeda in November 1952, (2) the Hatoyama-JSP cooperation to amend
the budget in December 1952, (3) the votes of censure and noconfidence against
Yoshida's name-calling in March 1953, (4) the stillborn attempt of Sohyo to
support a Shigemitsu-JSP coalition in May 1953; and (5) the Hatoyama-
Shigemitsu-JSP cooperation to take the speakership and vice-speakership from
Yoshida in May 1953. As long as Yoshida was in power, conservative-JSP
cooperation would center on Hatoyama or Shigemitsu. But Yoshida-JSP cooperation against Hatoyama would soon begin—in defense of the constitution and
pacifism.[10]

So the only thing to do was to unite all the conservatives into one party
(*hoshu godo*). The architect of this scheme was Miki Bukichi, an old Minseito
veteran who joined former Seiyukai because of his friendship for Hatoyama.
Miki felt by 1953 that no matter how many elections were held, there could not
be a stable conservative government as long as the Yoshida-Hatoyama issue
remained unresolved.[11] He was supported by Kono, Hatoyama's close adviser,
and Kishi. But they were no babes in the woods; they knew that the attempt to
reconcile Hatoyama with Yoshida was to beg the question. So they had to get rid
of Yoshida. Until then constitutional revision, rearmament, and independence
had been ideological issues for Ashida and Hatoyama. When the real power
brokers adopted this agenda in the wake of the Name-Calling Dissolution, the
"ideology" became the platform of a movement with muscle. This was the
thrust that produced the Liberal Democratic party.[12]

At the minimum, the merger had to end the JSP intervention in the conservative politics and that also meant that the Socialists would be kept out of power
and even decimated. But the merger scheme did not reckon with the difficulty
of containing Yoshida after his overthrow.

In November 1953 Yoshida swallowed his pride and asked Hatoyama and the
breakaway party to return to former Seiyukai. Hatoyama consented on the
condition that the Constitution Investigation Commission be established in the
party. But early the next year, a bribery scandal implicating the Yoshida faction
was exposed. When an arrest warrant was issued for Sato Eisaku, secretary
general of the party, Yoshida had the justice minister restrain the prosecution
and let Sato off the hook, without a breach of the law. A quarter-century later,
in the late 1970s, Prime Minister Tanaka Kakuei, implicated in the Lockheed
scandal, failed in the same legal maneuver because of the public's outrage. It
seems that the power of the press had grown enormously in the interim. Back in
1954 the media did not cause Yoshida's immediate downfall but pushed the
merger ahead one notch.

Even Ogata, Yoshida's heir-designate, abandoned him and joined all the other conservatives moving in unison toward the establishment of a new party. No longer able to coopt a faction of former Minseito, Ogata declared it was the "urgent task of the moment" to have a merger of the two parties as equals (April 1954). Hatoyama's return to former Seiyukai enabled him to blast Yoshida from inside. On the outside, the directorate of Japan's business community called on Yoshida to stand down in November.[13] The Bloody Mary Day (the attack on American GIs) and the JCP's revolutionary war on behalf of Cominform forced the issue on Keidanren. Since this was to be a movement for conservative renewal, it seemed fitting that the conservative politicians should juxtapose themselves against the radical-liberals, the constitution, and the bureaucratic politicians, all legacies of the occupation.

What emerged in the fall of 1954 was the Democratic party, which consisted of (1) former Minseito, (2) the Hatoyama faction of former Seiyukai, and (3) the faction of former Seiyukai led by Kishi, an anti-Yoshida bureaucrat. The union of Kishi and Miki Bukichi carried weight. Immediately, the Democrats joined hands with the two wings of the JSP to vote Yoshida out of office (November 1954).[14] Yoshida faced a dire prospect—unless he could split the Socialists from Hatoyama, all his work would be undone. Washington, too, braced itself for a deteriorating Tokyo connection. Hatoyama, Kishi, and Shigemitsu, were rated as undesirable—all were purgees, Kishi was Tojo's minister of munitions, and Shigemitsu was a war criminal.[15]

Ironically, Hatoyama Ichiro was perhaps the best educated of all postwar prime ministers in the political culture of democracy. Hatoyama's father, Kazuo, was born in 1856, three yeas after the coming of the Black Ships, into the family of a samurai bureaucrat in southern Japan. He availed himself of the first round of precious government fellowships to study abroad at the tender age of 20. He chose to go to Columbia University. Upon graduation, he entered the predecessor of Yale Law School, from which he graduated with a master's in law and a doctorate in jurisprudence. Altogether he spent five years in the United States.

The three aspirations of young Hatoyama Kazuo were the establishment of the legal profession, of a private university, and of constitutional government in Japan—all of which were obviously the outgrowth of his experience in the United States. Upon returning home in 1881, he taught briefly at Tokyo University before entering the Foreign Ministry's treaty bureau. As parliamentary government was founded under the Meiji constitution, Hatoyama was elected to the first session as a Dietman. He inclined toward the opposition and the people's rights movement, though he was a moderate. He deplored the confusion in parliamentary procedure in the nascent assembly and wrote a manual, which immediately became the standard in the Diet as well as in all local assemblies. In 1882 he collaborated with Okuma Shigenobu, another Meiji founding member, to create Waseda University, a major private institution, and he later became its president. He died in 1911.

Hatoyama Ichiro, Kazuo's first son, was born in 1883 and was raised under comfortable circumstances with the best of maternal care. Throughout his adolescence he imbibed the tradition of political discussion and public service to which his father devoted himself. The year after his father's death, the first year of the Taisho era, he was elected to the Tokyo City Assembly, succeeding to his father's profession at the age of 33. Four years later he was elected concurrently to the Diet. He was befriended by Hara Kei, the leader of the Seiyukai party, which he later joined. Hara, a contemporary and a friend of his father, was the man who established parliamentary democracy in Japan.

In 1927 Hatoyama was appointed chief cabinet secretary of the Tanaka government. About the same time, he and Yoshida, then a foreign-service officer, struck up a friendship. Politically, they shared the same convictions, though in personality and style Hatoyama was more open and egalitarian. In 1931 Hatoyama was appointed education minister of the Inukai cabinet.[16]

By upbringing and profession, he was thoroughly wedded to parliamentary democracy and constitutional government. His defense of constitutional government brought him into a collision course with the militarists and their parliamentary supporters. He was shunted aside and spent most of the war years in a self-imposed exile away from Tokyo. For a brief while in 1945, he worked in the shadows with Konoye and Yoshida to end the war.[17] When the war was over, he, Miki Bukichi, Kono Ichiro, and others—all professional politicians who came of age in the Taisho democracy period, and who were penalized for resisting the militarists and their collaborators—reorganized the remnants of Seiyukai into the Liberal party. Unquestionably, Hatoyama was the leader.

Hatoyama's inclination to be outspoken—somewhat incongruous with his gentle personality—may be traceable to his personal integrity and his Christian convictions. Nothing shows his streak better than the two public statements he made as soon as the occupation began. In September 1945, as mentioned earlier, he denounced the bombing of Hiroshima and Nagasaki. This may have hastened the imposition of SCAP censorship.[18] Shortly thereafter he also denounced communism with quixotic indiscretion at a press conference at the Foreign Correspondents' Club. In so doing, he walked into a trap set by Mark Gayn, a reporter for the *Chicago Sun,* who collaborated with the Japanese Communists to see to it that Hatoyama was purged.[19] This was the earliest and most controversial case of purge for "democratization" rather than demilitalization purpose, the original justification for purge. Having spent upward of five years in banishment, he was outraged by the fact that his depurge was delayed by Yoshida's shenanigans. Just as the purge was lifted, he suffered a stroke and became paralyzed from the waist down.

Hatoyama's coming to power coincided with a shift in the Cold War that was traceable to the death of Joseph Stalin, the Korean truce, and the Soviet acquisition of the hydrogen bomb—all in 1953. After some twists and turns, Stalin's successors fell in line behind Nikita Khrushchev's leadership. Confident in the efficacy of the Soviet system, Khrushchev chose to go on a "peace offensive," which presupposed superpower coexistence, but which was much more daring and bellicose than anything that Stalin had practiced. In close collaboration with the Chinese Communists, the Soviet Union sought to lead the anticolonial struggle in the Third World.

The Soviets and the Chinese lent their support to the Vietminh War, the Huq rebellion in the Philippines, the Algerian insurgency, the rise of Colonel Nasser to the presidency in Egypt, and the worldwide peace movement that culminated in the meetings in Vienna and Helsinki. The Vietminh War ended in French defeat and retreat at the Geneva Conference of July 1954, attended by China's Chou En-lai and John Foster Dulles. At the same time, the Kremlin accommodated itself to the division of Europe and to America's major allies. It issued a joint declaration with China in October 1954 calling for normalization of diplomatic relations with Japan;[20] agreed to Austrian neutrality in May 1955; and recognized Adenauer's West Germany in September. Peking conceded that "the government of Japan represents the people of Japan" and began to seek normalized relations through expanded trade. Playing up the theme of "peaceful coexistence," Khrushchev actively sought and arranged the four-power summit meeting of the United States, the Soviet Union, Britain, and France in Geneva in July 1955. The Sino-American dialogue also commenced at the ambassadorial level in August. Whereas Stalin had confined his intervention in Japan to the Cominform hierarchy, Khrushchev and the Chinese leaders sought to influence both the government and the JSP directly.

The United States, in contrast, did not slacken the pace of its Cold War buildup. In early 1954 Secretary Dulles unveiled with much fanfare the strategic New Look, conducted a series of thermonuclear tests in Bikini (resulting in the deaths of Japanese fishermen), and further expanded regional alliances for containment. Starting with South Korea (October 1953), the United States enlisted the Ngo Dinh Diem regime in South Vietnam, West Germany in NATO, the SEATO and Baghdad Pact partners, and the Chinese Nationalists. The French defeat in Indochina and the communist peace offensive combined to create the impression that the United States was on the defensive and truculent.

It was against the backdrop of the "thaw" and its pressure on Washington that Hatoyama and his depurged friends displaced Yoshida, and called for "revisions" and "autonomy." Hatoyama dissolved the Diet for a general election in February 1955, as he had promised the Socialists in exchange for their support in voting against Yoshida. There was a widespread sense that politics in Japan was at a turning point. The two wings of the JSP were gearing up for a merger of their own with Sohyo's endorsement. The Sino-Soviet joint declaration of October 1954 triggered this event.[21] The Socialists were eager to put their new strength to an electoral test at a time when the economy was still in the grip of a post-Korean War recession.

Much yearning for a change filled the land, and both the Socialists and the revisionists took heart. Hatoyama vowed, "I'll do everything the opposite of Mr. Yoshida,"[22] and he campaigned on two issues: constitutional revision and a peace treaty with the Soviet Union. He was more interested in rapprochement with China, but he bowed to the weight of circumstances, created by the San Francisco treaty, and scaled down his China plank to the opening trade opportunities. The Socialists warmly endorsed his "peace diplomacy," ushering in the brief and only period of "bipartisan" foreign policy in postwar Japan. Hatoyama basked in the glow of the so-called Hatoyama boom that swept the country.

At no other time did Japan come so close to constitutional revision as it did under Hatoyama. Voters were tired of Yoshida's double-talk and sophistry. Washington was dissatisfied with the 180,000-man army Yoshida had promised and kept up the pressure for more. Anti-Yoshida revisionists were close to forging a union of the conservatives pledged to write Japan's own constitution. Among the newspapers, *Mainichi* supported it, though *Asahi* opposed it.[23] According to *Asahi*'s poll of December 1954, 30 percent of respondents supported revision, 25 percent opposed, and 45 percent had no opinion.[24] *Chuo Koron,* a respectable journal of intellectuals on the center Left, supported it in principle but felt that Japan was not free enough of American influence to be able to write a constitution of its own liking.[25]

But beneath the good feeling on the surface yawned the chasm of dissent. Thirteen out of 17 members of the Hatoyama cabinet were depurgees. The merger commotion in the Diet and among the revisionists naturally provoked the opposition. For the rightwing Socialists, January 1954 was the turning point on the constitutional issue—the revisionist Socialists fell silent before the rising tide of antirevisionism.[26] The National Union of Constitutional Defense (Kenpo Yogo Kokumin Rengo) was organized at Sohyo's urging in late 1954. It was an umbrella for 135 organizations, which together boasted a total membership of 5 million.[27]

In the progressive wing of former Minseito, now in Hatoyama's Democratic party, was a young Dietman by the name of Nakasone Yasuhiro from Gumma prefecture in the mountain fastness of central Japan. He had been a first lieutenant and paymaster in the imperial navy when the war ended. An inveterate patriot, he was offended by the demoralization of the countrymen and decided to do something about it through public service. He ran successfully for the lower house in 1947 and has never lost his Diet seat since. He objected strongly to the anti-Japanese policy of the occupation and had several run-ins with Americans. He took exception, for instance, to SCAP's policy of banning the display of the rising sun emblem and the singing of the national anthem. One day he had the flag hoisted high in the front yard of his house, only to have a jeep-load of American MPs drive up and take it down.

Realizing quite correctly that the future of Japan was being decided by the peace treaty negotiation with John Foster Dulles, Nakasone went to see him at MacArthur's headquarters. He presented to Dulles a petition critical of occupation policies. On a visit to Washington in the early 1950s, he came to know Vice President Richard M. Nixon, who he found shared his views. Nakasone says he persuaded Nixon to make the speech against the constitution in 1953.[28] Known as "young officer" for his daring and unconventional views, which used to be further to the Left than they are today, young Nakasone could not have been happier in 1955. Now that Hatoyama was in power and calling a general election, he felt his time had come. He composed the Constitutional Revision Song and sought to popularize it through personal appearances on television.[29]

The Hatoyama boom seemed to have considerable coattail effect for his party in the February 1955 election; Hatoyama's Democratic party won 185 seats, an increase from 127; Yoshida's Liberals 112, down from 180; the leftwing JSP 89, an increase from 72; and the rightwing 67, an increase from 64. The Socialists together gained 20 seats, of which 16 went to the leftwing. The rightwing muffled its strong objection to the leftwing's pro-communism when the election resulted in further gains by the Left and the conservatives began to move toward merger. The only clear-cut mandate was that the constitutional naysayers, the Socialists, managed to retain the one-third minority needed to block revision. Hatoyama needed the support of the Liberals, now under Ogata's leadership, to run the government. Instead of retiring as many people had expected, Yoshida ran successfully for the Diet, but, with his following drastically reduced, he appeared to be contained.

But he was still a threat, for his strength was always in his ability to read Washington's mind. And in early 1955 it was not difficult to see which way the wind was blowing in the U.S. capital. In March *Time* magazine featured a cover story on Hatoyama and his Japan. It was translated and read widely in

Japan. *Bungei Shunju,* the conservative magazine that published it, gave it a tongue-in-cheek title: "Disobedient Japan under Hatoyama Ichiro: A criticism of Hatoyama's Japan, which talks of terminating subservience to the United States and of autonomy and independence."[30] Because it gives us an insight into America's view of its relations with Japan at this time and a clue to what happened subsequently, I quote from the American magazine at length:

> Once upon a time, goes a story, there was an Emperor who was particularly fond of cherries. When he discovered one day that the sparrows were eating his cherries, he decreed that all sparrows must be killed or driven away. But with the birds gone, the beetles abounded. They overran the orchards and devoured the crop. The Emperor, rueful of his error, ordered the sparrows back.
>
> It is now ten years since the Allies drove the Japanese back to the cage of their meager islands and forbade them ever to bear arms again. It is three years since the West ruefully reversed course, gave the Japanese their independence, and bade them rearm and join in the defense against Communism. . . .
>
> [Hatoyama's] mandate went far deeper than a change of personalities. In sweeping out the Liberals, the Japanese were sweeping away a regime that represented to the majority of Japanese a decade of meek complaisance to the commands and suggestions of the U.S. occupiers. . . .
>
> Like cheap cosmetics, many of the conquerors' customs have rubbed off on the conquered. . . . There is still much that the Japanese would like to discard . . . but they cannot. Though they have found their way back to sovereignty, the Japanese have not found the way to stay alive without the help of the U.S. . . .
>
> So far, to judge by the campaign appeals that proved most powerful, the dominant wish of the Japanese, ten year after Hiroshima and surrender, is to have the best of two worlds. They yearn to be neutralist. . . . But being what they are and where they are, the Japanese can hardly hope to avoid the angry winds around their wood and paper houses.[31]

Washington's displeasure with Hatoyama that *Time* reflected was given a visible demonstration as he assumed office. To the amusement of Yoshida's followers, Hatoyama had his first run-in with Washington in connection with his first budget, for 1956. Japan's defense budget consisted of two major categories: appropriations for the Self-Defense Forces (SDFs) and appropriations for a share of the U.S. garrison's cost. It had already been established under Yoshida that a decrease in the U.S. garrison appropriation should be offset by an increase in the SDFs, so that the total defense outlay would not shrink.[32]

Moreover, through the MSA agreement, the U.S. Military Assistance and Advisory Group (MAAG) was stationed in Japan, and defense-budget requests were to originate in a mutual consultation of MAAG and Japan's Defense Agency. Where a government policy impinged on defense outlay, an American concurrence was required. Through practices such as these, the Pentagon was keeping an eye on Japan's defense efforts. But during the election campaign, Hatoyama promised a cutback in defense to provide for an increase in housing construction. An impasse ensued. "If worse came to worst," Hatoyama recollected, "we faced the prospect of being forced to resign for our inability to work out a budget."[33] In the event, the problem was solved through an American concession arranged by Ambassador Allison. But the damage was done—the public saw that the government did not control its own budget. Someone in the Yoshida camp sneered at the "blundering compradors."[34]

*Time* and the budget wrangle were bad auguries for Hatoyama. Having eased Yoshida out for lack of "national spirit," Dulles was having second thoughts about his successor. To the Japanese, Washington appeared to be drifting and playing both ends against the middle in Japan.[35] Washington's trouble was that it could not trust Japan, not that it disagreed basically with Japan. When Dulles sought him out in 1951, Hatoyama personally assured the envoy of his friendly intentions to the United States.[36] Kishi, a leader of the anti-Yoshida movement, and Ikeda also assured Ambassador Allison that Hatoyama will stay the course in foreign policy.[37] Still, Washington was not reassured. It seems to have become captive to the fear of a militarist restoration. Hatoyama did not help matters either. For instance, he was the only prime minister since the peace conference (with the exception of Ishibashi who was in office for less than two months) who did not pay a visit to Washington.

He stood mostly on principles, which were impeccable. He did not question Japan's need for U.S. military protection. But that did not mean that Japan did not owe itself an honest self-help. It was inconceivable that Japan should regard defense as a favor for America and demand a quid pro quo, as Yoshida was doing. Hatoyama saw Japan's inner corruption down that path. For him and the other revisionists, rearmament itself was less important than political-diplomatic equality that came with it. That equality was attainable only if Japan revised its constitution and entered into a collective security arrangement. Diplomatic equality also meant Japan's having a window on Moscow and Peking. It was inconceivable that Dulles, the champion of equality and mutuality, should deny that to Japan.

For Dulles and the State Department, it was the moment of truth: at last they had to define the content of equality for Japan they have been championing in their conflict with the Defense Department. Did State mean that? Or was State not really different from Defense after all? Recent precedents were not promising for Japan. After the peace treaty with China was denied, Yoshida resumed diplomatic probes to seek rapprochement with Peking once again, but the United States saw to it that nothing came of it.[38]

But Hatoyama was going ahead anyway. His agenda was a tall order. Some called for a two-thirds majority in both chambers of the Diet, others called for a majority at home plus Washington's support. They were all hard to come by. It must be said, however, that Yoshida's counsel to improve the Washington connection first was disingenuous: it was he who spoiled that connection with his defense policy. It was also the Yoshida-Dulles conflict that radicalized Japan's politics in the previous few years. The conservatives' merger gave Hatoyama a fighting chance to articulate the national will, but that was only a chance.[39] The election result immediately forced Hatoyama to shift his short-term priorities. The constitution had to take the back burner, though he had not given it up by any means. If he succeeded on Soviet rapprochement, he could bring greater power and popularity to bear on the revision.[40]

In order to keep the issue alive until an opportune moment arrived, he decided to establish the Constitution Investigation Committee in the prime minister's office. Composed of Diet members of governing and opposition parties and independent scholars, the committee was to recommend appropriate revision. But the bill failed to pass in 1955. This was the second occasion for Liberal-JSP collaboration against Hatoyama.[41] The first occasion had come immediately after the lower house election. Hatoyama's choices for lower-house speaker (Miki Bukichi) and vice speaker lost to the candidates of the Liberal-JSP coalition: Masutani Shuji, a former Hatoyama follower who switched to Yoshida's side, became speaker.[42]

Hatoyama's first postelection priority was diplomacy. On December 10, 1954, immediately upon taking office, he answered the Soviet-Chinese joint declaration of October calling for rapprochement. A mere six days later Foreign Minister Molotov announced that Moscow was ready to enter into negotiations and that the San Francisco treaty did not stand in the way of normalization. On January 25 Andrei N. Domnitsky, head of the Soviet mission, visited Hatoyama's home and delivered a similar message. Such an irregular procedure was necessary because both Foreign Minister Shigemitsu and the Foreign Ministry had strong reservations about Japan-Soviet rapprochement, and they frequently sabotaged the prime minister's efforts. This was a classic case of conflict between professional politicians and the bureaucracy. Shigemitsu's defiance of Hatoyama was made possible by the fact that he represented a sizable faction (former Minseito) in Hatoyama's new party. On February 4, however, Shigemitsu announced the decision to commence negotiations.

Coming on the heels of the defense budget cut, Hatoyama's Soviet courtship produced a predictable result in Washington. In early April, Foreign Minister Shigemitsu requested an appointment to visit Washington to ask for a reconsideration of the security treaty and to consult on the pending Soviet negotiations, but Dulles rebuffed him with a transparent excuse—a deliberate public snub. Shigemitsu felt the tension was comparable to the one on the eve of Pearl Harbor.[43] Under Dulles's long shadow, the peace negotiation was slated to start in London in June between Matsumoto Shun'ichi, Japanese plenipotentiary and confidant of Hatoyama, and Jacov Malik, Soviet ambassador to Britain.

Japan had a choice between two paths to normalization. It could negotiate a formal peace treaty, which came to be called the "London formula" in Japan. It was a quick, comprehensive decision. The alternative was the Adenauer formula, named after the West German settlement with Moscow of September 1955. Because of its divided status, the German rapprochement was limited, involving the repatriation of German prisoners of war and an exchange of ambassadors, postponing the formal peace treaty and territorial settlement to future negotiations. There was a long-standing territorial dispute between Tokyo and Moscow, and its settlement was predicated on the "London formula."

In addition, there were several nasty problems pending between Tokyo and Moscow. The Soviet Union had committed aggression against Japan in violation of the nonaggression pact, had tried Japan for "war crimes," and continued to hold many troops prisoner in unspeakable conditions in Siberia. Moscow had used its veto to deny Japan's admission to the United Nations as a pointed reminder of the cost of "separate peace." Then there was a nagging dispute over fishing rights in the northern Pacific.

But Hatoyama and the revisionists in the Democratic party were adamantly in favor of a peace treaty. Hatoyama undoubtedly wanted his Soviet treaty to outshine Yoshida's San Francisco treaty. The opposition to Hatoyama, both in his party and among the Liberals, were concerned with Washington's reaction. The United States was very ambivalent on the peace treaty. The paucity of archival material makes it difficult to probe the reason for it.[44] Neither Washington nor the domestic opponents of Hatoyama could argue against the treaty. It is conceivable that Dulles counseled consolidation of Hatoyama's domestic strength first (Hatoyama wanted to consolidate his domestic position with a diplomatic feat), or that he preferred the Adenauer formula falling well short of a normal friendship treaty, for the sake of Japanese-German parity.

Opposition to Hatoyama divided the conservatives roughly into two equal halves. The opponents included Yoshida and the Liberal party; the Foreign Ministry bureaucracy; Shigemitsu, now Hatoyama's foreign minister; and Shigemitsu's former Minseito followers minus the progressive wing (e.g., Miki Takeo). At the outset, the business community was divided pro and con, parallel with the division among the conservative politicians.[45] In the Diet, therefore, the JSP could tip the scale. Both the JSP and the JCP endorsed Hatoyama.

Foreign Minister Shigemitsu posed a major problem for Hatoyama's rapprochement. He was personally named a class A war criminal at the insistence of Moscow, the real aggressor in the one-week war, and convicted. Shigemitsu never forgave that. In addition, he had developed an intense dislike of Kono, Hatoyama's adviser.

Since 1945 Japan had been in continuous dispute with the Soviet Union over southern Sakhalin, the Kurile Islands, and what Japan began to call the northern territories since 1956, consisting of the Habomai Islands, Shikotan, Etorofu, and Kunashiri, lying immediately to the north of Hokkaido. The origin of the dispute was the unfounded allegation in the Cairo Declaration that Japan had stolen the territories.[46] On that ground, President Roosevelt had ceded them to Stalin at Yalta as the price for Soviet entry into the war against Japan. The Potsdam Declaration imposed a territorial settlement on Japan that honored the Cairo Declaration. The Soviet Union occupied southern Sakhalin, the Kurile Islands, and, in addition, all the islands lying between the Kuriles and Hokkaido in August 1945.

Japan accepted the territorial provision of the Potsdam Declaration when it surrendered. Therefore, it would have been imperative for Dulles to define the boundaries of southern Sakhalin and the Kuriles, have Japan renounce its claim to them, and name the Soviet Union as the legal claimant at San Francisco, as Soviet Foreign Minister Molotov demanded. For reasons not yet fully explored, however, Dulles did something different: he left the boundary of the Kuriles ambiguous; he had Japan renounce the two territories but named no claimant. The question of why Dulles did not define the boundary of the Kuriles has given rise to two inferences. One has to do with fact that the United States was making a commitment to defend Japan's territory at San Francisco. If Japan was allowed to claim a territory under Soviet occupation, that would have brought the United States into direct collision with the Soviet Union. Dulles, it is argued, wished to avoid such consequences.[47] But this inference is negated by the fact that he did later encourage Japan to expand its claim against the Soviet occupied areas. The other inference, an insidious one, argues that Dulles wanted to sow a seed of territorial dispute between Tokyo and Moscow, so as to prevent a formal peace treaty.

The Japanese government and the Foreign Ministry, in particular, had been incensed by the Cairo Declaration. They were sorely tempted to object—for the record—to ceding southern Sakhalin and the Kuriles, resting their case on the principle of nonaggrandizement, stated in the Atlantic Charter, but they bowed to the fact of having accepted the Potsdam Declaration. Nonetheless, Yoshida's speech in San Francisco included a full-dress rebuke of the Soviet land-grab, a rebuke directed as well at the United States for having acted on the Cairo principle at Yalta. In other words, Gaimusho at this stage was concerned (1) with keeping the historical record straight rather than with reclaiming part of the lost territories, and (2) with preserving Japan's residual sovereignty over Okinawa and the Bonins, under American control.

Yoshida maintained in the same speech that Kunashiri and Etorofu had never been a part of the Kuriles Islands and that Shikotan and the Habomai Islands have always been an integral part of Hokkaido administration. But his definition of what is not included in the Kuriles was at odds with that of the United States. Dulles, on the same occasion, took note of the dispute over whether the 'Kurile Islands" included the "Habomai Islands," and stated the American position that the "Habomai Islands" were not included in the Kurile Islands.[49]

For reasons that remain unknown, the Japanese government unilaterally retreated from the claims made by Yoshida at San Francisco. During the parliamentary ratification of the San Francisco peace treaty in October 1951, Nishimura Kumao, the director of the treaty bureau of the Foreign Ministry—with the obvious consent of Yoshida as prime minister—went on record saying that the Kuriles it had abandoned included the southern Kuriles or Etorofu and Kunashiri. A lower house resolution of July 1952, sponsored by former Seiyukai, former Minseito, and the two wings of the JSP, called for the return of the Habomais and Shikotan alone.[50] Indeed, the working assumption and consensus of the Japanese officials when the London talk began was that the return of the Habomais and Shikotan alone would be a satisfactory settlement, but that the Soviets would reject even that. Both Shigemitsu and the foreign ministry were so interested in delaying the peace treaty that they might have balked at commencing the negotiation, had they not been sure of a Soviet rejection.[51]

Being Republican, the Eisenhower administration was at greater liberty than its predecessor to criticize the Yalta agreement. In September 1954, the United States chose to resurrect the dispute over the Soviet Union's shooting down of an American military aircraft over Habomai back in October 1952, and Secretary Dulles took the case to the UN Security Council to renew the protest against this minor incident. Clearly the point was not to protest Soviet military conduct, for the 24-page memorandum distributed to the Council members by U.S. Ambassador Henry Cabot Lodge was almost exclusively a defense of Japan's territorial claims to the Habomais and Shikotan. One may add that in September 1954, it was public knowledge that the Yoshida cabinet would soon be toppled by the Democrats headed by Hatoyama (it happened in December) and that the Soviets were wooing Hatoyama. In early November, another U.S. aircraft strayed into the same airspace and it, too, went down. The United States protested the incident and demanded an answer to the September memorandum as well. A National Security Council meeting of November took up the matter for discussion, and in reply to the president's inquiry Dulles sent a memorandum on "sovereignty of the Habomai Islands." He concluded, "I do not know anything we can do to get the Russians out short of war."[52] Intended or not, the tension over the Habomais and Shikotan would have the effect of making it difficult for the Soviet Union to relinquish them.

Formal negotiation began in London in June 1955 between Japanese Ambassador Plenipotentiary Matsumoto Shun'ichi and his Soviet counterpart, Jacov Malik. During their talk on August 9, Malik surprised Matsumoto with an offer to return the Habomais and Shikotan as a territorial settlement.[53] With one stroke, the obstacle to a peace treaty was removed. Matsumoto reported the offer to Gaimusho. Then, in an incredible act of malfeasance, Shigemitsu and the foreign ministry bureaucracy sat on the report, refusing to pass it on to the prime minister or the cabinet.[54] Faced by the prospect that the peace talk might succeed on Hatoyama's terms, senior Gaimusho officials went into a huddle with Shigemitsu. Among them were Tani Masayuki, adviser; Kadowaki Suemitsu, administrative vice minister; Shimoda Takezo, chief of the treaty bureau; Tanaka Mitsuo, chief of the information and culture bureau; and Teraoka Kohei, councilor for European affairs. Having served as Prime Minister Yoshida's secretary, Teraoka was now in charge of the peace negotiation.[55] There is a strong presumption that Teraoka was acting in close concert with Yoshida. As an organization, postwar Gaimusho subscribed to the policy of Yoshida, an illustrious alumnus, and toed a line that was pro-American to a fault in everything except defense.[56]

Stung by the disloyalty of the foreign ministry, Hatoyama dispatched Kono, minister of agriculture, to London to serve as a back channel. Arriving in London on August 11, he was debriefed on the Soviet offer of the Habomais and Shikotan. He was elated but told Matsumoto to hold off substantive negotiations because of the uncertainty in the political situation back home. Kono was on his way to meet Dulles later in the month in Washington, where he was to be joined by Kishi, the Democratic party secretary general, and Shigemitsu.[57] This was the meeting that the Japanese side had originally asked for in April but had been refused by Dulles. Knowing the foreign minister's objections to the peace treaty and wary of the charge of "two-headed diplomacy," Hatoyama had ordered Kono and Kishi to accompany Shigemitsu to keep an eye on him.[58]

But before he left Tokyo for Washington on August 23, Shigemitsu had decided to raise the ante against Moscow: to demand (1) the return of all four islands (Etorofu, Kunashiri, the Habomais, and Shikotan), and (2) an international conference to determine the Soviet claim to southern Sakhlin and the

Kurile Islands. Did Shigemitsu feel that, now that the Soviets were in a concil-
iatory mood, he could get further concessions for the asking? But Teraoka and
other Gaimusho officials certainly intended to stall the negotiations. One may
note that Shigemitsu met with Yoshida and U.S. Ambassador Allison before
departing for Washington.

For the trio of Japanese officials in Washington, the priority item on the
agenda was the request for American consent to revising the security treaty
toward greater equality. Shigemitsu led off with a rather stuffy reading of a
prepared text for half an hour. Then Dulles rose to his feet and gave the Japanese a barbed lecture. As long as Japan keeps its constitution and is thereby
prevented from dispatching its army overseas, he pointed out, it cannot enter
into a collective security arrangement. His position had remained the same
since 1950: "How can you ask for a treaty revision when your own institutions
are not ready?"[59] Dulles, like Yoshida, had a proprietary interest in his treaty.

Dulles's reported reaction to the peace negotiations already underway was
mixed.[60] Shigemitsu went before the National Press Club and denied any intention of concluding a friendship treaty with Moscow, Japan wanted a merely
"technical" relations, he said.[61] The joint communique created an uproar in
Tokyo by saying that Japan would contribute to peace and security in the "Western Pacific," i.e., toward regional security. Shigemitsu made the concession to
draw out Dulles on treaty revision, but the uproar caused him to disown it.[62] As
the chilly reception in Washington became known in Tokyo, Yoshida's hand was
strengthened.

At this time the Japanese conservatives in the Democratic and Liberal parties
were in the midst of extended talks and maneuvers, begun in July, looking
toward merger. The major motives for the merger were (1) the desire to create a
stable party enlisting all the conservatives, (2) the desire to contain the expanding JSP, also about to have a merger of its own, and (3) the revisionists' design
to contain Yoshida and to carry out a basic reorientation in domestic and foreign
policy. But the U.S. reaction to the Soviet offer of August had given Yoshida a
new lease on life. Instead of resolving the Yoshida-Hatoyama conflict, the merger itself became an arena for the conflict.

In the race for the presidency of the new party, Hatoyama had the edge over
Ogata, the Liberal president. Ogata favored constitutional revision, and he carried his party toward the merger, shelving Yoshida upstairs. But when the Soviet question was injected into the merger, the alignment shifted. Ogata was
inclined to side with Yoshida on the peace treaty. Within the Democratic party,
Ashida reversed himself and joined Shigemitsu. The "domestic 38th Parallel"
now emerged among the conservatives.[63]

To clear the air, the Hatoyama government sent an inquiry to Washington in

early fall, and a reply was received in late October. It said (1) that the United
States was not aware of the allegation that Yoshida had reserved Japan's rights
to the "southern Kurile" (the four islands) at the San Francisco peace conference, (2) that the boundary of the Kuriles remains undefined, and (3) that Japan
was at liberty to negotiate a territorial settlement it chose.[64] Immediately the
prime minister issued a statement calling for a settlement on the basis of the two
islands.[65]

Meanwhile, the two wings of the Socialists finally merged in October at the
leftwing's initiative. Another victory in the February election convinced them
that they were on the way to political power. Sohyo pressured the leftwing to be
accommodating toward the rightwing, and the leftwing obliged. The sense of
proximity to power was working wonders. A joint party program was patched
together,[66] and the merger was accomplished in October. Suzuki Mosaburo of
the leftwing became chairman and Asanuma Inejiro of the rightwing secretary
general.

On the critical national issue of the Soviet peace treaty, however, the JSP was
too ideological to be of any help for Hatoyama. The JSP's platform called for
the restoration of the southern Sakhalin and the entire Kuriles.[67] This amounted
to rejecting the peace treaty, which was Yoshida's stand.

One month later the Liberals and the Democrats merged into the Liberal
Democratic Party (LDP) at a convention in Tokyo. The proceedings showed,
however, that, the whole purpose of the merger had been seriously compromised. On the one hand, the platform committee succeeded in writing constitutional revision into the party program. The LDP's "mission" was defined as if
it were a criticism of Yoshida:

> While democracy and liberalism, stressed during the occupation, should be re-
> spected and defended as the guiding principles of new Japan, the initial occupa-
> tion policies were directed mainly to the end of weakening Japan, with the result
> that in the reform of several institutions—starting with the constitution and the
> education system—the concepts of state and patriotism were unjustly suppressed
> and state power was excessively fragmented and reduced. The ensuing gap [in
> state power], together with the recent shift in the international situation, lent itself
> to exploitation by forces beholden to class society and enabled them to rise
> rapidly.[68]

On the other hand, the platform committee delivered a blow to Hatoyama
with a resolution instructing the government to demand the return of the four
islands.[69] Unable to overcome the Yoshida faction, the Hatoyama government
had to accept the LDP resolution as binding. Instead of naming the incumbent
prime minister president, a collective leadership consisting of Hatoyama,

Ogata, Ohno Banboku (an old-timer in the former Liberal party), and Miki Bukichi was installed. It was agreed that the LDP would let Hatoyama stay in office until the Soviet treaty was concluded before letting Ogata succeed him.[70] Kono intimates that Hatoyama was partly responsible for this defeat: Hatoyama was so absorbed in constitutional revision and the Soviet question that he entrusted party politics entirely to his lieutenants and acted more like a chairman of the board than a CEO.[71]

Showered with toasts, back-slappings, congratulatory telegrams, and accolades, Miki Bukichi kept up the upbeat appearance at the LDP convention, but he was disappointed by what the merger had wrought. Hatoyama was compromised, and Yoshida came back to life. But then Miki had been down and out more than once, and each time he rebounded into the ring. Undoubtedly, his thoughts dwelt on Kishi and Kono, the remaining revisionists who were moreover endowed with great political savvy. The two struck up a friendship during their trip to Washington to meet with Dulles. They swore mutual support after Hatoyama's retirement, expected soon: Kishi would succeed Hatoyama and later pass power on to Kono. Miki supported the idea;[72] so did Hatoyama. If Kishi and Kono could maintain a long tenure in office between them, they would be in a position to implement and consolidate the revisionist line of policy Hatoyama had barely embarked on.

But how could the treaty negotiation be rescued? The Soviet ambassador had recessed the negotiations in September 1955 when Matsumoto, his counterpart, demanded four islands as instructed. Early the next year, Kono volunteered for the task of resurrecting the talks. He was quite like Tanaka Kakuei, later to be prime minister, in being a politicians' politician. He was short of stature but amazingly energetic, gregarious, talkative, quick of mind, deadly in heckling, loyal to his friends through thick an thin, formidable to his enemies, and above all fully endowed with the virtues of a political man—courage and decisiveness.

Born in 1898 into a well-to-do farming family, Kono began his career in 1923 as a crusading cub reporter for *Asahi,* which explains a great deal about his subsequent devotion to fighting bureaucratic politics, of the imperial or the postwar variety. In 1931 he entered politics, and before long Hatoyama took him under his wing in the Seiyukai party. They and Miki Bukichi were kept out of politics by their enemies—the military and the bureaucracy—even before war came. When the remnants of Seiyukai organized the Liberal party in November 1945, Kono was appointed secretary general. Following Hatoyama's purge in 1946, Kono arranged the meeting between him and Yoshida for the transfer of power.

Kono and Miki, in actual control of the party in power, defied both SCAP GHQ and Yoshida. They were convinced that GHQ-Yoshida shenanigans were to blame for their purge shortly thereafter.[73] While in banishment, he and Hatoyama were investigated for allegedly running afoul of the Government Section's campaign for clean elections.[74] Hatoyama was cleared of suspicion, but Kono was not. He was tried and found guilty, appealed that decision all the way to the supreme court, but lost.[75]

He entered a Yokohama prison in the summer of 1949, but was transferred to another soon thereafter. While the truck ferrying him and other inmates was chugging through his election district in Yokohama, it stalled. To his consternation, the guard ordered the inmates to get off the truck and push it. While he was at the chore in his prison uniform, he recalled with gallows humor, the good people of his district spotted "Kono sensei" (Mr. Kono). He put the best possible face on the situation, enlisted their help, and the truck was off and running.

Hatoyama, Kono, and Miki returned to public life in 1952, determined to displace Yoshida. Although their wish was granted in late 1954, the Hatoyama government was soon bogged down. Again Kono and Miki found a way out through the creation of the LDP. But contrary to their plan, the LDP itself now stood in the way of a peace treaty with Moscow. By then Kono and his friends were accustomed to seeing Yoshida use his liaison with the Americans to his advantage. So why not enlist the Soviets for his own? Kono needed to undo the resolution of the LDP that called for the return of the four islands as a condition of peace, and a timely Soviet intervention to accomplish that end materialized in March 1956. There is no proof that Kono arranged that intervention—all we have are rumors and innuendoes. But then it would have been out of character for Kono not to try to outdo Yoshida at his own game.

The Hatoyama-Kono group had plenty of contacts—both direct and indirect, through conduit organizations—with the Soviet representatives. These contacts served Kono's interest quite independently of the peace treaty. To begin with, Kono was the chief spokesman for the fishing interests, which were heavily dependent on the catch of salmon, trout, and cod in the Bering Sea and northern Pacific off the Siberian coast. He was also the minister of agriculture, with jurisdiction over fisheries and forestry.[76]

Meanwhile, Nikita Khrushchev, who had taken personal charge of rapprochement with Tokyo and Bonn and had a political stake in it, was getting impatient. Soviet officials often pointed out to the Japanese that Chancellor Adenauer had visited Moscow and normalized diplomatic ties in five days' negotiation (September 1955), a sharp contrast to Tokyo's indecisiveness. After the London talks recessed in September, another session was held in London from January to March 1956 without any progress.

Then, on March 21 Radio Moscow broadcast a bulletin by Tass news agency announcing the decision of the Soviet government to ban salmon fishing in the wide arc of open sea stretching from the Sea of Okhotsk to the Bering Sea for the 1956 season. The Soviet move was designed to nudge Japan out of its impasse on the peace treaty, and it created quite a ripple in Tokyo and in the fishing industry, the mainstay of the Soviet lobby. The Japanese government decided to send to Moscow a delegation headed by Kono to settle the dispute in late April. Before his departure Kono reportedly said, "Who in hell would go all the way to Moscow to fiddle around with fish? I'm going to reopen the Japan-Soviet rapprochement talks."[77] In a private conversation with Kono in the Kremlin, Premier Nicolai Bulganin declared that the settlement of the fishing rights question was tied to the rapprochement, and he pressed Kono to choose between the London formula and the Adenauer formula.[78] Kono was more than happy to agree to reopen the peace talks, slated for late July, and take the credit for getting the fishing ban lifted. The Soviet demarche, it appeared, might succeed in removing the deadlock in the LDP.

Kono should have been riding high in May. But returning home, he was subjected to a heavy barrage of criticism, undoubtedly orchestrated by Yoshida, alleging that he was "red" or that he had sold out Kunashiri and Etorofu in his meeting with Bulganin. Kono says he almost became neurotic because of public criticism, an incredible fact in light of his nerves of steel.[79] In reality there were plenty of reasons for Kono to be depressed in May. Miki Bukichi, his comrade-in-arms, had been stricken with a brain hemorrhage in January, and at the age of 71 was not expected to recover. In addition, the Hatoyama camp suffered a mortal defeat in May: the electoral reform bill—designed to replace the multi-member election district with a single-member-district, winner-take-all system—went down to defeat.

Japan had had a single-member-district system until 1925, when universal male suffrage was instituted. However, to stultify Seiyukai, which agitated for the suffrage extension, the Interior Ministry discarded single-member districts in favor of multimember districts, because the latter tends to encourage minor parties, which were expected to vie with Seiyukai. The idea of returning to the single-member district had been on the minds of Japanese politicians ever since then. But the electoral reform pushed by SCAP was designed to undercut Seiyukai and Minseito. The first reform bill of 1945 had established the large-district (coinciding with prefecture), multiballot system, even more conducive to the birth of minor parties, and 386 of them came into existence. Shortly after the general strike of February 1, 1947, was countermanded by SCAP, Interior Minister Uehara—with the obvious blessing of Prime Minister Yoshida—began a campaign to restore single-member districts, so as to keep the Communists under control. But SCAP would not countenance such a scheme; so Uehara settled for medium-size multimember districts as a way station to a single-member, winner-take-all system.[80]

The single-member district was resurrected by Miki Bukichi and Kono, the two samurai who engineered the conservative merger, and Kishi, the secretary general. Their real purpose in supporting the scheme remains shrouded in secrecy and can only be tentatively assembled piece by piece as in a jigsaw puzzle. It was part and parcel of their search for a stable but vigorous political system, for which the conservative merger turned out to be a disappointing answer. Yoshida, though weaker, carried weight in the LDP. It was healthier for Yoshida and the revisionists to be in separate political parties that could alternate in power. But the JSP stood in the way. It had just voted with Yoshida to take away speakership from Miki.

It seemed that Miki, Kono, and Kishi wanted a two-party system. This was no mere moralizing on democracy but a matter of hardheaded calculation. These men were born to command other men. They knew that the party leader's power rested on the threat of dissolving the Diet on an issue that could be put to the judgment of the voters. But the LDP could not be thrown out of power no matter how many elections were held. Thus LDP leaders were denied the disciplinary power of dissolution—unless there was a functioning two-party system. In the parlance of political scientists today, the revisionist trio was working toward the so-called responsible party system.

A functioning two-party system, said Kishi, must be made up of Tweedledum and Tweedledee, with overlapping constituencies in the middle.[81] This was inconceivable since the JSP was committed to the constitution and the LDP was committed to its revision. Being revisionists, the trio's diagnosis of the Japanese problem, I infer, went to the very heart of the matter. Creating a system of Tweedledum and Tweedledee had to coincide with revision of the constitution. Unless everyone adhered to the same constitutional framework, it was impossible to agree to disagree. To make that revision possible, the Socialists must be reduced in strength to under one-third of both houses. According to the widely accepted lore of electoral dynamics, the single-member, winner-take-all system fosters a two-party system by penalizing minority parties, whereas the multi-member system does the opposite. However, depending on the way the district boundary is drawn, a single-member district as such may on the contrary entrench a minority party. By itself it is inadequate for the revisionists' purpose. Behind the small district bill lurked the lure of a blood-curdling scheme to gerrymander the Socialists to impotence.

That done, the two-party system would establish a government that had eluded Hatoyama, Kono, and Miki for so long. They wanted nothing less than a

made an enormous difference for subsequent history.
'the biggest loss of the Hatoyama government.''[98] But it was
two-party system was shelved. The constitution survived.
ity learned how to prevail over the Diet with its hidden
we shall see. However, whether Yoshida masterminded the
district bill remains moot.[99]

ounched together for Hatoyama. Miki Bukichi died in July.
ction of July was a defeat for the revisionists. The merged
1 seats, an increase from 66, and managed to hold one-third
he first time, although the conservatives also expanded, from
ends of the spectrum were gaining at the expense of the third
as the 1955 system spread to the upper house.
olated and his banner tattered. But he never lost his compo-
upgrade and resume negotiations in Moscow by sending his
igemitsu, as the chief negotiator, assisted by Ambassador
oice of Shigemitsu, an avowed Russophobe, rested on do-
sideration rather than on his four-islands-or-nothing stand.
ter said little to Shigemitsu before departure, giving him to
was given a wide latitude.[100] Without any foreknowledge of
ished a rather shrill anticommunist letter addressed to

it has frequently declared that it is the cornerstone of our diplo-
in friendship with the United States. At the same time, it has just
its pro-Soviet designs by proclaiming the Japan-Soviet rapproche-
the most critical policies of the present cabinet. This will not win
e free nations. Is the government prepared to see the U.S. Far
nd as well as the United Nations Command transferred to Hawaii

enced on July 30 in a cool atmosphere, and the talks stalled
n with Shigemitsu standing pat on his previous demands. In
-by-blow accounts of the hard bargaining were reported to
ce back home, with the result that public opinion visibly
the astonishment of Hatoyama, Shigemitsu carried out a
ed down to a demand for two islands and asked for Tokyo's
n August 12. The prime minister rejected Shigemitsu but
ntinue negotiating with his Soviet counterpart in London,
nal conference to deal with the Suez crisis was to be held.

system of majoritarian political supremacy that would yield a strong, unambig-
uous mandate in the conduct of foreign and domestic policy. Their desire was
reinforced by their recent disappointing experience. The Japanese political system was too fragile and unstable to be seaworthy in the world of superpower
conflict.[82] Being foreign policy activists, the revisionists wanted unified public
opinion and a system that would yield a clear, rational decision, pro or con, on
major issues. But that was not all.

Hatoyama, Kono, and Miki, who had been contending for decades with the
imperial bureaucracy, resented its revival under the occupation. The Foreign
Ministry's sabotage of the Soviet peace negotiations outraged them, as did the
Finance Ministry's reluctance to spend money on defense. They wanted to put
the central ministry bureaucracies back to the place prescribed in the constitution. That called, first, for keeping bureaucratic prime ministers out of power
and, second, for a periodic change of government to insure political neutrality
of the bureaucracies.[83]

Kono Ichiro was particularly irritated by the budgetary power of the Ministry of Finance, a power that should by right belong to the Diet. I have touched
above on the budget cut of 1955, which brought the Hatoyama cabinet into
conflict with the U.S. government. Kono was behind that idea. In his scheme
the budget cut was tied to administrative reform. And the crux of the reform
was to move the power over budget from the Ministry of Finance to the prime
minister's office, an arrangement identical to that prevailing in the Office of
Management and Budget in the White House. With the consent of Miki and
Hatoyama, Kono started maneuvering toward this end in 1956, about the time
the small district bill was being introduced.

A consultative council (*shingi-kai*) consisting of journalists, scholars, and
businessmen was duly appointed, in accordance with the usual procedure, and it
was expected to produce a report endorsing Kono's scheme by January 1957.
But by then the Hatoyama government had already been retired following grave
setbacks, and there was no way to pull off Kono's OMB scheme.[84] It was the
last hurrah for Seiyukai's antibureaucratic politicians.

Another group that stood to be downgraded in status in the system of political supremacy was big business. The old Seiyukai professionals had a natural
dislike of big business, a sentiment that dated back to the days when they had
been at the beck and call of *zaibatsu* financiers, Mitsui for Seiyukai and Mitsu-
bishi for Minseito. Their discontent kept smouldering as Yoshida, well connected with big business, sought to starve them into submission on occasion.
The "Surprise Dissolution" of the Diet in 1952 was a case in point. Their
sensibilities were rubbed the wrong way once again at the time of the conservative merger and the peace negotiations with Moscow, when the business com-

munity intervened in politics with an audacity rarely seen since. They saw the nascent triumvirate of business, bureaucracy, and government working against them, and they did not like it.[85] This story was a small blip long since erased from memory in the establishment of Kono's enemies. But side by side with the conservative merger and the small district bill, it provides an important piece of the puzzle, one without which the origin of today's Japan may never be understood.

With such a picture of Japan somewhere in their minds, the LDP leaders decided to go for the small district bill in December 1955.[86] This was the final solution and a high stakes game. Surprisingly, many of the Socialists responded rather calmly at first, because the bill was presented as a measure to restore a two-party system. Katayama Tetsu, the former Socialist prime minister, was in favor of the bill, provided it did not favor constitutional revision.[87] But then the Socialists knew that Kono and Miki always had a trick or two up their sleeves; the Socialists looked them over like Little Red Riding Hood surveying granny to see if she was licking her chops or growing a tail under her skirt.

The bill was introduced in the lower house in March 1956, one month after the bills to set up the Constitution Investigation Commission and the National Defense Council were introduced for a second time; the latter passed without a hitch this time. But the small district bill ran into serious trouble. A regularly scheduled upper house election was coming up in July, and the LDP commenced a propaganda campaign for the avowed aim of winning two-thirds majority control. It was plain for anyone to see what the LDP was up to.

Even without an ulterior motive, redrawing election district boundaries is difficult enough for a popularly elected assembly. To achieve forward momentum, it has to reward enough legislators. Therefore the LDP decided to increase the total number of seats from 466 to 497.[88] But gerrymandering was precisely the ulterior motive. The Socialists assailed the irregularly shaped boundaries, such as the "hop-skip-jump district" and the "eel's bed district." Within the LDP, the Yoshida faction and the progressives from former Minseito led by Miki Takeo objected to the bill. To split the Yoshida faction, the party leadership tried to win over Ikeda by gerrymandering in his favor.[89]

The JSP denounced what it called "Hatomander," and the party headquarters composed versus for "The Hatomander Song" and "The Song Against Constitutional Revision" to be sung to popular tunes. The latter went this way: "Hear ye, traitorous LDP / The hurrahs of 80 million / Rising up to smash constitutional revision and rearmament." It was a riposte to Nakasone's "Constitutional Revision Song" of the year before. In the Diet the Socialists fought a bitter rearguard action to delay the vote. A filibuster in the Japanese Diet is an effec-

tive weapon because, as a l⎸ cracy sought to curtail the D⎸ days a year, unless it is exte⎸

Still, it was difficult to s⎸ Some major newspapers ass⎸ majority vote and encourag⎸ struction to stall the bill.[91] T⎸ most recent exercise in viole⎸ before—had been so unpop⎸ walk" toward the end of the⎸ devised originally by the re⎸ 1947.[92] It called for a slow⎸ per man—to the speaker's⎸ Dietman would tease senile⎸ food from the speaker, and ⎸ a succession of motions de⎸ interminable delays.[93]

The Socialists moved suc⎸ dence against six cabinet m⎸ proached, tension mounted⎸ for the Socialists materiali⎸ Shuji, elected speaker of t⎸ against Miki Bukichi in earl⎸ opposition, ostensibly to pr⎸ for democracy.

Senile and inactive, Mas⎸ time Lamp," (*Hiru-andon*),⎸ He was warming the seat in⎸ cause. He held off to the l⎸ vote and "allowed ample ti⎸ allegedly to avert a fistfig⎸ standing committee for fur⎸ broke out between the spea⎸ are you on?"[95]

Finally the LDP agreed t⎸ lated the bill. It was then se⎸ gratefully, "I'll never spea⎸ who was identified only as⎸ been Ikeda, was reported⎸ Japan-Soviet negotiations—⎸

involved, this ⎸
Hatoyama calle⎸
more than that.⎸
The Socialist n⎸
partner, Yoshida⎸
coup over the s⎸

Bad news ca⎸
The upper hous⎸
Socialists captur⎸
of the chamber f⎸
108 to 124. The⎸
party in the mid⎸
Hatoyama wa⎸
sure. He decided⎸
foreign minister,⎸
Matsumoto. The⎸
mestic political ⎸
But the prime m⎸
understand that ⎸
that, Yoshida p⎸
Shigemitsu, sayi⎸

The governm⎸
macy to ma⎸
as often sho⎸
ment as one⎸
the trust of⎸
Eastern Con⎸
or Korea?[101]

The parley co⎸
as soon as they be⎸
the meantime, bl⎸
the cheering audi⎸
hardened. Then ⎸
volte-face: he cli⎸
approval by radi⎸
instructed him to⎸
where an interna⎸

So, for several days following August 12, the Japanese government seemed to teeter on the brink of accepting the Soviet terms and a fullfledged peace treaty.

But John Foster Dulles would not let Japan succumb to the Soviet intervention. At a private London meeting with Shigemitsu on August 19, Dulles tried to block the peace talk with a threat of a U.S. counterintervention. Whereas in the October 1955 reply to the Hatoyama government Dulles had said that it was up to Japan to define the boundary of the Kurile, he now insisted that: (1) Japan merely renounced its claim to southern Sakhalin and the Kuriles in the 1951 treaty, and it did not have the right to unilaterally name the Soviet Union as the claimant to those territories; (2) Kunashiri and Etorofu are not part of the Kuriles and belong to Japan, along with the Habomais and Shikotan; and (3) for Japan to cede Kunashiri and Etorofu to the Soviet Union in a peace settlement would run afoul of Article 26 of the San Francisco treaty, which stated that "Should Japan make a peace settlement . . . with any State granting that State greater advantages than those provided by the present Treaty, those same advantages shall be extended to the parties to the present Treaty." Dulles threatened that if Japan ceded Kunashiri and Etorofu to the Soviet Union, the United States would claim Okinawa and the Bonin Islands.[102]

When the story of the Dulles demarche appeared in the press in Japan, Tokyo was shocked and the Diet began an inquiry. Then Dulles went public in softer tone, saying, "I have merely stressed the existence of Article 26. I said nothing as to the position Japan should take or what is necessary."[103] He also maintained that his endorsement of the recovery of all four islands was intended to strengthen Japan's negotiating hand with Moscow.[104] The door to the peace treaty was now closed. This left the Adenauer formula as the only viable formula for normalization.[105]

By then even Kishi, the LDP secretary general, deserted Hatoyama and sided with Yoshida. The entire business community deserted Hatoyama and, to Kono's chagrin, called for Hatoyama's immediate resignation. Yoshida published another diatribe against Hatoyama. But mollifying Washington entailed a different problem. Now that the Adenauer formula was the only mode of normalizing Tokyo-Moscow relations, Japan was in danger of forfeiting the Habomais and Shikotan as well—a formal peace treaty was the precondition for the return of those islands.[106]

After a month and a half of bitter factional wrangle in the LDP, the party leaders agreed to let Hatoyama go to Moscow personally, to see what he could do to salvage the two islands. The Soviet Union in the meantime had had some second thoughts about the Adenauer formula in view of Japan's hypersensitivity about the territorial question. It wanted to settle the question once and for all rather than postpone it, as under the Adenauer formula. But it agreed to declare its willingness to return the Habomais and Shikotan when the peace treaty was concluded at some future date. On this basis, it agreed to (1) end the state of war with Japan, (2) exchange ambassadors, (3) return all prisoners of war immediately, (4) put the fisheries agreement into effect, and (5) support Japan's admission to the United Nations.[107] Arriving in Moscow in October, Hatoyama tried to extract an acknowledgement from the Soviets that additional territorial issues (Kunashiri and Etorofu) remained, but in this he failed. It was the Adenauer formula to the end. (Subsequently, the Soviet Union decided to keep Habomai and Shikotan as well.)

In December 1956 the LDP held its first open election to choose a successor to the retiring Hatoyama (actually there had been an election in February, but Hatoyama had had no competitor since Ogata had died in January). The December 1956 election of an LDP president was a landmark in the party's history because it was on this occasion that factions as they exist today made their debut—each with an aspirant to the prime ministership as leader, independent headquarters, a campaign organization, seniority ranking among members for cabinet and party appointments, and more or less stable sources of funding. The "seven divisions and three regiments," or "eight divisions," that became the talk of the Nagatacho district (around the Diet), became fullblown and vied with one another for the prime ministership.[108]

The election was noted for being "dirty," involving the use of "bullets," or cash with which votes of Diet members were traded. Three candidates ran, and in the first round of balloting, the results were Kishi, 223; Ishibashi Tanzan, 151; and Ishii Kojiro, 137. In the runoff between the first two, Ishii—with Ikeda's prompting (and possibly with Yoshida's as well)—supported Ishibashi. Kishi lost by seven votes, 258 to 251, to Ishibashi. Lacking a strong factional base of its own, however, the Ishibashi cabinet was the first in history to be based on a factional balance of power.

Factionalism is supposed to mean the kind of politics in which the interests of factions take precedence over those of the party. Indeed, the LDP factions possess the trappings of a political party and behave like one. Hence the LDP should have resembled a coalition, creating the kind of politics for which the Fourth Republic in France was noted—with short-lived cabinets, incoherent decisions, and immobilism. The following chapters fully substantiate these characterization of LDP factions. However, one peculiar trait distinguish LDP factions. They never grew into fullfledged parties to rival the LDP. The LDP has never experienced an open split. It retained its powers in its own right and kept the factions subordinated to it on some vital issues. It is this duality that marks the Japanese system.

The duality stems from the fact that the three-way division of politics was prior to factionalism: Yoshida and the revisionists could never unite, nor could they forego cooperation to maintain the security treaty against the Socialists. Factionalism could enjoy a field day on many noncritical issues; but it could not be allowed to jeopardize the LDP's control of the security treaty. Factionalism could come into play even over the terms of the treaty, but never over the treaty itself. In this sense, factionalism has been peculiar to the 1955 system, as indeed the three-way division of Japanese politics has been.

The point can be illustrated by asking, why did LDP factionalism come to full bloom in *December 1956*? My answer is speculative and hypothetical, since most major actors have passed away without leaving a record.[109] The role of the multimember election district must be minimized, since it had been in existence since 1925 without any discernible impact. The theory that holds that caucusing, rather than open balloting, to choose a LDP president would stifle factionalism is at best of dubious validity. Open balloting and factionalism merely coincided in 1956, in my view. A caucus has selected several LDP presidents since without diminishing factionalism.[110] The true answer might be highly politico-strategic: as Yoshida successfully beat back the revisionists' challenge by December 1956, the modus operandi of the U.S.-Japan security tie was finding an equilibrium.

Within the preceding months, the conservative merger failed in its anti-Yoshida purpose; the small district bill was doomed; the two-party system went under with the small district bill; constitutional revision became a mirage; Yoshida returned from banishment to a commanding position; having lost its window on Peking in 1951, Japan lost its window on Moscow; Hatoyama's foreign polity initiative was buried; the power of the pro-Yoshida bureaucracy in the government was affirmed; the JSP acquired a permanent tenure but only because it was completely contained by the one-third barrier; neutralism suffered a setback when Japan's window on Moscow was half closed. All this was tremendously reassuring to the Yoshida faction and its hopes of hitching a "free ride" on America. The LDP no longer faced a threat to its monopoly at home or an external threat to Japan. It could afford to break up into factions and quarrel among themselves about lesser matters.

## NOTES

1. Kiichi Miyazawa, *Tokyo-Washington no mitsudan* [The Tokyo-Washington secret talks] (Tokyo: Jitsugyo no Nihon-sha, 1956), pp. 131–32.

2. Masataka Kosaka, *Saiso Yoshida Shigeru* [Prime minister Yoshida Shigeru] (Tokyo: Chuo Koronsha, 1968), p. 121.

3. Otake Hideo of Tohoku University has been inquiring into this subject. See *Adenaua to Yoshida Shigeru* [Adenauer and Yoshida Shigeru] (Tokyo: Chuo Koronsha, 1986). Such a Japan would certainly have behaved differently. For instance, much of trade friction with the United States stems from the sense that it has been exploited by Japan all through the Cold War, but this could have been averted.

4. Ogata Taketora denki kanko-kai, *Ogata Taketora* (Tokyo: Asahi Shimbunsha, 1963), pp. 210–11.

5. Tatsuo Mitearai, *Miki Bukichi den* [Biography of Miki Bukichi] (Tokyo: Shikisha, 1958), p. 446.

6. On Ogata's willingness to work with the rightwing JSP, see *Ogata Taketora*.

7. His friendship with Miwa Juso of the JSP was the key connection. Ikuzo Tajiri, *Showa no yokai Kishi Nobusuke* [Kishi Nobusuke: the spectre of Showa] (Tokyo: Gakuyo Shobo, 1979), p. 139.

8. Again he used the Miwa connection. Tajiri, p. 147–48.

9. Mitearai, p. 432. Others included Kitamura Tokutaro, Nakasone's mentor. Tokutaro Kitamura, "Ichi hoshu giin no kuchu" [A conservative Dietman's concern], *Bungei Shunju* (June 1956), pp. 88–93.

10. I use the word "collusion" to refer to the Yoshida-JSP cooperation only because they always concealed the purpose of common efforts, constitutional defense.

11. Mitearai, p. 443.

12. Ibid.

13. Kobayashi Naka, president of the Development Bank, Uemura Kogoro of Keidanren, Fujiyama Aiichiro of the Japan Chamber of Commerce, Sakurada Takeshi of Nisshin Textile, and Shikanai Nobutaka of Nikkeiren. Kosaka, p. 106.

14. See the Diet resolution calling for Yoshida's resignation in Kenzo Uchida, *Sengo Nihon no hoshu seiji* [Postwar Japan's conservative politics] (Tokyo: Iwanami Shoten, 1969), p. 66.

15. *FRUS,* 1952–54, XIV, 1743–44.

16. Takashi Itoh, "Jiyushugi-sha Hatoyama Ichiro: sono senzen, senchu, sengo" [Liberalist Hatoyama Ichiro: His prewar, wartime, and postwar career], Ryuichi Nagao, ed., *Taiheiyo senso* [The Pacific war] (Tokyo: Tokyo Univ. Press, 1967), pp. 51–79.

17. Kosaka, p. 21.

18. Ichiro Hatoyama, *Hatoyama Ichiro kaikoroku* [Memoirs of Ichiro Hatoyama] (Tokyo: Bungei Shunjusha, 1957), pp. 43–48.

19. Mark Gayn, *Japan Diary* (New York: William Sloane, 1948), pp. 161–64. Later, Prime Minister Tanaka met his demise in the same forum; since then the club has been anathema to Japanese politicians.

20. This declaration stimulated not only Hatoyama but the JSP, which began to move toward a merger. *Nihon Shakaito no sanjunen,* II, 43.

21. See Note 20.

22. Cited in Shigeto Tsuru, "Keizai gaiko no tenki" [The turning point in economic diplomacy], *Chuo Koron* (October 1955), p. 64.

23. According to one statistic, of the 40 editorials written on the issue in 1954, 25 favored revision. Haruhiko Fukui, *Jiyu Minshuto to seisaku kettei* [The Liberal Democratic Party and policy making] (Tokyo: Fukumura Shuppan, 1969), p. 262.

24. *Asahi Shimbun,* December 12, p. 3.

25. Editorial, January 1956, p. 25.

26. Koken Koyama, *Nihon Shakaito-shi* (Tokyo: Haga Shoten, 1965), p. 123.

27. Fukui, p. 261.

28. Nakasone, "Beikoku no atsuryoku to Nihon no teiko" [American pressure and Japanese resistance], *Bungei Shunju,* (January 1954), p. 70.

29. *Kempo Kaisei no Uta.* Cited in an autobiographical account given to this author by the Nakasone office.

30. *Bungei Shunju,* May 1955, pp. 84–91.

31. *Time,* March 14, 1955, pp. 34–37. I detect the theme of race and power here.

32. Through the Okazaki-Rusk talks during the negotiations for the Administrative Agreement. See "Hatoyama naikaku no chokumen suru yottsu no mondai" [The four problems facing the Hatoyama cabinet], *Chuo Koron,* (June 1955), pp. 44–48.

33. *Hatoyama Ichiro kaikoroku* (Tokyo: Bungei Shunju, 1957), p. 159; Fred Dickinson, "Nichi-Bei anpo taisei no henyo" [The transformation in the Japan-U.S. security system], *Hogaku Ronshu* (Kyoto: Univ. of Kyoto), 121, No. 4, 60–131.

34. *Chuo Koron,* June 1955, p. 49; John M. Allison, *Ambassador from the Prairie or Allison in Wonderland* (Boston: Houghton Mifflin, 1973), p. 275.

35. Ambassador Robert Murphy's dismissing of Ikeda but saving Okazaki was another instance. See Chapter 3.

36. *Hatoyama Ichiro kaikoroku,* pp. 85–92; Kiyotada Tsusui, *Ishibashi Tanzan: ichi jiyu shugi seijika no kiseki* [Ishibashi Tanzan: the track record of a liberal politician] (Tokyo: Chuo Koronsha, 1986), pp. 8–43.

37. *FRUS,* 1952–54, XIV, 1805.

38. See ibid., p. 1251, for Richard Finn's report that Yoshida is seeking to mediate between Peking and Washington; ibid., p. 1300, for NSC 125/1, directing that Yoshida's efforts be discouraged.

39. Donald C. Hellmann has been rightly critical of Japanese factionalism. See *Japanese Foreign Policy and Domestic Politics: The Peace Agreement with the Soviet Union* (Berkeley: Univ. of California Press, 1969). However, he viewed Japanese politics in isolation, as if it were independent of American influence. He overlooked the fact that the American connection was the very issue that was dividing Japan as it debated rapprochement with the Soviet Union.

40. This point was lost on many observers but not on Professor Kosaka (p. 104). For a sample of Hatoyama's "backtracking" remarks, see Kiyoaki Tsuji, *Nihon naikaku shiroku* [History of Japan's cabinets] (Tokyo: Daiichi Hoki, 1971), V, 282–83.

41. *Nihon naikaku shiroku,* V, 322–23.

42. Ibid., pp. 308–09.

43. Ashida, V, 411.

44. *Foreign Relations of the United States* has not extended beyond 1954 as of now.

45. See Hellmann, pp. 94–98, for a good discussion. Fujiyama Aiichiro, president of the Japan Chamber of Commerce and later Kishi's foreign minister, was in favor of rapprochement at first.

46. Southern Sakhalin and the northern Kuriles were inhabited by Japanese and Russian nationals, until in the settlement of 1875, Russia was given exclusive possession of all of Sakhalin in exchange for Japan's possession of all the Kuriles. Southern Sakhalin reverted to Japan's possession as a part of the settlement of the Russo-Japanese War, to which President Theodore Roosevelt lent his good offices.

47. Haruki Wada, "Sanfuranshisuko kowa to Chishima retto" [The peace of San

Francisco and the Kurile Islands], *Sekai,* (November 1988), pp. 233–49; Haruki Wada,
"Chishima retto no han'i ni tsuite" [On the boundary of the Kurile Islands], *Sekai,*
(May 1987), pp. 147–61; Haruki Wada, " 'Hoppo ryodo' mondai no hassei" [The ori-
gin of the 'northern territories' issue], I, *Sekai,* (April, 1989), pp. 153–69; Haruki
Wada, " 'Hoppo ryodo' mondai no hassei," II, *Sekai,* (May 1989), pp. 205–23.

48. See note 105 below.

49. Kashima Heiwa Kenkyujo, *Nihon gaikoshi* [Japan's diplomatic history], Vol.
27, Kumao Nishimura, *Sanfuranshisuko heiwa joyaku* [The San Francisco peace treaty]
(Tokyo: Kashima Heiwa Kenkyujo, 1971), p. 204; Haruki Wads, "Sanfuranshisuko
kowa to Chishima retto" [The peace at San Francisco and the Kurile Islands], *Sekai,*
November 1988, p. 245; Nanpo doho engo-kai, *Hoppo ryodo mondai shiryo-shu* [Data
related to the Northern Territory issue] (Tokyo: Nanpo doho engo-kai, 1966), p. 88; see
also Dean Acheson's letter, in *FRUS,* 1951, VI, Pt. 1, 1235.

50. *Asahi Shimbun,* August 1, 1952, p. 1. After the fact Yoshida stated that Japan
was then not in a position to make an irredentist claim because the ratification of the
peace treaty by the allied governments were pending. Kubota Masa'aki, *Kuremurin eno
shisetsu: hoppo ryodo kosho, 1955–1983* [The emissary to the Kremlin: the northern
territories negotiations, 1955–1983] (Tokyo: Bungei Shunjusha, 1983), p. 69. Along
with Matsumoto, Kubota is the most authoritative source.

51. JCP Central Committee, *Chishima mondai to Nihon Kyosanto* [The Kurile
question and the JCP] (Tokyo: Central Committee Publishing Bureau, 1974), p. 24. See
the statement by Shigemitsu in January 1955, in Kashima Heiwa Keynkyujo, *Nihon
gaikoshi* [Diplomatic history of Japan], Vol. 29, Seijiro Yoshizawa, *Kowago no gaiko*
[Posttreaty diplomacy] (Tokyo: Kashima Heiwa Keynkyujo, 1973), p. 152.

52. *FRUS,* 1952–1954, XIV, Pt. 2, p. 1793.

53. Shun'ichi Matsumoto, *Mosukuwa ni kakeru niji* [The rainbow over Moscow]
(Tokyo: Asahi Shimbunsha, 1966), pp. 42–43; see also Hellmann, pp. 34, 59.

54. Haruki Wada, " 'Hoppo ryodo' mondai no hassei" [The origin of the "northern territries" question], *Sekai,* April 1989, pp. 166–67.

55. Kubota, pp. 76–81.

56. Or pro-American in nondefense matters because it refused to cooperate on
defense.

57. Matsumoto, p. 46.

58. The conservative merger was about to jell at this moment, with both Kono and
Kishi masterminding it. Kono feared vacating Tokyo leaving Kishi in charge. So he
asked Hatoyama to send both of them to Washington. See Yoshihisa Hara, *Sengo Nihon
to kokusai seiji* [Postwar Japan and international politics] (Tokyo: Chuo Koronsha,
1988), p. 80.

59. Ichiro Kono, *Imadakara hanaso* [Now I can talk] (Tokyo: Shunyodo, 1958),
p. 100; Martin E. Weinstein, *Japan's Postwar Defense Policy, 1947–1968* (New York:
Columbia Univ. Press, 1971), pp. 78–80; Hara, pp. 80–85.

60. Matsumoto says he was displeased, (p. 54); but Kishi says he concurred, in
*Kishi Nobusuke kaisoroku* [Memoirs of Kishi Nobusuke] (Tokyo: Kosaido, 1983),
p. 205.

61. Matsumoto, pp. 52.

62. Weinstein, p. 79; see also Kono, *Imadakara hanaso* pp. 103–6.

63. "Why the conservatives cannot merge," *Asahi Shimbun,* October 23, 1955, p. 1.

64. Ibid., October 22, 1955, p. 1.

65. Ibid., October 26, 1955, p. 1.

66. *Shakaito no sanjunen,* II, 23. The biggest obstacle lay in differences over foreign policy. The leftwing asserted that Japan was a "subjugated country" (*juzoku-koku*), that the Soviet Union and China had "no need to export revolution," and that they "would not invade Japan at the risk of nuclear war." Ibid., pp. 56, 87. On the critical definition of the U.S.-Japanese relationship—around which most other important issues revolved—the rightwing Socialists maintained that while Japan was "legally and formally independent," its independence was "incomplete." For the sake of unity, the leftwing conceded the point.

On foreign relations, the rightwing moved to the left by endorsing the demand for "autonomous and independent diplomacy" and agreed furthermore with the judgment that the nations of Asia supported such diplomacy. For Japan's security, the new program called first for separate nonaggression pacts with China and the Soviet Union, to be superseded ultimately by a collective nonaggression pact involving the United States, the Soviet Union, China and Japan (a "Locarno type pact"). The security treaty with the United States was to be phased out accordingly.

67. Because the JSP and the JCP objected to the San Francisco peace treaty, they do not consider themselves bound by it. The JCP initially echoed the Soviet policy, but later switched to claiming the Kuriles for Japan. It agrees with the Cairo Declaration's contention that Japan *stole* southern Sakhalin in a war of aggression, but disagrees with the charge of theft with regard to the Kuriles.

68. Masumi, p. 444. At its founding, the LDP clearly was not what Seizaburo Sato says it is today: a party of weak nationalism. See Seizaburo Sato, *Jimin-to seiken* [The LDP regime] (Tokyo: Chuo Koron, 1986), pp. 4–16.

69. Matsumoto, p. 70; see also *Asahi Shimbun,* November 10, 1955, p. 1.

70. Masumi, II, 442–43.

71. Kono, *Imadakara hanaso,* pp. 5–6.

72. Kono, *Imadakara hanaso,* pp. 110–13.

73. Ichiro Kono, *Kono Ichiro jiden* [Autobiography of Kono Ichiro] (Tokyo: Tokuma Shoten, 1965), pp. 201–4.

74. Yuzo Tamura, *Sengo shakaito no ninaitetachi* [Postwar Socialist Party's rank and file] (Tokyo: Nihon Hyoronsha, 1984), p. 168.

75. *Kono Ichiro jiden,* pp. 216–17.

76. Hellmann, pp. 98–102.

77. Cited in Uhei Arimura, "Hatoyama gaiko no jittai" [The truth about Hatoyama's diplomacy], *Chuo Koron,* (August 1956), p. 40.

78. Matsumoto, pp. 90–91; Kono, *Imadakara hanaso,* pp. 30–47.

79. Kono, *Imadakara hanaso,* pp. 48–50. Yoshida's charge that Kono abandoned Kunashiri and Etorofu in the Kremlin meeting cannot be substantiated, but it does not seem to be cut from the whole cloth either. See Kubota, pp. 151–56.

80. The Social Science Research Institute, University of Tokyo, ed., *Sengo kaikaku* [Postwar reforms], vol. III, *Seiji katei* [The political process] (Tokyo: Univ. of Tokyo Press, 1974), pp. 105–12, 130–38.

81. See Nobusuke Kishi and Kazuo Yatsuji, "Hoshu godo eno michi" [The road to conservative merger], *Chuo Koron* (December 1979), pp. 298–313. See also the letter by Miwa Juso, Kishi's friend in the JSP, in ibid., (January 1980), pp. 392–93.

82. Interviews with two senior LDP members of the Diet, who prefer to be anonymous, September 1988. Nakasone Yasuhiro, then a young follower of Kono, much admired the presidential system because it articulated a unified national will seemingly independent of partisan politics.

83. There is a contrary thesis that frequent turnover of politicians would strengthen the bureaucracies, but the thesis does not apply to Japan's case. A government change instills the fear of a new master. This is what happened during the Socialist cabinets in 1947–48.

84. Kono, *Imadakara hanaso,* pp. 192–200; Tadao Okada, *Seiji no uchimaku* [Inside politics] (Tokyo: Yuki Shobo, 1959), pp. 219–21.

85. See Kono, *Imadakara hanaso,* pp. 192–200.

86. *Asahi Shimbun,* December 18, 1955, p. 1.

87. Soichi Oya, "Kokkai senjutsu-ron" [On parliamentary tactics], *Chuo Koron* (June 1956), p. 180.

88. Rei Shiratori, *Nihon no naikaku* [Japan's cabinets] (Tokyo: Shin Hyoron, 1986), II, 172.

89. Hideya Homma, "Masa ni kuzen no gerimanda" [This is gerrymander without parallel], *Chuo Koron,* (May 1956), p. 95.

90. See Mochizuki, p. 375.

91. *Yomiuri Shimbun,* April 29, 1956, p. 1, asked for physical obstruction to stop the bill if necessary.

92. Mochizuki, p. 380. Ohno Banboku was the inventor.

93. Okada, pp. 168–70.

94. Soichi Oya, p. 180.

95. *Asahi Shimbun,* May 1, 1956, p. 2.

96. Ibid., May 6, 1956, p. 1.

97. Uhei Arimura, "Hatoyama gaiko no jittai" [Truth about Hatoyama diplomacy], *Chuo Koron,* (August 1956), p. 40.

98. *Hatoyama Ichiro kaikoroku,* p. 188.

99. Miyazawa Kiichi feels that Yoshida might well have been behind the opposition to the bill. Interview with this author, May 1990.

100. Kubota, pp. 117–18.

101. *Asahi Shimbun,* July 22, 1956, p. 1.

102. See *New York Times,* August 28, 1956, p. 1; *Asahi Shimbun,* August 29, 1956, p. 1. Dulles's position was spelled out in greater detail in a memorandum handed by U.S. Ambassador Allison to Shigemitsu on September 10, 1956. Kubota, pp. 64–66.

103. *Asahi Shimbun,* August 29, 1955, p. 1.

104. *New York Times,* August 29, 1956, p. 1.

105. There is a school of thought in Japan, associated with the Foreign Ministry, that maintains that Dulles deliberately drafted the San Francisco peace treaty with a view to perpetuating a Japan-Soviet Union dispute (Ken'ichi Ito, "Nakasone tai-So gaiko eno chumon" [Requests for Nakasone's Soviet diplomacy], *Bungei Shunju,* December 1986, p. 120). One recalls Dulles's remark to British ambassador Oliver Franks soon after San Francisco: "The facts of [the] US-Japan relationship were such that it was unthinkable,

for the next several years at least, that Japan would pursue a policy in the Far East which was counter to that of the United States," in *FRUS, 1952–54,* XIV, 1076.

106. Matsumoto, p. 140. The LDP passed a new resolution in September taking account of the Dulles demarche. It called for immediate return of the Habomais and Shikotan and reserved Japan's right to Kunashiri and Etorofu, to be realized in negotiations after a peace treaty. Kubota, pp. 197–98.

107. Matsumoto, pp. 121–28; Kubota, pp. 189–218.

108. Tsuneo Watanabe, *Habatsu* [Factions] (Tokyo: Kobundo, 1964), p. 106.

109. Hatoyama left a well-kept diary, but it is not open to public scrutiny.

110. Watanabe (pp. 147–50) offers the standard theory of the origin of LDP factionalism: that the multimember district and the open balloting for the LDP presidency create factions.

# Chapter 7

# A Gaullist as an Adenauer

Two months into his administration, Prime Minister Ishibashi was stricken with a brain hemorrhage that left his speech impaired, and he resigned. Kishi, who had been Ishibashi's foreign minister in order to balance the faction-laden cabinet, was appointed his successor in March 1957, Ishibashi's brief tenure concerns us only for these facts: a liberal economic journalist, he advocated the small Japan alternative before the war, and he got on well with SCAP officials at first. But while serving as Yoshida's finance minister in 1946–47, he collided with them over major fiscal policy. The dispute concerned whether producers of war material and munitions should forfeit government guarantees, and if so, how to cope with foreclosures and bankruptcies across the entire economy.

Ishibashi, an advocate of what he called positive finance, argued that guarantees should be made good through deficit financing, if reconstruction efforts were not to be crippled. The Economic and Science Section of SCAP GHQ overruled him because of its opposition to anything connected with Japan's war efforts. The New Dealers were even willing to see forfeiture of bank deposits. This was to be part of a running dispute between SCAP and the Japanese government over balanced budget vs. positive finance that was to culminate in the imposition of the Dodge Line of belt-tightening. Ishibashi was purged simply for defiance. It may be recalled that Ikeda, who succeeded Ishibashi, went to Washington to seek relief from the Dodge Line in 1950. Basically, Ikeda was to preside over Japan's return to Ishibashi's policy when he became prime minister in 1960, to usher in the decade of high-speed growth.[1] Ishibashi in the meantime became a revisionist, owing perhaps to his purge experience, and was among the men canvassed by Dulles as a possible alternative to Yoshida. When he was elected prime minister in 1957, he championed the cause of Sino-Japanese detente. He barely put the issue on the political agenda before he fell ill.[2]

Like Hatoyama, Miki Bukichi, and Kono, Kishi was a Gaullist at heart. It was precisely this trait that prompted him to cut for himself the Adenauer role

in Japan—involving full-scale defense efforts in cooperation with the United
States. For the first time, Washington found in him a prime minister it was
looking for to fight the Cold War (Nakasone was the last). Unfortunately for
Kishi, even the Adenauer role for Japan presupposed a constitutional revision.
How he coped with his predicament deserves close scrutiny.[3]

Nobusuke was born in 1896, the second son of Sato Hidesuke, who also
fathered Sato Eisaku, the third and youngest son. Nobusuke was later adopted
through marriage by the Kishi family. Eisaku was to succeed Ikeda as prime
minister in 1964. Nobusuke and Eisaku were born and raised in Yamaguchi
prefecture in southern Japan, the domain once ruled by the lord of Choshu and
one that had given birth to some of the founding fathers of the Meiji Restoration. In those early modern days, Nobusuke's grandfather was the governor of a
neighboring prefecture. But such traditional ties seemed to matter much less in
the Japan of the 1930s, when Kishi began to climb up in the world. A bright
child, he had no trouble passing the rigorous entrance examination to the First
High School. Then he entered the Faculty of Law of Tokyo Imperial University,
earning an education prerequisite to his career in the imperial civil service. He
was to be typecast later as a bureaucrat and wore the label like a cross. He
would also strike some people later as an intellectual, another fact that counted
against him as a politician.[4] Cultivation of his intellect began at the First High
School, where he read Hauptmann, Ibsen, Tolstoy, Dostoevsky, Wilde, Scho-
penhauer, Nietzsche, Kant, Natsume Soseki, Tanizaki Junichiro, and the like, a
standard fare for extracurricular reading in prewar high schools.

It was at Tokyo Imperial University that he struck his own intellectual vein,
to which he remained faithful. World War I was about to end and the roaring
twenties about to begin, unleashing a floodtide of faddish leftism in Japan. The
choice before Nobusuke and his generation was either that or some variant of
the Japanese tradition. He chose the latter but distinguished himself with his
thoroughness and coherence. He enrolled in the classes of Professor Uesugi
Shinkichi, a nationalistic constitutional lawyer who set his ideas up against
those of Professor Minobe, with his theory of the emperor as an organ of state
rather than the embodiment of the state itself. Nobusuke interested himself in
the ideas of such ultranationalist thinkers as Kita Ikki and Okawa Shumei, the
latter later tried as a war criminal. But Kishi leaned in the direction of Kita, a
national-socialist. Nobusuke is said to have toyed with the idea of abolishing the
peerage and reforming the system of private property. Thereafter there always
remained in him a streak that inclined him to favor the public weal over the
private, a tendency that could easily be typecast as "statism" by hostile critics.[5]

As a top graduate, he was promised a place in the sun. He entered the

Ministry of Commerce and Industry, the predecessor of today's MITI, and distinguished himself in drafting statutes and ordinances in the secretariat. Here he mastered the ins and outs of organizational life in the bureaucracy, at the same time becoming an expert in industrial development through administrative guidance. Undoubtedly he owed his approach to problem solving—his second nature, as it were—to his bureaucratic experience. He was good at deferring to someone else's authority while he remained in control behind the scenes. He was also good at *nemawashi*—rooting or preparations; that is, he had a good sense of ends-means balance, and he made sure that everything he did would minister to his desired end. He had the reputation of having a "razor-sharp" mind and of being "free of improprieties," this being a condescending description of a clever bureaucrat.

In 1936 he was banished to Manchuria after an altercation with a minister. The colony, then only five years old, was the imperial army's domain and was in need of administrative talents to foster heavy industry within the framework of a guided economy. He became one of the new breed, called "radical bureaucrats" (*kakushin kanryo*), who threw in their lot with the empire and its destiny.

Manchurian development was based on a grandiose scheme, which was primarily Kishi's achievement. Foreigners who are used to today's inward-looking Japan would be stunned by its sheer pretension. He drew on his intellect in conceptualizing the scheme, and he drew on his skill in politicking to implement it. The empire was founded by two groups: the Kwangtung Army and the South Manchurian Railway Company. Matsuoka Yosuke, his maternal uncle and the man who was to conclude the Axis pact later, was there as the president of the railway company. In the Kwangtung Army, he had a friend in Tojo Hideki, a staff officer. Kishi used a third organization, the state of Manchukuo, to emasculate the SMRC by establishing new *zaibatsu* groups.[6]

Recalled to Tokyo in 1939, he was offered the post of administrative vice minister of the Military of Commerce and Industry, which was already involved in reorganizing the Japanese economy on a wartime footing. Shortly thereafter he was offered the ministership but declined on the ground that the appointment would unduly alarm the business community, with its dislike of state control. When General Tojo formed his cabinet in October 1941, Kishi was asked to take charge of Commerce and Industry, now renamed the Ministry of Munitions. Hence he was a minister of state when the war with the United States began. After the fall of Saipan in 1944, however, Kishi played a critical and successful role in the movement among imperial advisers to bring Tojo down. Three months after Japan's surrender, he was incarcerated on suspicion of class A war crimes. He languished for three years in Sugamo Prison, but was re-

leased without charge in 1948. While his trial was pending, he made preparations for a spirited defense of Japan's war policies.[7]

Having been at the top of the Japanese government before, during, and after
World War II, like Emperor Hirohito, he had to account for his conduct ever
since. In a memoir published long after his retirement, he freely admits that a
minister of state prior to and during the war, he is answerable to his own
countrymen for the ruin of the nation. But he bristled at the idea that responsibility for the war was the sort of thing the victor could or should put to a trial.
His return to government after the war seemed to have been occasioned by a
strong desire to compensate for his part in the war.[8] As soon as he was released
from Sugamo Prison in 1948, he began casting about for contacts and connec-
tions, with a view to an eventual reentry into politics when the purge was lifted.
In this he enjoyed a head start—during his career at Commerce and Industry, he
had collected a dazzling array of industrial and commercial tycoons as personal
friends, who were now willing to contribute to his cause. An outstanding benefactor was Fujiyama Aiichiro, owner and president of Japan's biggest sugar
producer.

When the purge was lifted in 1952, Kishi became hyperactive. By then he
was already convinced that Yoshida had outlived his usefulness to the country,
and that the constitution and the security treaty had to be revised.[9] The depth of
his conviction was rivaled only by that of Hatoyama, and it found its way into
the program of the Japan Reconstruction League, which he organized in 1952.
He intended to enlist the rightwing Socialist leaders in the league to oppose
Yoshida. But the league fared poorly in the election of 1952. The prewar caucus
politics of the notables, with which he was familiar, did not work in postwar
Japan. When Kishi learned that, he switched the venue with alacrity.

In 1953 his brother Sato, a bureaucratic politician and a trusted lieutenant of
Yoshida, arranged Kishi's admission to LDP membership. Kishi ran successfully for the lower house in the election following the Name-Calling Dissolution. Then, while enticing the business community with the lure of rearmament,
he persuaded the conservative parties to jointly organize the Constitution Discussion Forum. When Yoshida asked for Hatoyama's return to former Seiyukai,
Hatoyama and Kishi prevailed on a reluctant Yoshida to establish the Constitution Investigation Commission in Yoshida's own party, with Kishi as the chairman.[10] From here on, Kishi and Miki Bukichi held the levers of power as the
conservatives moved toward the merger. When the anti-Yoshida forces organized the Democratic party, Kishi became the secretary general. In 1955 he kept
pushing for the creation of a two-party system. When the LDP was born, he
remained in the party, again as secretary general. In the same year, he, Kono,
and Shigemitsu were sent to Washington to broach the subject of treaty revision

with Dulles. When the American secretary of state intervened against the peace treaty with the Soviet Union, Kishi wavered over the wisdom of Hatoyama's visit to Moscow and earned the epithet "Both Shores" (Kishi means "shore"). At a critical moment, he would rather be a Hamlet than a gutter fighter.

Kishi came to power with a concept of Japan's role that was identical to Hatoyama's, and he tried to implement it with greater intensity, care, and with less of Hatoyama's quixotic quality. He knew that one reason for Hatoyama's failure lay in Washington. Hatoyama was outflanked by Yoshida in Washington, which favored Yoshida's anticommunism. Kishi had once told Kono that the "red label" would be fatal to his ambition to be prime minister.[11] This was a reference to the public knowledge that Yoshida had once told Ambassador Douglas MacArthur II, nephew of General MacArthur who replaced Allison, that the LDP was so disunited on the Soviet issue because of "procommunists" like Kono.[12] Kishi tried to live up to his own advice to Kono—by taking a strong anticommunist and pro-American posture. But that proved to be his undoing. He was perceived as even more subservient to Washington than Yoshida. Ironically, Kishi, the nationalist, was forced to retire in the face of the biggest nationalistic upheaval in postwar Japan.[13]

For a long time before his death in 1987, he was the forlorn preeminence and chairman of the National Congress for the Establishment of An Autonomous Constitution, a cause today's LDP has seemingly abandoned in favor of money, power, and selfish gains.

One surmises that Kishi watched the U.S.-Japanese connection with enormous intensity. Kishi seems to have agreed and disagreed with Dulles. He saw that the ties between the two countries were deteriorating, as Dulles destabilized and radicalized Japanese politics. Washington's biggest mistake was that, disagreeing with Yoshida but mistrusting the revisionists, it was pitting them against each other and going nowhere. Behind this was Washington's succumbing to the temptation to coast along with the occupation–bred micromanagement. Unless Japan was given greater autonomy and equality, the future was uncertain.

> Japan was occupied by the United States for a long time after the war [Kishi said], and even though she recovered political independence of sorts with the San Francisco treaty, unequal relations between Japan and America persisted everywhere. The occupation period had left behind a stiff muscle, as it were, and the Japanese carried the psychological debt of the occupation. . . . Though it was over formally, we carried its residue in our heads. . . . To build friendly ties between Japan and the United States, that residue should not remain. We had to eliminate it and place Japan on an equal footing with the United States. As a

practical proposition, we had to deal with the treaty revision and the Okinawa issue.[14]

Kishi saw that Dulles, too, wanted an alliance and equality, not a protectorate arrangement. Kishi wanted to consolidate his power against Yoshida, build an alliance, and move on to constitutional revision. That much was required for an Adenauer of Japan to measure up to equality promised by Dulles. And beyond that, he would have been glad to have a truly equal alliance in which Japan would undertake the obligation to go to America's rescue if it were attacked by the Soviet Union.

Kishi's prime ministership was received politely, neither with a "boom" nor with hate by which he was swept out of office later.[15] The only exception was young Nakasone's vote against Kishi in the LDP presidential election because of his alleged "bureaucratism."[16] The country was at peace with itself and fascinated by the spectacle that had engulfed it for two years already—the incredible economic boom. No one knew at the time how it happened, nor that Yoshida would steal the credit for himself later. Those who were in its midst thought it was just a bubble that would soon burst. But it began in 1955, under Hatoyama. Having felt only the year before that Japan was at the end of its rope—what with the Yoshida government's failure to secure a large American loan, and with the politicians squabbling among themselves—the whole thing was miraculous to the Japanese. But Japan's economy shuddered, heaved, and began to move—in *1955 under Hatoyama.*

Government economists at the Economic Planning Agency, in its annual *Economic White Paper* on the state of national economy for 1955, said without a trace of irony, "it is no longer postwar." They meant that mining and industrial production, average income, and stocks of capital goods had exceeded the prewar level. Recovery had been completed in 10 years, and it would no longer be the prime mover of economic growth. Regarded as something of a masterpiece of bureaucratese, the *White Paper* seized on Schumpeter's concept of "innovation"—that mother of creative destruction—as the engine of future growth. Then it used "innovation" interchangeably with "modernization" to plead the case for the creation of the Keynesian desideratum: effective demand.

Actually nothing that can be called government planning, strictly speaking, existed then or since, and Keynesian fine tuning perhaps did more damage than good by exacerbating the boom-and-bust cycle pegged to the foreign exchange balance.[17] Naturally, it did not occur to anyone then that high–speed economic growth would become a partisan political issue between the revisionists and the Yoshida school. The thesis—later elevated to political doctrine—that Japan's economic prosperity was possible only because it fended off arms expenditure by means of the constitution would undoubtedly have struck anyone as preposterous. At the time Japan was spending close to 3 percent of its GNP on defense—in contrast to 1 percent today, and was none the worse for it. Kishi, the architect of the Manchurian economy and a MITI man, was obviously aware of the explosion of the economy under his care. But neither he nor anyone else believed that economic prosperity was incompatible with national defense.[18]

Besides economic prosperity, there was a more obvious reason why Kishi was viewed more positively at the time. In the three-way alignment in politics, the revisionist-JSP "bipartisanship" that began under Hatoyama continued under Ishibashi because he favored China trade, and Kishi inherited it. On the question of treaty revision, the Left and Right had a prima facie agreement. The agreement was reinforced in early 1957, as the Kishi cabinet was installed, by the so-called base struggle (*kichi-toso*) that had begun in 1953, two years after San Francisco, and now spreading across Japan.

It is little known that, beating the deadline of the peace treaty, the U.S. military expanded the bases in 1951. "Base struggles"—communitywide campaigns to resist landseizure and evictions to make room for military bases or to demand better compensation—had started in Uchinada, a firing range on the coast of the Sea of Japan, and reached a crescendo in 1956–57 with the campaign in Sunakawa, a small town in the suburbs of Tokyo located near Tachikawa air base, an U.S. installation. In May 1955 the Tokyo city government notified the town that it had to vacate a part of its domain for runway expansion. At the time, there were 200 disputes pending throughout Japan.[19]

When the town of Sunakawa rebuffed the Tokyo government, an army of riot police descended on the town to evict property owners. Close enough to Tokyo for an easy commute, Sunakawa was tailor-made for the radicals. In short order, the JSP, Sohyo, radical intellectuals, and Zengakuren decided to put their muscle behind the town in the violent collision. For the JSP it was a "Tennozan," a battle of do or die, that did wonders for rallying support for the leftwing. It must be noted that politics of pacifism was not institutionalized until well after the San Francisco peace treaty. It originated in the 1951 reaction to the "reverse course," and drew its sustenance from the Washington–Yoshida conflict of 1952–54. The movement became full-blown in the wake of the "ashes of death incident" of 1954, in which a Japanese fishing vessel, *Lucky Dragon No. 5,* became the victim of radioactive fallout from the hydrogen bomb testing near Bikini Atoll. By the time the base struggle began to coalesce with the peace movement, the latter had fully professionalized organizations, which were funded in all likelihood by the communist-bloc countries, and which responded actively to the cue from Moscow and Peking.[20]

Media reporting, exaggerated and sympathetic to the evicted, played up the notion of a "domestic 38th parallel" between the people and the government acting on behalf of the foreign army. Base struggles became a difficult issue for the conservative government, because the LDP's rightwing sympathized with the radicals' protest against foreign bases, while the center was colluding with the radicals from time to time to restrain the rightwing. Under public—or media—pressure, the Japanese government therefore began to bend over backward to pay generous compensation. The government became hostage to the most recalcitrant landlord who held out for the best "payoff," which then became the compensation standard for the community as a whole. Slowly, the "consensus" approach began to emerge at the grassroots at the same time that it made its appearance at the center. The cost to the public can be seen in the stupendous expenditure called for in the construction and maintenance of Narita airport outside Tokyo, and in finding a home port for the atomic–powered ship *Mutsu.*[21]

The base struggles had their cause celebre during the short-lived Ishibashi government. On January 30, 1956, Specialist Third Class William S. Girard, U.S. Army, was on guard duty on the firing range of a military base in Gumma prefecture. To ward off junk dealers collecting spent shells, he fired a blank and killed a Japanese farmer's wife. By then the extraterritorial privileges enjoyed by U.S. military personnel and their dependents had been surrendered to Japanese jurisdiction, and the Japanese courts were empowered to try crimes committed in off–duty hours. In the Girard case, however, a dispute over Japan's right to trial arose between the two governments, and inflamed public opinion turned the incident into a major international issue.

The point at issue was whether the suspect was in the line of duty when he shot a civilian to death. The city of Aurora, Illinois, from which Girard hailed, innocently petitioned the emperor for a pardon. The Illinois state legislature resolved to demand U.S. jurisdiction over his case. And Girard took the jurisdictional dispute to the U.S. Supreme Court. The Japanese public was equally adamant because of the testimony by witnesses that the suspect threw out spent shells to entice the victim before taking aim at her. The settlement, which came during the Kishi cabinet, was transparently political but satisfactory to both sides: the Japanese court tried Girard and gave him a suspended sentence, whereupon he left for home with a Japanese bride.[22]

The Girard case came on the heels of another incident created by a news dispatch from Washington quoting a State Department spokesman as saying that the United States was considering a plan to station nuclear-armed units both on Okinawa and in Japan proper.[23] But under the original security treaty, Japan had no say over the movement of U.S. nuclear ordnance nor, indeed, over a war that might be waged from the U.S. bases in Japan. That, too, was grist for the opposition mill; the ongoing runway expansion at several air bases seemed to fit in with the strategic New Look. Feeding on all these events and a few more important ones to be mentioned below, the radical opposition gradually built up and kept in readiness a large network of extraparliamentary mass organizations; through trial and error it was also accumulating know-how on the use of the media; and it was developing political tactics for coordinating parliamentary, extraparliamentary, and media campaigns for maximum effect.

Open agitation for revising the security treaty came originally from the radical-liberal camp, although the opposition reversed itself later. Kishi made much of the fact. It would not be surprising if he waited until they publicly committed themselves before responding with sympathy. Suzuki Mosaburo, on the leftwing of the JSP and JSP chairman, first pressed the new prime minister with the need for revision, though Suzuki used the word *kaihai,* or "revise and abolish."[24] "Revise the Security Treaty," ran the *Asahi* headline reporting on the gathering of over 500 "scholars and culture persons" in February 1957.[25] The faces and names were more or less the same as in the Peace Problem Symposium of 1950, but bloody riot suppressions at Sunakawa were creating public sympathy.

Professor Shimizu Ikutaro, who organized the gathering, revealed later that he had called for "revision" rather than "abolition" of the treaty in order to mobilize a wider constituency.[26] The JSP plank, "revise and abolish," drafted at the 13th congress in January 1957, was a compromise and fence-straddling. As far as the leftwing was concerned, "revision" was the first step toward eventual "abolition."[27]

The issue Kishi and the JSP were raising at this stage had to do with Japan's status, not security. For instance, at one point during the treaty negotiations with Ambassador MacArthur, Kishi quipped, "That's just like Manchukuo," in commenting on a provision in the security treaty.[28] The security issue—the danger to Japan of getting involved in an American war—was raised later, during the crisis over the islands of Quemoy and Matsu in the Formosa Strait in 1958, ending the Kishi-Socialist cooperation.[29] Yoshida, Ikeda, Miyazawa, and their friends scoffed at the status issue. No matter how the treaty was reworded, they assured, the basic inequality between the United States and Japan could not be gotten rid of.[30] There was sophistry in this argument: Yoshida, too, sought a mutual and equal treaty, and he settled for an unequal one by refusing Dulles's terms. That was Kishi's point.

However, a revision was a two-way proposition. Dulles climbed down considerably from his initial demand of 1951 for Japan's role in regional collective security: he resigned himself to constitutional status quo and the role of the Self-Defense Forces (they were no longer constabulary and capable of dealing with external threat but only on Japanese soil) in the Ikeda-Robertson talks. But it was one thing for him to ignore the inequality of the old treaty, and something else to write another that is "equal" only to Japan. No, if it came to a revision, he wanted to bring up regional collective security once again. Kishi's heart was in going with the American secretary of state all the way, to regional security. In fact, he seems to have envisioned for Japan an even bigger role in the midterm to distant future. He was dissatisfied with Yoshida's peace treaty with Taiwan, and he intended to get back to the China question. So he appointed Fujiyama Aiichiro, his progressive businessman friend, foreign minister in the second cabinet (June 1958).[31] He also took care not to close off the nuclear option for the distant future. It was one thing, he thought, to abide by an external constraint against offensive weapons and something else for the Japanese to reinforce it.[32]

But the constitution, Yoshida, and the Socialists were blocking overseas deployment of troops, the sine quo none of regional security. Thus, Kishi appeared to be damned if he sought a revision and damned if he did not. On the other hand, the treaty was so glaringly unequal and the Japanese radicals were so restive about it that Washington may be persuaded to accept a revision in exchange for greater Japanese cooperation that fell short of regional security. Kishi was going for the "equality" that Yoshida sought for himself but did not get. Hence, Yoshida should have been his ally in this venture. Instead, he had to rely on the feckless Socialists as he moved in closer to Washington. Although Kishi was the prime mover behind the treaty revision, personally drafting the new treaty and masterminding the political strategy, there was an independent and parallel move in the foreign ministry, a move that Shigemitsu represented before Dulles in the 1955 meeting.[33]

Upon becoming prime minister, Kishi ushered in with considerable hoopla what he called the "new U.S.-Japanese era." He became a very close friend of the new American ambassador, Douglas MacArthur II, nephew of the general, who presented his credentials as John M. Allison's successor in February 1957. MacArthur, quite possibly the greatest U.S. ambassador ever to be posted to Tokyo and also the least appreciated by the Japanese, fully shared Kishi's convictions on the need to put the U.S.-Japan relations on a more equal footing. Kishi brought up the topic in a private conversation within six to eight months of MacArthur's arrival. MacArthur enjoyed Kishi's confidence, so much so that the prime minister was probably closer to the ambassador than to his own cabinet ministers. It was fortunate that the envoy had once been a political adviser to Eisenhower at SHAPE and had a direct access to the president. It was also fortunate for Kishi that the president, having been allied commanders in war and peace, fully understood the need for mutuality in alliances.[34]

As a first step in his venture, Kishi personally energized diplomacy. Suddenly he became a globe-trotting diplomat. He instituted what has come to be called with tongue in cheek *sankin kotai*—a trip to pay homage to the overlord—to Washington upon assuming the prime ministership. Though by inclination pro-Taiwan, he became pointedly antimainland in order to assuage Dulles's suspicions toward the China plank he inherited from Ishibashi. Taiwan was on his itinerary in the spring, and he and Chiang Kai-shek embraced each other warmly, with Kishi issuing a statement supporting the Nationalists' desire to return to the mainland. With condescending sarcasm, one of Yoshida's lieutenants noted, "Though in the past Kishi has exhibited a dangerous attitude as if he were a neutralist, he has now demonstrated a clear anti-communist stance and support for the freedom camp. We are indeed back to the period of Yoshida government."[35] But by taking a pro-American stance, Kishi was taking a chance with the JSP and Peking. The Chinese government, which was restrained during Hatoyama's Soviet overture and Ishibashi's Peking courtship, retaliated with a broadside. But no matter. Kishi concluded a reparations agreement with the government of South Vietnam, putting off Hanoi. China unveiled a scheme to use the $150 million annual two-way trade as a lever to split Japan's public opinion and isolate Kishi. In July the JSP organized the National Congress for Sino–Japanese Rapprochement, with some leftwing LDP participation.[36]

Kishi's grand design for treaty revision called first for a trip to Southeast Asia to work out a role enabling Japan to mediate between that region and Washington, on the basis of a rather nebulous plan being worked out by the Eisenhower administration. Having cut Japan off from the China market, Dulles despaired of Japan's prospect for selling its "shoddy goods" in America, and settled on Southeast Asia as a substitute. Kishi wanted to forge the Asian tie with economic aid, but, alas, Japan is the 1950s was too poor for that. He met howling protests in Canberra and Manila, but was heartened in India by Nehru, who told Kishi that India's independence movement was inspired by Japan's victory over Russia in 1905. More important for treaty revision, Kishi spruced up the defense establishment at home. He had the National Defense Council adopt the Basic Direction for National Defense (Kokubo no kihon hoshin) and go ahead with the "first defense buildup," with the promise of more to come.[37] His message to Washington was that, starting from zero in 1951, Japan has built up its armed forces, which deserved to be honored in an equal treaty.

Fully armed for an encounter with Dulles, Kishi was ready for his official visit to Washington in mid–June. Two days before his departure, Yoshida wrote a newspaper column titled, "Hopes for Prime Minister Kishi's U.S. visit," and said:

There seem to be opinions demanding a revision of the security treaty and the Administrative Agreement. But I am convinced that there is no need to touch them at all. They are quite acceptable as they are. . . . There are treaties that are equal and others that are unequal. I would gladly conclude a treaty if it serves my nation's interests. Politics is not made of legalistic bullsessions in dormitories.[38]

On the first day of Kishi's visit, he was surprised by an unexpected show of friendship and attention by Dwight Eisenhower, who invited him to the Burning Tree Country Club for golf. What struck Kishi most, it seemed, was the shower he and the president took together afterward: "becoming naked" is a metaphor in Japanese for openness and candor. He was also surprised to find Secretary Dulles, who had been so brusque with him in 1955, being coy and respectful toward the president. Kishi was pleased by an invitation to address a joint session of Congress, which gave him a standing ovation. In this speech, another at the National Press Club, and in the joint communique of the two governments, he took a strong anti-communist stance.[39] In the meetings with Eisenhower and Dulles, Kishi discussed treaty revision, the reversion of Okinawa, Japan's defense efforts, reduction of U.S. forces in Japan, and loans from the International Monetary Fund and the Export-Import Bank in Washington.

Kishi wanted reversion of Okinawa and the Bonins in due course, and, failing that, he wanted to extend the coverage of the revised treaty to those islands. Washington refused reversion of Okinawa and the Bonins, as expected, but it agreed to let Japan contribute fiscally to their civil administration, as a way of affirming Japan's residual sovereignty. On the treaty question, Eisenhower seemed to have talked Dulles into yielding in form but not in substance. The joint communique stated that the treaty was provisional and agreed to appoint a joint committee to study problems arising from the treaty, starting with a session in August. What was denied Kishi and Shigemitsu during their 1955 visit to Washington was granted—in principle. This and the grant of loans made the trip a success for Kishi, even though in a separate press interview Dulles put a damper on speedy revision.[40] Kishi returned to Tokyo amid the violent collision at Tachikawa air base.

In July, after his return from Washington, Kishi carried out a reshuffle of the cabinet and the three major party posts (secretary general, chairmen of the policy and research committee and the executive committee) to consolidate his power. He swept out most of the carryovers from the Ishibashi government and replaced them with members of revisionist or allied factions. Ikeda left the Ministry of Finance. The new foreign minister was Fujiyama Aiichiro, Kishi's old friend from the business community and his benefactor during the purge. Kono, Kishi's sworn comrade-in-arms who was too ambitious to be left out of sight, was brought into the cabinet along with four of his followers. Kishi's brother Sato, a close lieutenant of Yoshida, was coopted so as to keep the Yoshida faction divided. Sato was placed in charge of the party's executive committee.

In August Kishi made an announcement that many contemporaries received with a grain of salt. He declared, "Liquidation of factions is the voice of heaven," and ordered LDP factions out of existence.[41] Such a "liquidation"— always coupled with party finance reform because money is what holds a faction together—has since become a ritual and farce in the LDP. Kishi, who had been intimately involved in the origin of the 1955 system and who knew the whys and wherefores of factionalism, might have been skeptical of what he was doing. But being the first prime minister to bear the brunt of full–blown factionalism, he was willing to try any nostrum. Specifically, he appeared to be having a problem persuading Kono and other faction leaders to go along with the idea of an early general election.[42]

Otherwise, everything seemed to be going Kishi's way as far as domestic politics was concerned. But in August and October 1957 two rockets were fired from the Soviet Union, marking the beginning of a shift in the international environment. One rocket carried an intercontinental ballistic missile that flew over Japan and landed in the Pacific. The other thrust the first man–made satellite, *Sputnik,* into orbit, from which it beamed a radio message to the earth. The political impact of the two rockets on Moscow, Washington, Peking, and the Japanese Socialists would have startling consequences for Kishi later.[43]

A prime minister has the power to call an election at a moment most opportune for himself, his faction, and his party. Kishi's chance to dissolve the Diet came in April 1958, when the Socialists—eager for the first test of strength since the merger—demanded it. Kishi did not feel he had a chance to aim for a two–thirds majority.[44] The JSP boasted of winning the governing majority.[45] But realistically it hoped to gain 20 to 30 seats and go on to wrest power in two or three more elections. In the May election, which saw the highest voter turnout of all postwar elections (at 76.99 percent) and whose issue was China, the LDP won 287 seats, for a decrease of three, but coopted 11 independents afterward. The JCP and another minor party won one each. The JSP expanded by seven to 167. These results struck the JSP as defeat and the LDP as victory. It turned out that 1958 was the height of the JSP's power and the beginning of its long-term decline. The "defeat" at hand cast a pall over the Socialists.

For subsequent JSP conduct, particularly its switch from support for treaty revision to opposition, there are two major explanations, political and sociological. The former, offered by Kishi, is that the JSP was responding to a change in tactics in Moscow and Peking over the Quemoy crisis. But more on this later.[46]

The sociological answer has to do with the JSP's predicament, as it came to light in the aftermath of the 1958 election.

"The one–third barrier," an expression that gained currency about this time, was one way of putting the JSP's problem. Having taken one third of the lower house in 1953 and of the upper house in 1956, the JSP stopped growing—as if ordered by an invisible hand. The barrier was to become a permanent fixture of Japanese politics, and the media would argue that it was erected by the collective intelligence of the body politic. Caught in the East-West conflict in the Cold War, the argument goes, Japan had to protect itself from the Russians and Chinese by means of the security treaty, and protect its autonomy from the Americans by means of the constitution. For this purpose, it was necessary to hold the Socialists at the "one–third barrier," neither more nor less.[47] If they command a majority, they can jeopardize the security treaty; if they lose one-third of the Diet, the constitution can be amended.

When the barrier materialized, the JSP divided itself once again along its Left–Right cleavage. A dispute over the current political situation and future policy orientation followed, and it had to take into account the far-reaching changes wrought in Japanese society in the more than 10 years that had elapsed since the defeat, and especially in the last few years of economic prosperity.

The Socialists were alarmed by the great strides the LDP was taking in building a new form of organization called *koenkai,* a personal vote-getting machine, for each Dietman. The LDP boasted of having 10 million *koenkai* members, in addition to one million dues paying party members. Controlled by a Dietman, rather than by the LDP, *koenkai* made him independent of the party, but its enormous expenses made him dependent on his faction.[48] In the rural areas, moreover, the land reform had wrought an amazing change in the style of politics. A vast number of proprietor–farmers, enriched by the frenzied production of subsidized rice, were recruited into Nokyo (the Japan Federation of Agricultural Cooperative Associations), which supplanted the landlord class as the most powerful conservative lobby in the countryside.[49] At the same time, industrialization was luring rural population into the cities, creating new urban voters with different needs. A Buddhist sectarian party (called Soka Gakkai, later renamed Komeito) was born in the Socialists' own bailiwick. The head-long rush of the economy had spread the sense among the majority of voters that they belonged to the middle class. Ideological politics was losing its appeal.[50]

The radical–liberals themselves were subject to the social changes around them. A little under half the JSP Diet members were elected by Sohyo, and they constituted a labor aristocracy of sorts, with a strong distaste for returning to the union locals and shops. The JSP was fast turning into a parliamentary party with but a very weak local organization of its own. But Sohyo itself was changing. In 1954 its radicalism spawned a breakaway labor federation called Domei, affiliated with the JSP rightwing. Domei began organizing second unions in the private sector in close cooperation with employers, who launched the Productivity–Enhancement Campaign. The landmark event was the victory of the company union at the Nissan Motor Corporation. Sohyo was forced to steer a little to the right. It dethroned its communist chairman in 1955, shifted its foreign policy from pro–Soviet to pro–third force, and launched the first of the vaunted "spring offensives" for pay hikes in 1956. But it remained the linchpin of the JSP leftwing.

During 1952–54, the Socialists surged ahead in strength by taking Yoshida's side in the Washington–Yoshida conflict over rearmament. They took credit for themselves as the defender of the constitution. But now Kishi took the wind out of their sails by softpedaling that issue. Suddenly, the Socialists' ideological slogans began to sound hollow and shrill. It was noted that they merely reacted to the conservatives and were fast becoming an "automatic safety valve" that lets off the steam.[51] As Japanese society began to undergo major transformation, the JSP was caught straddling two constituencies, which were diverging from each other: the radical Sohyo unions and the voters at large on the center Left. If the JSP was to grow beyond the "one–third barrier," it had to capture the independent voters by steering further to the right. Yet it was too dependent on Sohyo to do that. The postmortem in 1958 concerned the strategy required to break out of the dilemma.

The two wings of the Socialists offered completely contradictory diagnoses and recommendations. The leftwing attributed the brilliant comeback of the JSP to the strength of the Left since the San Francisco peace conference, noted the success of recent base struggles, blamed current setback on the unprincipled merger of 1955, and demanded unswerving allegiance to socialist revolution. Sohyo upheld the leftwing. Among other things, it advised the JSP: "We are opposed to the two-party system based on persuasion and dialogue. . . . The current setup, which decides everything on the majority principle, means that the LDP is law."[52] Professor Sakisaka Itsuro, ideologue of the leftwing, struck the keynote with his call to recapture the socialist "soul."[53]

In vain Nishio Suehiro and the rightwing JSP demanded moderation. But the 1958 election was the "final blow" to the two-party thesis, according to the JSP's official history.[54] The JSP did not thereupon abandon the parliamentary system and take to the streets. It decided to lean more and more on extraparliamentary mass struggle to make up for its weakness inside the Diet. The modus operandi of this approach can be traced back to the JSP victory in defeating the small district bill. Schematically, it had several components, in emerging trends: (1) the Socialist Diet members were becoming rowdy, violent, and willing to disregard parliamentary protocols, (2) the rules of Diet proceedings, characterized by so-called viscosity, could be manipulated to frustrate the legislative process, (3) the LDP's party cohesion was undermined by the Yoshida-Kishi division and factionalism, (4) extraparliamentary mass organizations controlled by the radical-liberal parties were on the rise, and (7) the media campaigns by the liberal newspapers against the "violence of numbers," or majority rule, was an incentive to create parliamentary deadlock.

In a straight partisan vote on ordinary legislation, the Socialists were completely impotent and outvoted every time. But skillful use of parliamentary procedures could enable a minority to stall a vote or to pigeonhole a bill. The occupation reform of Dietary procedure effectively dispersed power by creating powerful standing committees and giving full protection to individual Dietmen and minority parties. The short duration of legislative sessions, a legacy of the imperial Diet, became a millstone around the government's neck in the postwar period because it could create a traffic jam. The role of traffic cop, played by the Ways and Means Committee in the U.S. House of Representatives, was assigned in the Diet to the House Management Committee of 25, on which every party was represented. The rule of the HMC was unanimity, and it controlled the agenda of the day-to-day legislative process. There were two ways of circumventing the power of the HMC. The speaker could set aside its ruling on a critical vote, or when a bill was stalled in a committee, the plenary session could vote an 'interim report" to force the bill to the floor.[55]

Voting in spite of physical obstruction was called a "forced vote" (*kyoko saiketsu*), On a good many occasions the JSP simply boycotted a committee or plenary session, which would compel the LDP to proceed with "lone legislation" (*tandoku shingi*) or "lone vote" (*tandoku saiketsu*). But as often as not the government would hesitate to take this course for fear of media reaction. A forced vote was as unnerving to the LDP leadership as a boycott was ineffective for the JSP, if repeated too often. Repeated boycotts turned it into crying wolf—it was no longer scary. A forced vote was a last resort and a government would squander its resources by using it too often. The success of a forced vote depended on the unity of the governing party, which—given the LDP's structure—was apt to be purchased at a dear price. At a critical moment, when a prime minister's political life was at stake, a faction leader might threaten to trade his support for an advantage.[56]

The problem in the Japanese Diet was that on certain critical votes, majority rule did not work. When a simple majority decision turned into a forced vote, the media came into play, attacking the "violence of numbers." If the majority rule was "violence," the only alternative was unanimity, or "consensus." But this problem cannot be treated simply as procedural peculiarity of the Japanese Diet. The rule of unanimity was only the tip of the iceberg. Underneath was the three-way division of Japanese politics and the Yoshida-Socialist collusion to cry wolf against the "militarist" bogey, as Miyazawa Kiichi conceded:

> In managing politics, we were much troubled by this question: how to dissuade autocratic, reactionary, or militarist demands by old politicians of the prewar persuasions. It is true that as a means to this end, we have often used emotional reactions of the people and the resistance potential of the radical-liberals: it was decisive leverage in restraining the hardliners.[57]

When parliamentary "consensus" system was skillfully combined and coordinated with extraparliamentary mass mobilization, one arrived at a potion that was seductively syndicalist for the Socialists and devastating for the LDP. Prime Minister Kishi was to have his first encounter with it in late 1958.

Kishi took the victory in the May election as a mandate to go ahead with treaty revision. He carried out another reshuffle of cabinet and party posts. In the second Kishi cabinet, the mainstreamers were the Kishi, Kono, Ohno, and Sato factions, which together filled 11 out of 22 cabinet posts. Ikeda was reinstated as minister without portfolio. Together with the enlisting of Kishi's brother Sato, the reshuffle had the effect of keeping the Yoshida-Ikeda faction in check. In addition, instead of letting the JSP take the vice speakership and committee chairmanships in proportion to its numerical strength, as had been the custom, Kishi decided to put all the parliamentary posts to a vote, and he won them all. Kono positioned himself as the chairman of the party's executive committee, a forum that ratifies all party decisions.

As Kishi veered away from his predecessor's pro-Peking policy and moved closer to Dulles, there were skirmishes with both Peking and the radical-liberals. One was with the Japan Teachers' Union over the summer, which ended in a draw.[58] Then, in October, Kishi sprang a bill to amend the Police Duties Law and dug his own grave, according to standard history. In the remainder of this chapter, I offer an account that heeds the interpretation of standard history and that has been unanimously accepted by the media and academics. The point of this interpretation is to view the police bill affair as a purely domestic event. In the next chapter, I put the event in the proper international context, to explain why Kishi had to act the way he did.[59]

The Police Duties Law parallels the Police [Organization] Law. The latter had been revised three times since San Francisco, but the former had not. Kishi felt its revision was long overdue. His bill was designed to expand policemen's power to routinely investigate, carry out searches, enter private property, and

issue warnings—in short, it was not the stuff of which the *Miranda* decision of
the U.S. Supreme Court was made.[60] At an LDP conference, weighing the
wisdom of pushing the bill against the trouble to be expected from the Socialists, Kono bellowed, "Get it in." And that was that.[61]

On October 8, four days after the start of the Fujiyama-MacArthur talks on
treaty revision, the police bill was introduced in the Diet. The Socialists immediately refused to take part in Diet deliberations and barricaded themselves in
the committee room. The media said nothing of this but reacted with hysteria to
the bill. It was portrayed as a threat to civil liberty and a return to the prewar
Peace Preservation Law, which had a symbolic value to the radical-liberals
equivalent to the Holocaust. It was alleged that the police would "barge in on
your date" or "break into your bedroom on your honeymoon." As the JSP
admitted later, the media took the initiative.[62]

The JSP, Sohyo, the National Federation of Constitutional Defense, and
other organizations, 66 in all, established the National Congress for Opposition
to the Police Duties Bill. In order to keep the moderates in, the JSP kept the
Communists and Zengakuren out.[63] "United action" by the National Congress
began on October 24 under Sohyo auspices, and it was repeated thereafter in
the form of general strikes. The climax of the event was to be on November 4,
the end of the session. If Kishi wanted to persist with the bill, he would have to
extend the session. The Diet building was surrounded by demonstrators num-
bering several tens of thousands for several days. A rumor that a "February
revolution" was in the offing spread around Nagata-cho.[64]

On November 4 Kishi decided to extend the session. But Socialist obstruction made it impossible for the speaker—he was reported to have written a will
before setting out for the Diet building—to approach the podium.[65] Tanaka
Kakuei, a young LDP Dietman, came up with the idea of a "surprise
extension"—the vice speaker would call for a vote by acclamation from the
floor.[66] Tanaka personally led the charge of young LDP Dietman past the cor-
don of burly Socialist secretaries to obtain an affirmative decision. The JSP
refused to recognize the "illegal" extension and boycotted the Diet. In protest,
Sohyo, Domei and another labor federation called a strike involving six million
workers for the following day.[67] This was the first political strike since 1952.

The morning papers of the following day began a massive campaign. The
issue had suddenly changed from the police bill to the "surprise extension"
itself. The media professed to believe that that extension was a breach of parliamentary democracy. Kishi could have gone on to obtain passage of the bill had
it not been for internal opposition: Ikeda, Masutani (the former speaker),
Hayashi, Ishii, and Miki Takeo would not agree to "lone legislation." That is,
they insisted on unanimity.[68] Kishi wavered, to the disgust of Kono. Ohno was

in favor of "lone legislation," but Hatoyama favored a compromise.[69] With a somersault, Yoshida came to Kishi's rescue, saying, "Don't fumble. You've had a taste of your own medicine, haven't you?"[70]

But the bill had to be abandoned in a stunning reversal for Kishi. The JSP-revisionist cooperation was dead; Yoshida's disciples were now flirting with the JSP; and Kishi was isolated. The concerted campaign to discredit him was under way, as if he was needed as an antihero. The machinery of extraparliamentary mass mobilization was now tested. In retrospect, the police bill affair was the dress rehearsal for the 1960 upheaval against the security treaty. But there was much more to the police bill fiasco than met the eye—Yoshida's strange move was the clue, as explained in the next chapter.

# NOTES

1. Hiroshi Masuda, *Ishibashi Tanzan: senryo seisaku eno teiko* [Ishibashi Tanzan: the resistance against occupation policies] (Tokyo: Soshisha, 1988), chapter 4.

2. An excellent analysis of his political career is Kiyotada Tsutsui, *Ishibashi Tanzan: ichi jiyu-shugi seijika no kiseki* [Ishibashi Tanzan: the track record of one liberal politician] (Tokyo: Chuo Koronsha, 1986).

3. Just recently, an excellent book on Kishi has been written: Yoshihisa Hara, *Sengo Nihon to kokusai seiji* (Tokyo: Chuo Koronsha, 1988). Like this book, it takes its cue from Hans J. Morgenthau, and its treatment of the LDP's factional struggle is very thorough and penetrating. I do have some serious differences with Hara on other matters, however.

4. This is noted by Sei Ito, "Kishi Nobusuke shi ni okeru ningen no kenkyu" [Kishi Nobusuke: a study in personality], *Chuo Koron* (August 1960), pp. 169–78.

5. Kosaka calls it "rational statism."

6. Masaya Ito, Prime Minister Ikeda's secretary, cited in Ikuzo Tajiri, *Showa no yokai Kishi Nobusuke* [Kishi Nobusuke: the spectre of Showa] (Tokyo: Gakuyo Shobo, 1979), pp. 146–47.

7. Tajiri, p. 125.

8. Ibid., p. 127; Ichiro Ohinata, *Kishi seiken: sen-nihyaku-yonju-ichi-nichi* [The Kishi government: 1241 days] (Tokyo: Gyosei mondai kenkyu sho, 1985), p. 9.

9. Tajiri, pp. 138, 143.

10. Uhei Arimura, "Kempo kaisei makari toru" [Constitutional revision on the march], *Chuo Koron* (May 1956), p. 57. It must be noted, however, that Yoshida told Kishi on this occasion that he did not object to constitutional revision as such.

11. Chiyoda-roshi, "Dara dara seiken no yume" [The dream of the lackadaisical government], *Chuo Koron* (October 1959), p. 127.

12. Tadao Okada, *Seiji no uchimaku* [Inside story of politics] (Tokyo: Yuki Shobo, 1959), pp. 191–92. See Kono's angry reaction to Yoshida's bad-mouthing, in *Imadakara hanaso* [Now I can talk] (Tokyo: Shunyodo, 1958), pp. 48–51.

13. See the orthodox treatment of Kishi by a student of Yoshida, in Masataka

Kosaka, *Saiso Yoshida Shigeru,* [Prime Minister Yoshida Shigeru] (Tokyo: Chuo Koron-sha, 1968), pp. 108–28.

14. Quoted in Hara, p. 35.

15. Uhei Arimura, "Kishi bumu wa naze okoranaika" [Why there is no Kishi boom], *Chuo Koron,* (December 1959), pp. 66–76.

16. Tsuneo Watanabe, *Habatsu* [Factions] (Tokyo: Kobundo, 1964), pp. 47, 88.

17. Takamitsu Sawa, *Kodo seicho: ri'nen to seisaku no do-jidai-shi* [High-speed growth: a contemporary history of theory and practice] (Tokyo: NHK, 1984), pp. 23–31.

18. See Kosaka, *Saiso Yoshida Shigeru,* p. 136, where he takes issue with Kishi.

19. Nihon heiwa iinkai, *Heiwa undo niju–nen undo–shi* [Twenty–year history of the peace movement] (Tokyo: Otsuki Shoten, 1969), p. 104.

20. Hitoshi Ashida, *Ashida Hitoshi nikki* [The Ashida Hitoshi diary] (Tokyo: Iwanami Shoten, 1986), V, 183, for confirmation of communist funding.

21. David Apter traces the origin of the Narita agitation to the tradition of peasant revolt, on the one hand, and to the structural strains of high-speed growth, such as pollution, on the other. But this sounds too much like the rhetoric of radical Zengakuren students at war with Japanese society. Apter should have looked closer to home—to base struggles against the U.S. military presence. David Apter and Nagayo Sawa, *Against the State: Political and Social Protest in Japan* (Cambridge: Harvard Univ. Press, 1984).

22. See an account by a defense counsel, Itsuro Hayashi, "Jiraado saiban no oshieru mono" [The lesson of the Girard trial], *Bungei Shunju* (January 1958), pp. 164–174.

23. *Nihon naikaku shiroku,* V, 372. It seemed that the Pentagon was testing the nuclear allergy in Japan. See Martin E. Weinstein, *Japan's Postwar Defense Policy, 1947–1968* [New York: Columbia Univ. Press, 1971), pp, 80–83.

24. See Tajiri, pp. 174–75, for Suzuki's interpellation on February 4 on the lower house floor against Kishi's "state of the union" address. On February 8, Hiroo Wada of the JSP made an identical demand in the Budget Committee of the upper house. According to Sakurauchi Yoshio, the JSP was agreeable to an improvement, rather than to abolition. See Hajime Terazawa, "Jiyuminshuto no gaiko kankaku" [The LDP's diplomatic sense], *Chuo Koron* (August 1959), p. 165.

25. *Asahi Shimbun,* March 1, 1957, p. 1.

26. "Anpo senso no 'fukona shuyaku' " [The anpo war's 'sad protagonist'], *Chuo Koron* (September 1960), p. 180. He even issued a qualifying statement on April 28 that a "review" of the treaty was to be based on the existing constitution. *Ibid.*

27. *Nihon Shakaito no sanjunen,* II, 148–52. Hitoshi Yamakawa, a firebrand of the JSP left, noted in an article most revealing of Japanese thinking at this time that Kishi's self-appointed task was "hopelessly difficult." See "San Furanshisuko taisei karano kaiho" [Liberation from the San Francisco system], *Chuo Koron* (May 1957), pp. 144–56.

28. Kosaka, *Saiso Yoshida Shigeru,* p. 121.

29. Yoshikazu Sakamoto, "Kakushin nashonarizumu shiron" [A trial thesis on radical-liberal nationalism], *Chuo Koron* (October 1960), p. 49. The *makikomareru* (getting involved) thesis existed from the beginning but the slogan had not yet been coined.

30. Professor Packard, who has written an outstanding account of the treaty revision on which this book has drawn for many insights, argues that there was no mandate for

treaty revision, and that Kishi imprudently tied his fortune to it. George R. Packard III, *Protest in Tokyo: The Security Treaty Crisis of 1960* (Princeton, NJ: Princeton Univ. Press, 1966), p. 152. He implies that Japan should have lived with the original treaty, but he also agrees with Christian Herter that it was very unequal. Packard reflects the view of Yoshida, who defended the treaty and postoccupation tutelage. He ignores the role played by Dulles in stimulating and mobilizing the coalition of the revisionists and Socialists.

31. Kishi in an interview, *Chuo Koron* (March 1980), pp. 294–95.

32. In May 1957 he said at a meeting of the Cabinet Committee of the upper house, "The Constitution does not ban nuclear weapons for self-defense." The JSP moved for a vote of noconfidence against Kishi, but was rejected. *Nihon naikaku shiroku*, V, 338. See also Ohinata, pp. 150–51. But then some of Yoshida's disciples were no different from Kishi in this respect. Ikeda wanted nuclear weapons some day. Kosaka, *Saiso Yoshida Shigeru*, p. 142.

33. Hara, pp. 85–88.

34. Douglas MacArthur II and Yoshihisa Komori, "Rokuju-nen anpo jyoyaku kaitei no shinso" [The truth behind the 1960 security treaty revision], *Chuo Koran* (November 1981), pp. 184–85.

35. Cited in Uhei Arimura, "Kishi to-Bei: sono go ni kurumono" [Kishi's U.S. visit: what lies ahead], *Chuo Koron* (August 1957), pp. 71–79.

36. *Asahi Shimbun*, July 27, 1957, p. 1. The JSP delegation visited Peking in April to pave the way. *Nihon Shakaito no sanjunen*, II, 180–83.

37. The Ground SDF was to be expanded to the authorized level of 180,000 men; the Maritime SDF was to increase its tonnage to 124,000; and the Air SDF was to expand to 1,300 aircraft. *Nihon naikaku shiroku, V. 391*.

38. Tajiri, p. 177.

39. Ibid., pp. 392–93.

40. It is said that Kishi agreed to the freeze on Okinawa in exchange for the U.S. concession on the treaty review committee. See Uhei Arimura, "Kishi to-Bei: sono go ni kurumono" [Kishi's U.S. visit: what lies next], *Chuo Koron* (August 1957), pp. 71–79.

41. *Nihon naikaku shiroku*, V, 405–6.

42. Kishi was aided by Keidanren. The business community, it may be recalled, intervened publicly against Yoshida to foster conservative unity in the face of the Socialist challenge. Within a year of the LDP's birth, however, it split into factions, and each and every faction began soliciting funds from business. Separate fundraising would solidify factions. In January 1955 Uemura Kogoro of Keidanren began to streamline and consolidate all political contributions. In 1959 a unified organization devoted to raising and distributing funds was created, though it has had no visible impact on factionalism. *Nihon naikaku shiroku, V. 405–6*.

43. See what looks like the precursor of the "makikomareru" (getting involved) thesis in the Socialist Dietman Okada Soji's speech on the occasion of Sputnik launch, in Ichiro Ohinata, *Kishi seiken: 1241 nichi* [The Kishi government: the 1241 days] (Tokyo: Gyosei Mondai Kenkyujo, 1985), pp. 123–24.

44. *Kishi Nobusuke no kaiso*, p. 195.

45. *Nihon Shakaito no sanjunen*, II, 208–9.

46. *Kishi Nobusuke no kaiso*, p. 235.

47. See Soichi Oya, a well-known writer and critic, in "Daigaku no nyu koroniarisumu" [New colonialism in universities], *Chuo Koron,* (August 1960), pp. 180–87.

48. Fukuji Taguchi, "Seiji jokyo no henka to Nihon Shakaito" [The change in the political situation and the JSP], *Chuo Koron,* (September 1959), p. 85.

49. Yu Ishida, " 'Sengo wa owatta' to iu koto no imi" [What 'the end of postwar' means], *Chuo Koron,* (September 1957), pp. 164–79.

50. Kotatsu Fujiwara, "Tenka taihei ron" [The world at peace], *Chuo Koron* (January 1958), pp. 54–66.

51. Fukuji Taguchi, *Chuo Koron,* (August 1959), p. 80. Numerous analyses were written by independent but sympathetic writers on the JSP predicament. See Fukuji Taguchi, "Nihon Shakaito ron" [On the JSP], *Chuo Koron,* (September 1958), pp. 124–43; Masaaki Takane, "Heiwa undo no kabe" [The barrier against the peace movement], ibid., pp. 154–61; Jiro Kamishima, "Seiji teki jiba no henka ni tsuite" [On the shift in the political magnetic field], ibid., (January 1959), pp. 56–64; Yasumasa Oshima, "Chukan teki kaigi chitai no rinri" [On the morality of the centrist-skeptic zone], ibid., pp. 142–52; Seihachiro Shimizu, "Genko senkyo seido no mujun o tsuku" [Criticizing the contradictions in the current electoral system], ibid., (March 1959), pp. 158–70; Seihachiro Shimizu, "San-in senkyo no kekka o bunseki suru" [An analysis of the result of the upper-house election], ibid., 60–77; Fukuji Taguchi, "Seiji jokyo no henka to Nihon Shakaito" [The change in political situation and the JSP], ibid. (August 1959), pp. 80–91; Keiichi Matsushita, "Shakai shugi no futatsu no tamashii" [The two souls of socialism], ibid., (December 1959), pp. 73–83.

52. *Nihon Shakaito no sanjunen,* II. 226.

53. Koken Koyama, *Nihon Shakaito shi* [History of the JSP] (Tokyo: Rodo Daigaku, 1973), pp. 147–82; *Nihon Shakai-to no sanjunen,* II, 204–12; Koken Koyama, *Nihon no hi-kyosan-shugi Marukusu shugi-sha* [Japan's non-communist Marxists] (Tokyo: San-ichi Shobo, 1962), pp. 221–25.

54. *Nihon Shakaito no sanjunen,* II. 210.

55. Mochizuki's dissertation gives the full details.

56. For the best account of Diet maneuvers between the LDP and the JSP at this time, see Tadao Okada, *Seiji no uchimaku* [Inside story of politics] (Tokyo: Yukishobo, 1959).

57. Kenzo Uchida, *Sengo Nihon no hoshu seiji* [Postwar Japan's conservative politics] (Tokyo: Iwanami Shoten, 1969), p. 10. The textbook controversy of 1982 reenacted this basic mechanism. Note that Miyazawa was the cabinet secretary of the Suzuki government in 1982.

58. *Nihon naikaku shiroku,* V, 421–2.

59. Unfortunately Hara's book, too, basically adheres to the orthodox interpretation.

60. Okada states that the idea originated with the chairman of the National Public Security Commission, the agency charged with domestic security. Okada p. 14. But I suspect it was Kishi's own.

61. Ibid.

62. *Nihon Shakaito no sanjunen,* II. 238.

63. *Nihon Shakaito no sanjunen,* II. 217. However, the chairman of Domei supported Kishi. See Koko Shinofuji et al., eds., *Nihon Shakaito* [The JSP] (Tokyo; Rodo Daigaku, 1973), p. 107.

64. "Nigatsu kakumei setsu to nana-jikan senryo setsu no shussho" [The origin of the February revolution rumor and the seven-hour-occupation rumor], *Chuo Koron* (January 1959), pp. 220–22.

65. Ibid. The rumor about the speaker's will is also reported in Chiyoda-roshi, "Keishoku-ho sodo: sono go ni kuru mono" [The police duties law incident: what comes next], *Bungei Shunju,* (January 1959), pp. 114–23.

66. Okada, p. 13.

67. *Nihon Shakaito no sanjunen,* II. 215.

68. Ohinata, p. 169.

69. *Asahi Shimbun,* November 8, 1958, p. 1; *ibid.,* November 9, p. 1.

70. Ibid., November 10, 1958, p. 1.

# Chapter 8

# To the Brink of Quemoy and the Disaster

In the summer of 1958, the configuration of forces surrounding Japan shifted rapidly toward confrontation. Correspondingly, the domestic alignment of forces surrounding Kishi, as he headed for treaty revision, went through a startling change. Kishi certainly knew this fact. His introduction of the police bill in October had something to do with it. So did Yoshida's sudden reversal of his role.

The thaw in East-West relations had been proceeding in zigzags. Khrushchev's secret speech denouncing Stalin at the 20th congress of the Soviet Communist party (February 1956) was followed by the revolts in Hungary and Poland and Soviet suppression. That was a setback both for him and for the thaw. But Khrushchev soon rebounded and added enormously to his confidence and prestige with the successful launching of an ICBM and *Sputnik* in 1957. In March 1958 he displaced Bulganin as premier. As the "missile gap" debate was rattling Washington, Khrushchev resumed the peace offensive with a foray into the Middle East. The combination of arms buildup and diplomatic pressure would lead to summits with Eisenhower and Kennedy on the one hand, and the Cuban missile crisis on the other.

Following Hatoyama's visit to Moscow, the Soviet Union was cordial and proper toward Japan. China was on a parallel track, seeking rapprochement with Ishibashi's Japan. Just as the Soviets used the fishing in the northern Pacific waters as a bait, the People's Republic expanded private trade with friendly Japanese firms, enticing Japan to move by stages toward recognizing the "one China." In the spring of 1957, however, a large-scale purge of the Chinese Communist party began, as China's foreign policy began to veer away from the "spirit of Bandung" toward an ideological hard line. It was learned later that when Mao intervened in the Eastern European crisis in the name of bloc unity, in 1956, he began to have doubts over Khrushchev's competence. Peking greeted Kishi's visit with Chiang Kai-shek in May of 1957 with diatribe. *Sputnik*'s launch in October seemed to confirm Mao's confidence in the superiority of socialism, and he sounded off with the slogans, "The East wind prevails over the West wind" and "American imperialism is a paper tiger."

In February 1958, Peking demanded U.S. withdrawal from Korea; in March and April, Peking denounced Washington over Vietnam and SEATO. In March the fourth Japan-China Private Trade Agreement, an annual occurrence, was signed, with a silent nod from Kishi and in spite of an angry protest from the Chinese Nationalist government. In April China demanded that its trade mission in Japan be given semidiplomatic privileges, but Kishi refused. Shortly thereafter China made an issue of a small incident—in which a Japanese youth hauled down the Chinese flag at a trade mission in Nagasaki—and revoked the trade agreement.[1] In May the CCP held the second plenum of the eighth central committee and decided to launch a nationwide movement called the Great Leap Forward to build the people's communes; Mao decided to leapfrog the Soviets in the race toward the final stage of communism. In August, Peking sided with the Arab League to oppose the dispatch of U.S. marines to Lebanon. Mao's headlong rush culminated in a military confrontation: It started with air and naval engagement in the Formosa (Taiwan) Strait in early August and reached crisis proportions with the artillery bombardment and blockade of the islands of Quemoy and Matsu that commenced on August 23. On the following day, the U.S. Seventh Fleet went on war-footing in the Strait.

Meanwhile, having politely shelved the treaty revision issue on the occasion of Kishi's visit to Washington in 1957, Secretary Dulles kept a close watch on Kishi. A revised treaty upgrading Japan was a big prize, and he had no reason to give it away to an unfriendly or unstable government in Tokyo. For one thing, Dulles would have to overcome the enormous objections of the Pentagon bureaucracy to abandoning the vested interests: the freedom to move troops and nuclear weapons in and out of Japan; the freedom to wage war against the Soviet Union or China from the Japanese soil without a "prior consultation"; and the privileges codified in the Administrative Agreement, modeled after the Philippine treaty rather than the NATO treaty.[2]

But on his visit to Washington in late 1957, Ambassador MacArthur had secured Eisenhower's consent to revision in principle. The president then told him to sound out the Senate to see if its leaders were agreeable to a treaty revision that honored the constitutional status quo, and that consent, too, was forthcoming.[3] Having sized up Kishi through his Southeast Asian trips and the May election, Eisenhower and Dulles were favorably impressed. For the first time, America had an ally who was neither a Yoshida nor a Hatoyama and who seriously contemplated a constitutional revision at some future date. Though Kishi could not commit himself to regional security for the present, he might make something of Japan given a chance and support.

Accordingly, at a meeting on July 18, some two months after Kishi's electoral victory, Douglas MacArthur told Foreign Minister Fujiyama (who had just been elected to the Diet) for the first time that his government was ready to negotiate a "mutual security treaty." On August 25, two days after the bombardment began, MacArthur visited Kishi and Fujiyama. The ambassador brought an inquiry from Secretary Dulles, asking whether Japan desired (1) a new treaty of "mutual security" that did not call for a constitutional revision, (2) a revision of the existing treaty, or (3) an addendum to the existing treaty. Kishi insisted on the first option. Gaimusho, which had been thinking in terms of a minimalist approach, was surprised by both MacArthur's offer and Kishi's reply.[4] In a joint communique of September 11, the governments of Japan and the United States agreed to treaty revision. With blessings from an *Asahi* editorial, the negotiations began on two tracks in Tokyo.[5]

Mao and Khrushchev were having serious disputes at the time over a wide range of issues, some ideological and others practical. The bombardment of the offshore islands was Mao's attempt to involve the Soviets in a confrontation with the United States. If Khrushchev came to China's defense, well and good; China would keep the initiative. If he refused, he could be shown to be a revisionist. Chiang Kai-shek was playing a similar game on his side by staking his political life on the defense of the exposed garrisons. Without resupply, Quemoy and Matsu could not be held. Chiang Kai-shek's plea for help was met by the dispatch of the carrier *Essex* from the Middle East. On August 31 Moscow entered the fray with a statement in *Pravda* that he who threatens the People's Republic of China "threatens the Soviet Union as well."[6] In August, Moscow and Peking began lumping Eisenhower and Kishi together for denunciation.

On September 4 a "high official," soon identified as Dulles, declared that American determination to defend the islands was "categorical." Internally, he was advising President Eisenhower to use tactical nuclear weapons for the purpose.[7] For Dulles Quemoy and Matsu were the test case of Eisenhower's "domino theory" as well as his own thesis of asymmetrical response to aggressions, i.e., retaliating with a means of America's own choosing. He was gambling that a U.S. hardline would split the Moscow-Peking axis.[8] The gamble would pay off.

It was in the context of his "brinkmanship" policy that Dulles decided to push treaty revision with Japan. It was a link in the multilateral American efforts to shore up the West's defenses against the Soviet-Chinese challenge.[9] He appeared to be angling for the possibility that an international crisis would be a crucible in which to recast and stiffen the Japanese ally. This was vintage Dulles and a replay of what he had tried to do unsuccessfully with Yoshida at the height of the Korean War.[10] In view of the postwar political tradition (the 1955 system) that was already entrenched—thanks in equal part to Yoshida, the JCS, and Dulles—revising the treaty would have been difficult enough. It would be even more so in the context of an international crisis. A crisis may uplift the Japanese, as Dulles implied, but it can easily do the opposite. In any case, the decision to go ahead amounted to a decision to sink or swim together. The responsibility for it must be shared between Dulles and Kishi, rather than being placed solely on Kishi.[11]

Kishi must have known that he was in an entirely new game by late August, with immensely greater risks for himself. For the Japanese, both Right and Left, treaty revision had been primarily a bilateral question having to do with Japan's "occupied" status. Now an honest-to-goodness security issue with multilateral implications was injected. To be America's partner, Japan would have to stand forward of it, facing China and the Soviet Union across the Formosa Strait.[12]

The Japanese Socialists, too, had been acting rather more than merely reacting to the international developments described above. They, too, were impressed by *Sputnik* and began to have second thoughts about Kishi. By the time the postmortem of the May 1958 election defeat was underway, the JSP's internal situation was quite fluid. It is virtually certain that it abandoned the entente with Kishi and decided to oppose the treaty revision during the Quemoy crisis of August, although the facts surrounding this turnaround—particularly the JSP's coordination with Moscow and Peking—have been concealed. The justification for opposing the revision, revealed shortly thereafter, was that it would result in a tighter military integration of Japan into the American alliance and Japan's involvement (*makikomareru*) in an American war.[13] Thus the JSP would have opposed Kishi's police bill of October under any circumstances. More to the point, Kishi proposed the police bill precisely because the JSP—now deserting Kishi and aligning itself with Moscow and Peking—posed a threat to the treaty revision. In reality the JSP understood the point.[14] Instead, the JSP's propaganda asserted that Kishi, the "reactionary," jumped the gun on the police bill and alienated the otherwise friendly Socialists, that is, without cause. This is the prevailing interpretation in standard history, introduced in the previous chapter.[15]

To return to the theme of the JSP's reorientation, it began with the Peking visit of a Socialist leader (Sado Tadataka) in July and August, two months after Kishi's wrangle with Peking over the flag-snatching incident in Nagasaki (May). The visit was arranged by Secretary General Asanuma of the rightwing who was cultivating a new constituency among the leftwing. The prime minister's office and the U.S. Embassy would have been remiss if they were not aware of these moves. But as late as early September, prior to Foreign Minister Fujiyama's departure for Washington to discuss treaty revision, the JSP Dietmen on the Foreign Relations Committee bade him godspeed. By the time another Socialist leader (Kazami Akira) issued a joint communique in Peking, in October, the JSP was calling for "abolition of the Japan-U.S. security treaty" and vowing, "American imperialism is the common enemy of the peoples of Japan and China." The Quemoy incident expedited a major reorientation of the JSP, and gave it for the first time an international ally, putting it in the company of the LDP and the JCP, with their respective allies.[16]

What sort of voting support did Kishi anticipate for the revision through the sea change in circumstances? After the May 1958 election, he had the four mainstream factions (Kishi, Sato, Kono, Ohno) in his pocket. That came to a little under 200 votes, short of a majority. His understanding with Eisenhower—not to touch the constitution—was designed to bring Yoshida and the JSP along. But the Socialist support grew uncertain after *Sputnik* and especially after the May election. As soon as he had returned from the Washington visit of late 1957, MacArthur was asked by Kishi to persuade Yoshida to change his mind.[17] Yoshida knew full well by the time of the Quemoy crisis that Kishi's treaty revision did not exceed the "equality" he himself had sought in vain and, moreover, that the name of the game had changed in Washington. With the Socialists and Communists bending in the "East wind" in the midst of treaty revision, the treaty itself—not merely its revision—was endangered. Yoshida even appeared to have had second thoughts about his past collusion with the radicals.[18] Hence, he went to Kishi's rescue over the police bill. At this point he began a hasty effort to talk his followers into supporting Kishi. But he could not carry them—they were envenomed in partisanship. It appeared that the LDP rebels in the Diet numbered in the 90s, and they cheered Ikeda on as he walked out on Kishi over the police bill.[19]

On November 13, 1958, following the setback over the police bill, Foreign Minister Fujiyama announced that the treaty negotiations were to be recessed pending Diet normalization. On November 19 Foreign Minister Ch'en Yi of China issued a statement calling on Japan to adhere to neutrality in the treaty revision.[20] On November 22, Kishi and JSP Chairman Suzuki agreed to shelve the police bill. On December 3, the Soviet government issued a statement identical to that of the Chinese.[21] In this blackmail against Kishi and a pat on the shoulder for the Socialists, the Sino-Soviet powers asserted that the proposed revision was at Japan's request, for which it must bear the full consequences. Last but not least, the JCP announced on December 11 that it was now switching to the support of neutralism for Japan, a switch that brought it abreast of the Socialists. This removed the obstacle to a united front of the two parties.

As the Socialists broke with Kishi and Yoshida moved over to him, Kishi's erstwhile friends were shifting uncomfortably also. Kishi's defeat over the police bill cast a pall over them, but their problem appeared to be elsewhere. The revisionists had been moved primarily by their concern for Japan's equality and autonomy, that is, status. Constitutional revision was a status issue. So was regional collective security. It had been an abstract issue until now. But the Quemoy war, waged by the imprudent ally on behalf of a tinhorn dictator, seemed so unnecessary and absurd in itself and more so for Japan. To participate in such a conflict might actually harm its status and interests. Japan still owed itself honest defense efforts, but, given its inferior position, it would not have an equal say in managing a collective security arrangement. Yoshida was right to be selfish about overseas entanglements. In fact, it was not implausible to say that autonomy was on Yoshida's side, autonomy of sorts.

Utsunomiya Tokuma, a member of the Ishibashi faction and a maverick on the leftwing of the LDP, wrote an essay that illustrated what was on the minds of the revisionists. He felt that the U.S.-Japanese relationship was a "protectorate arrangement" whereby Japan surrendered diplomatic autonomy. He felt the treaty had to be revised, but he did not think inequality could be eradicated. Stipulating a U.S. obligation to defend Japan in the new treaty would change nothing. So he counseled going slow.[22] As Utsunomiya saw it, the only justification for going through with treaty revision had to do with "international confidence in Japan," that is, saving Kishi's face.[23]

Dulles's unfortunate choice of Quemoy as a touchstone of Japan's loyalty had inadvertently produced a foreign policy consensus across the entire political spectrum by early 1959. Forced by political necessity, Kishi first took aim at Yoshida's equality as an interim goal, without forsaking Dulles's equality or constitutional revision. But the Quemoy imbroglio demonstrated the futility of seeking Dulles's equality altogether. In a manner of speaking, the Socialists had also de facto endorsed the existing treaty when they decided to oppose its revision. This was a decision of major importance, but its implications escaped public notice for some time because the Socialists remained adamantly opposed to the security treaty *in rhetoric.*[24]

As Japan lowered its sight from mutuality, genuine equality, allied interests, and national defense to self-interest (noninvolvement), the glue that held the revisionists together came unstuck. There were troubles ahead, troubles that were common to all military dependencies. Military protection dulls the perception of external threat; the lack of autonomy inhibits a dependency from taking military initiatives or responsibilities against any but the most direct threat to its home land; if such responsibilities are imposed on by the protector, their discharge then becomes a favor; for which a payoff should be expected.

From here on, whoever pushed the revision had to pay in the coin that satisfied mundane domestic interest. First and foremost was the United States, which had just staked its prestige on the revision in the face of Sino-Soviet challenge. Washington had abandoned mutulity for itself by accepting the constitutional status quo and by offering "mutuality" to Japan. Now Kishi's foes would cannibalize the American interest, as Ambassador MacArthur stood by helplessly. The other prime mover was Kishi, whose face was involved in the revision. Yoshida with his "I told you so" stood a step removed from Kishi. His value to Kishi and Washington would be enhanced as the Socialists, Peking, and Moscow assailed the revision. Incredibly, everyone—Kishi, Dulles, Khrushchev, and Chuo En-lai—was playing into his hands, and he waited for the opportune moment to name the price for his assistance.

The sudden cooling of LDP leaders toward revision was painfully evident during the government-LDP liaison conference in early December, scarcely a fortnight after the truce with the JSP in the Diet. The item on the agenda was what kind of revision to aim for. The JSP had discovered that by virtue of America's defense pacts with Taiwan, South Korea, and the Philippines, Okinawa and the Bonins were also involved in the defense of these countries. For Japan to share the defense obligation of Okinawa and the Bonins would create the Northeast Asia Treaty Organization, a collective defense treaty. As the Socialists raised this charge, Miki Takeo, Matsumura, and Ishibishi, all on the leftwing of the LDP, chimed in.[25] Foreign Minister Fujiyama—nicknamed "Silk Handkerchief" because of his fabulous personal wealth—felt Kishi no longer had the power to stick to an ambitious revision and began to distance himself from Kishi. Kono, in contrast, demanded not only the inclusion of Okinawa and the Bonins but, shortly thereafter, a revision of the Administrative Agreement as well. His intent apparently was to embarrass Fujiyama's ministry. Ohno, with his domestic orientation, was now almost neutral toward revision. Ikeda was pointedly vague on Okinawa. Kishi had to drop Okinawa and the Bonins from the treaty coverage. With Kishi not taking any initiative, the meeting adjourned without a further decision.[26] From this point on, until Kishi's fortunes improved in the June 1959 upper house election, Kishi drifted, spending a better part of his time plugging holes in the dike. He let the foreign minister and his bureaucracy carry the ball, a technique a prime minister uses when he wants to distance himself from an issue.

Perhaps most ominous for the prospects of treaty revision was the attitude of Kono, Kishi's righthand man. In an interview conducted in early 1959, he said of the government, "There's no vision of how *anpo* [the security treaty] should be, nothing." "Constitutional revision is the ideal but impossible," he said, "There'll be no wars, so we'll slough off."[27] A superb politician, he understood better than anybody the change in stake after Quemoy. Nationalism was no longer needed, yet his politician's instinct demanded a satisfaction. So Kono was beginning to talk like Yoshida. He had come a long way from being a sworn comrade of Kishi to a purely partisan renegade.

What helped Kishi pull through the crisis was the announcement from the imperial household in late November 1958 that the crown prince was engaged to wed Shoda Michiko, a commoner. The news of the Cinderella story swept the nation off its feet, and the festive mood lasted well past the following April, when the wedding took place.

Kono still stood by Kishi, wavering between "Both Shores." Kono might have lost interest in treaty revision, but with enough enemies in the party, he could not win the prime ministership without Kishi's support. He had to go all the way with Kishi, and he knew it. He gave Kishi hard-nosed advice to hang tough. On Kono's suggestion, Kishi decided to move up to January 1959 the LDP presidential election scheduled for March. This would reaffirm the party's support for Kishi. But Ikeda, Miki, and the antimainstreamers objected to the idea and demanded instead bloodletting in the LDP leadership to pay for the police bill fiasco. They wanted Kono's ouster as executive committee chairman.

Kishi was caught between Ikeda and Kono, who were as incompatible with each other as water is to oil, as the Japanese saying goes. The bedrock of Kishi's support was in the four-faction alliance of Kishi, Sato (his brother), Kono, and Ohno. But now that the Socialists were deserting Kishi, he needed the support of Ikeda, the linchpin of the antimainstreamers in the LDP.

But Ikeda held fast to his stand, and in December 1958 he, Miki, and Nadao (the education minister) resigned their cabinet posts. Kishi was forced to replace the LDP secretary general (Kawashima with Fukuda Takeo) and executive committee chairman (Kono). Kishi was in a dire strait. In order to soothe Kono's ruffled feelings and to revamp his four-faction alliance, Kishi, Sato, Kono, and Ohno entered into a secret agreement in early January 1959; Kishi would first relinquish power to Ohno and then help Kono succeed Ohno. The point was to make Kono Kishi's successor, but a direct transition to another hawk, it was feared, would be a bit too unsettling.[28] But Kishi and Kono, it turned out, were drifting apart, and the secret agreement would become a dead letter. The LDP presidential election was held in January, and Kishi was reaffirmed, 320 to 166, over Matsumura. Yoshida and Ikeda voted against Kishi.

As Kishi regrouped the cabinet and the LDP in early 1959, he announced the resumption of the treaty work, hoping to have a draft approved by the Diet by March or April. He disclosed that the U.S. side was agreeable to keeping the constitutional framework intact.[29] The point was to assuage the LDP, which became cool toward the treaty revision, that Kishi would steer clear of collective security. In order to elicit intra-LDP consensus, Foreign Minister Fujiyama presented what purported to be his "private outline" of a draft revision in February. But he failed to muster unanimous support. Two issues divided the LDP. One was whether the new treaty should extend its coverage to Okinawa and the Bonins. Kono, Ikeda, and Sato insisted on it, but the LDP had to exclude Okinawa and the Bonins. The other issue, raised by Kono and seconded by Ikeda, was whether to amend the Administrative Agreement simultaneously. This was the Pentagon's big plum, and its objections to amendments had to be overcome. Kono and Ikeda hoped to delay the signing of the treaty and to embarrass Kishi.

At the end of March, the Tokyo district court ruled affirmatively on the suit brought before it by the town of Sunakawa, charging that U.S. military bases were unconstitutional. And that, too, provided ammunition to the dissenters. On April 11, the LDP's executive committee adopted the "Outline of Treaty Revision" and the "Outline of an Administrative Agreement," with difficulty.[30] The latter simply agreed to a revision without specifying the content. This was all the LDP could do before the resumption of the Fujiyama-MacArthur talks two days later.[31] Six months had gone by at this point since the start of formal negotiations, and the LDP was still vacillating in full view of the opposition. It was necessary to establish the Subcommittee for Adjusting Party Views on the Administrative Agreement, chaired by Funada Naka, chairman of the executive committee, on April 11. Kono, Ikeda, Miki, and Matsumura reserved their attitude. The official LDP position was finally announced on May 25, 1959, and it was close to the original Fujiyama draft. But the extent of amendment to the Administrative Agreement was yet to be resolved. So Fujiyama negotiated simultaneously with MacArthur and the LDP. But at last the government and the LDP were close to unity in time for the upper house election.

In the meantime, the leftward drift of the JSP—feeding on its victory over the police bill—was continuing. In March 1959 Asanuma Inejiro, secretary general of the JSP, led a Socialist delegation to Peking to confer with Foreign Minister Ch'en Yi. In a speech that startled the Japanese, Asanuma—who hailed from the rightwing of the party—repeated for public consumption what had been an obscure party stance: that "American imperialism is the common enemy of the peoples of Japan and China." This was the signal that commenced the reorganization of the antipolice bill movement for antitreaty purposes.

With Sohyo's backing, the leftwing Socialists insisted on including the JCP as an "observer" in the united front, in open break with existing policy.[32] This was a declaration of war against the rightwing of the JSP. Zenro and Shinsanbetsu, both moderate labor federations, objected to further cooperation with the JCP and left. The radicals, including the Communists, wanted the title of the united front to be the National Congress for the Overthrow of the Security-Treaty System. The JSP-Sohyo leadership conceded it was indeed their goal to abolish the treaty, along with the military clause in the Sino-Soviet treaty directed at Japan. This was the first step, it was maintained, toward the conclusion of a four-power guarantee of Japan's neutrality. But for the current tactical purpose of the united front, JSP-Sohyo wanted to concentrate on opposition to treaty revision and on rapprochement with China.[33] Even so, the departure of Zenro meant that it was only a matter of time before the rightwing Socialists who were affiliated with it would find it difficult to remain in the JSP.

To complete the picture on the radical-liberal side, we must deal with the JCP, whose power had reached the all-time high in the election of 1949 (35 seats in the lower house), but lost everything in the election of 1952, following the JCP's turn to armed insurgency. At the 6th congress, in July 1955, the JCP carried our self-criticism of its past failures, and in July 1956, five months after the 20th congress of the CPSU, at which Khrushchev had criticized Stalin, the Japanese party fell in line by acknowledging that transition to socialism could take place by peaceful means.[34] Forging a united front with the JSP began at the local level in 1956. In December 1958 the JCP aligned itself with the JSP on neutralism. In March 1959, Sohyo nudged the JSP into sitting jointly with the JCP in the National Congress for Opposition to Security Treaty Revision, a move that openly endorsed a limited united front. During the ensuing months of joint struggle, the JCP was openly anti-American and chose to demonstrate against the U.S. embassy, whereas the JSP was more anti-Kishi and preferred to encircle the Diet.[35]

The National Congress was an umbrella organization that presided over 13 leftwing groups, including the JSP, the JCP, Sohyo, the Neutral Labor Federation, the National Federation for Constitutional Defense, Zengakuren, the National Federation for the Base Struggle, Gensuikyo (against nuclear weapons), the National Congress for Sino-Japanese Rapprochement, and the Japan-China Friendship Society. Sohyo acted as the bridge between the Socialists and the Communists, and vigorously expanded the local branches of the National Congress across the land from a mere 97 in June 1959 to 1,633 in March 1960.[36] The Communists were no mere "observers" but active participants—70 out of 300 delegates to the Congress were JCP members.[37] All the tributaries and side currents in postwar Japan's pacifist-neutralist movement were coming together for a showdown. April 15, 1959, was designated as the first National Unified Action Day, to be held monthly thereafter.

With such a massive number being assembled against treaty revision, one might be misled into believing that the government was totally isolated. Actually, the international tension of late 1958 had given way to the national euphoria created by the forthcoming imperial wedding. The Left was in the doldrums because a large majority in the public were hardly affected by the Quemoy crisis and content with what they had: they were neither for nor against China, neither for nor against the security treaty.[38] In local elections held in April 1959, the LDP scored major victories in gubernatorial, mayoral, and local assembly races.

Then the upper house election of June 1959 turned into a sort of referendum on the treaty revision. The LDP expanded by 10 seats, to 132. The JSP won five more seats, to reach 85. The Green Breeze Society shrank from 31 to 11; Soka Gakkai gained nine seats. The parliamentary balance of power was not affected, but the JSP's party vote fell from 38 percent to 34 percent.[39] For the second time in 13 months, the "one-third barrier" thwarted the JSP. The defeat reopened the old internal wound.

There was a small episode during the election campaign that went unnoticed at this time. Earlier in 1959, a newspaper column by an economist named Nakayama Ichiro advocating the idea of doubling or even tripling Japanese wages struck Ikeda Hayato's fancy. He met with Nakayama and developed the idea into a speech that he used on the stump. Kishi noted Ikeda's speeches, and felt the idea was compatible with his own plank of purging the "three evils," one of which was poverty. When Kishi decided to recruit Ikeda as MITI minister shortly thereafter, he sweetened the offer with a promise to accept "income doubling" as cabinet policy.[40] Although no one had thought about it until then, doubling average income over a 10-year period was based on a simple projection of the current rate of growth of the gross national product, which had exceeded 10 percent annually since Hatoyama's time. Within a year, Ikeda turned the idea into an all-consuming national goal that would sweep everything else before it, transforming Japan into something that had been only a pipe dream in his mentor's mind in 1949.

The LDP "victory" in the upper house election, fought on the treaty issue, ended Kishi's vacillation. He carried out a major cabinet reshuffle. Kono insisted on the LDP secretary generalship. By far the most important function of a secretary general is to be the chief strategist, tactician, and manager of an election campaign, an experience through which an incumbent is said to come into full control of the party, thereby paving the way toward his prime ministership. But once again Kishi had to accommodate both Kono and Ikeda on the team, and for reasons that remain obscure to this day Kono was miffed and walked out, in spite of Kishi's entreaties. Ikeda, who had walked out on Kishi just six months before, came on as MITI minister. Ohno left. Miki and Matsumura were on the outs with Kishi. Kishi was now dependent on Sato and Ikeda, both of the Yoshida school. Kishi recalled later, "Yoshida was behind the move and told Ikeda of the importance of the American connection."[41] It was later speculated that at this point Kishi had reached an understanding with Yoshida to appoint Ikeda as successor.[42]

Miyazawa, Ikeda's former secretary, who had just been re-elected to the upper house, where he had been the lone opponent of treaty revision, also reversed himself at this time. In a highly revealing postelection interview, he said that he did not feel the security treaty was "honorable"; that "we've come too far to turn back" on the revision; that he anticipated "trouble" in the revision; that "you can never revise the constitution" and that if someone tried, "I'll see that he is stopped"; and that he understood well the decision-making process in the United States.[43] Now that Kishi was dependent on Yoshida and Ikeda, Ikeda's confidant was predicting "trouble" ahead!

After all the consensus-building and the upper house election, Kishi still had difficulty carrying the LDP. Kono, now the eye of the storm, was openly and willfully obstructionist. Ikeda, did not help Kishi either, for he straddled the mainstream and antimainstream to play hard-to-get. For the third time, the signing of the treaty was put off, beyond April, with MacArthur protesting in vain.[44] Once again the government was drawn into a debate on the definition of the "treaty area" to which the U.S. forces in Japan might be deployed. Whereas the 1951 treaty left Japan out of consultation, Japan was now demanding it. Hence the "treaty area" question. But the United States would or could say only that the treaty area covered the "western Pacific." The opposition raised a sensitive question: whether the "treaty area" included Quemoy, Matsu, Kunashiri, and Etorofu. Kishi at first said yes, with regard to Quemoy and Matsu. Later he backed away from geographical definition altogether.[45] It was in these 1959 debates that the Japanese decided that their right of self-defense was confined to the three-mile limit of their country's territorial waters. Anything that might happen beyond that was America's responsibility, not theirs.

Kono insisted that the 10-year extension of the proposed treaty was too long, and that the Administrative Agreement should be identical with NATO's. The latter point was finally complied with.[46] He nearly caused heart failure in Kishi when he said he wanted to visit Moscow in the fall, since a breakthrough on the Soviet peace treaty at this juncture would end treaty revision. Then Miki went to Moscow while Matsumura and Ishibashi visited Peking, without consequence.

No one in the LDP objected to treaty revision, after the Kishi-Yoshida-Washington entente came into being. The conservatives' chief concern shifted to whether Kishi would be replaced and by whom. The warm glow of nationalism that animated the revisionists following the San Francisco peace conference had died. There was nationalism on the Left, but it, too, would slowly wither on the vine as a result of the JSP's decision to attack both the existing treaty and its revision. That decision, or nondecision, to be exact, struck Nishio Suehiro of the rightwing as utterly irrational and irresponsible. In October 1959, he led a walkout of 24 rightwing Dietmen and organized the Democratic Socialist Party (DSP). This, needless to say, was a major blow to the JSP. The Unified Action Days in the summer and fall of 1959 were not impressive, falling short of the JSP' hopes. Japan was at peace in 1959 and interested primarily in itself. After a brief recession in 1957–58, caused by a mistaken government policy, the economy resumed its exuberant growth, and the balance of payments showed a healthy surplus. Kishi had successfully passed the minimum wage bill and the national pension bill, major pieces of welfare legislation, stealing the thunder from the Socialists. Toward the end of 1959, the radical-liberals were heard saying to themselves, "Anpo is heavy." With unusual haste, the Supreme Court in December overturned the lower-court ruling on the constitutionality of U.S. military bases. It maintained that national defense was a "political question," beyond the province of judicial review.

It was the lack of heroics in JSP-JCP leadership that prompted the hotheads in Zengakuren to turn one of their rallies into the first act of violence on November 27, 1959. The trouble with the united front was the JSP's unwillingness to go for straightforward "Yankee Go Home" neutrality; instead it was de facto defending the older treaty. Swallowing its pride, the JCP fell in line with the JSP and branded the Zengakuren mainstream as Trotskyites. After seven Unified Action Days with little to show for them, the pent-up energy of student radicals found an outlet in the slogan "To the Diet." November 27, the eighth Unified Action Day, was to be the day for massive though orderly demonstrations to petition the Diet. But by prearrangement, the Zengakuren demonstrators broke ranks, charged through the police barricade, and entered the Diet compound to produce a violent clash. The media blamed the JSP rather than Zengakuren, and the LDP pressed its advantage. The incident caused the JSP's leftwing to demand expulsion of Zengakuren from the National Congress, and to begin to steer away from the united front. That in turn added to the frustration of the radicals.

Kishi began his final push to secure the LDP decision in September 1959, and did secure it at a general meeting of the party members of both houses on October 26.[47] But the final draft took until January 1960 to finish. In it, the United States relinquished the domestic intervention clause without a murmur. It was also agreeable to keeping Okinawa and the Bonins out of the "treaty area" until they reverted to Japan's administrative control. But there was some hard bargaining. Ambassador MacArthur insisted on Japan's contribution to regional security and the Kishi government agreed to "self-help and mutual aid."

But its content was truncated. In Article IV of the new treaty, entitled Treaty of Mutual Cooperation and Security between the United States and Japan, the two parties agreed "to consult together from time to time regarding the implementation of this Treaty, and, at the request of either Party, whenever the security of Japan or international peace and security in the Far East is threatened." Article VI grants the United States the use of "facilities and areas in Japan for the purpose of contributing to the security of Japan and the Far East." But the Japanese armed forces would not go to the aid of U.S. counterparts unless the latter were fighting on the Japanese soil. This was to honor the principle of passive defense (senshu boei) that was already evolving out of the original treaty.

It was with reluctance that the Pentagon agreed to "prior consultation" for the movement of U.S. forces. In separate letters exchanged between Kishi and Christian Herter, who replaced Dulles in April 1959 (Dulles died on May 24), the United States agreed that major changes in the deployment of U.S. forces *into* Japan and *out of* Japan to other parts of the Far East, as well as major changes in their equipment, were subject to prior consultation with Japan. "Consultation" meant Japan's agreement and "equipment" referred to nuclear weapons.[48] Ambassador MacArthur made an enormous contribution toward bringing the Pentagon around to accepting Japan's truncated equality. That "mutuality and equality" that eluded Yoshida in 1951 were all conceded.[49]

On January 16, 1960 Kishi and his retinue took off for Washington. He was warmly received in America, and *Time*'s cover story on him was in sharp contrast to its earlier story on Hatoyama. The treaty and the Administrative Agreement were signed on January 19. It was announced that President Eisenhower and Crown Prince Akihito would exchange visits in 1960, Eisenhower arriving in Japan on or about June 20. Kishi was buoyant, and he vowed to stay in power beyond the ratification of the treaty. He wanted to usher in the "new era in U.S.-Japanese relations" personally, alongside a smiling Ike. He wanted a third term as prime minister. "The fear among the free nations that Japan might tilt toward neutralism will be eradicated by treaty revision, and we can henceforth open a dialogue with communist powers," he said.[50] He had a rapprochement with China in mind.

Looking back over the disaster that followed, Kishi regretted that he did not call a general election for treaty ratification in early 1960. The JSP and DSP wanted one. If he were to have an election, ratify the treaty, and be ready for Ike in June, he would have to dissolve the Diet during the first few days in February. But Kishi was persuaded against the idea by the LDP secretary general, Kawashima, who knew of major objections to it among the party bosses, most notably Ikeda. Without party unity on dissolution, Kishi could not be sure of winning an election. He let the chance slip by. Having abandoned the right of dissolution, the prime minister was in a weaker position. His only bargaining chip after that was an offer not to run for a third term.[51] And that was exactly what the dissenters wanted. Kishi might have acted differently had Kono been at his side.

The media became visibly hostile to the treaty as the 34th regular session of the Diet opened in January 1960 for ratification.[52] *Asahi,* the largest and most prestigious newspaper, with a daily circulation of 7.5 million, made demands that amounted to a total rejection of the treaty just signed.[53] Yet *Asahi* did not expect Washington to give in—the treaty would pass. On the other hand, Japan had made an excessive investment of time, energy, and frustrations into the revision, and the investment demanded a return. By early 1960 the momentum of the struggle had carried the opposition to the point where it was straining at the harness. On the streets the rhetoric of immediate "abolition" or "smashing" of the treaty could be heard and seen. A picture-perfect ratification leading to Kishi's third term would not defuse the situation. Somehow the system had to make a statement to America. But if the treaty could not be touched, Kishi was the only thing that might give. From the *Asahi* editorial one could surmise that the political system was going for a replay of the police bill fiasco. The major actors in this play were the LDP (Yoshida, Ikeda, and Kono) and the media.[54]

As the 34th regular session, scheduled to sit through March 26, was about to open, the Soviet Union delivered a fresh demarche and a nuclear blackmail. It announced that the islands of Habomai and Shikotan, which were to revert to Japan upon conclusion of the future peace treaty, would remain under Soviet control until Japan renounced the security treaty with the United States and became neutral.[55] Then, it fired a test missile almost directly over Japan into the Pacific Ocean down range. The Chinese Communists chimed in with their peculiar brand of invectives against the "Kishi clique of war criminals." Once again the opposition in the Diet recited the litany of charges against Kishi's involving Japan in war over Quemoy, Matsu, and Korea. And all the controversial points had to be gone over again.[56]

Having been chastised by the November 27 incident, the JSP confined itself to parliamentary debate for the time being. Whether in or out of the Diet chamber, the JSP's goal was to prolong the deliberations and to table the treaty, as it succeeded in doing with the small district bill. The JSP carried out a reshuffle of its leadership at the extraordinary congress on March 25, 1960, to reunify itself after the break with the rightwing the previous fall. Asanuma

Inejiro of the rightwing, who reciprocated Dulles's "brinkmanship" with his "American imperialism is the common enemy of the Japanese and Chinese peoples," was elected chairman. China's influence could be perceived in his victory.[57] The DSP, having cut itself off from the JSP on the issue of a united front with the JCP, was determined to stick to parliamentary rules in order to score points with the public. But that did not necessarily make the DSP a friend of Kishi's or of the revised treaty—it stood for eventual "phased" abolition of the treaty.[58] All the same, it was the only opposition that respected the normal parliamentary procedure. It was in the splendid position of being wooed by both the LDP and the JSP.

For all the threatening noise it made, the JSP was sensitive to the media's strictures against violence. So, when all was said and done, the Diet was still the seat of power. And here was the distribution of power in it. The JCP had one seat in the 467-seat lower chamber. The JSP started out with 167 after the 1958 election, but lost 32 to the DSP during the split of October 1959. That left the JSP with 135 parliamentary members. The LDP had 298 seats.

When the ratification debate began in the 34th regular session, the LDP factions did not divide simply along the customary mainstream-antimainstream line. It was the hallmark of Kishi's predicament that the LDP divided three ways: mainstream, middle factions, and antimainstream. Kishi, with 78–80 followers and Sato, his brother, with 35–40 followers, together constituted the mainstream. With 113–120 members, this was the biggest bloc but was not big enough to be decisive. The middle factions that rallied around Ikeda and Kono included the Kono (35–40 members), Ikeda (45–50), Ishii (20–25), and Ohno (35–40) factions. Ikeda and Kono were in the middle because they had to cooperate enough with Kishi to succeed him and obstruct him enough to make him relinquish power.

Kono, who had felt jilted when Kishi reappointed Ikeda to the cabinet a year earlier and who had begun to explore his chances with the antimainstream, veered back toward Kishi when the JSP split, because the weakened JSP strengthened Kishi's hand. Kono still held Kishi accountable to the secret agreement of the year before, whereby Kishi promised to hand over the reins of power to Ohno and then to himself. Ikeda, too, felt that the JSP split turned the treaty into less of a lever against Kishi. Under instructions from Yoshida, Ikeda was helping Kishi in spite of himself. Ikeda was also flirting with the Miki-Matsumura faction in the antimainstream, and because the Miki-Matsumura group was interested in the China connection, Ikeda surprised his conservative colleagues with a sudden show of interest in China in 1960. The Ishii faction was off in a corner because it was against Kishi, Kono, and Ikeda. In the antimainstream with pronounced interest in China were the Miki-Matsumura group with 30–35 followers, and former prime minister Ishibashi, with 10 to 15 members.[59]

The JSP mauled Kishi and Fujiyama badly in Diet interpellations, but Kishi appeared to be self-confident in March as the session passed the midpoint and the end was in sight. Yoshida's stock was suddenly rising in the early spring of 1960, and no one could ignore him. On the way back from a weekend outing in the Hakone Mountains in March, Kishi stopped by Yoshida's cottage in Oiso for a courtesy call. In his usual puckish mood, Yoshida, who was 81 years old, said, "Lately my old friends have been passing away, . . . and I am running out of condolence money [given in honor of the deceased at Japanese funerals]. It'll be my turn to rob them clean next time."[60] Kishi was momentarily nonplussed. The visit was obviously occasioned by a week-old report that the old man had had dinner with Ikeda and Sato, at which he instructed his disciples "not to pull Kishi's legs" because power would pass from Kishi to Ikeda to Sato.[61]

For the time being, no one could challenge Kishi, and he organized a "commando squad" to push through the treaty and related legislation, which were stalled in the Ad Hoc Committee for the Security Treaty. With almost the entire media cheering for "democracy," "respect for the minority," and "satisfactory debate," the JSP had been proceeding at a snail's pace since January. The session was to end on May 26. If the lower house were to pass the treaty by April 26 and let it stand before the upper house for a full month, the treaty would be automatically ratified. Hence April 26 was the absolute deadline— unless an extension could be voted on, which was difficult. In any case, the treaty had to be ready by the time Eisenhower was to arrive, on June 19.

On April 20 the LDP leaders moved for cloture. The LDP chairman of the Ad Hoc Committee moved to hold a public hearing, a step preceding a vote on a bill. The opposition refused and immediately resorted to physical obstruction. The Diet guards could not escort the chairman to the podium. The motion carried in a "forced vote," and the opposition immediately began a boycott. Two days later, the LDP decided to have the plenary session demand an interim report from the Ad Hoc Committee, thus forcing the bill out on the house floor. The JSP declared an "emergency," and the DSP closed ranks.[62] The scene began to resemble the police bill affair. The Miki-Matsumura and Ishibashi factions threatened to absent themselves, whereas the Ikeda, Kono, and Ishii factions objected to the forced vote. Kishi could not even be sure of a quorum. The speaker, Kiyose Ichiro—handpicked by Kishi for his ironclad integrity proven in legal defense of a Communist against the imperial government and Tojo against the Americans—and the DSP worked out a compromise whereby the LDP withdrew its motion for an interim report and agreed to resume the committee debate until "May 10 to 15," by which date the DSP agreed to a vote. In this way, the April 26 deadline passed. The compromise settlement was a defeat for the government, caused by internal disunity. Now an extension of the session became necessary.[63]

Tension began to mount in early May as the treaty headed for a vote. A timebomb was ticking away. Of all things in the world, another East-West confrontation intervened and gave the opposition fresh ammunition. On May 7 Nikita Khrushchev disclosed that Francis Gary Powers, pilot of a U-2 spy plane shot down near Sverdlovsk, was in Soviet custody. President Eisenhower had to own up to the operation while reassuring the allies of U.S. protection against Soviet threats.[64]

Kishi was in a no-win situation. The DSP, whose votes–never mind yea or nay—were needed in order for the LDP to avoid the opprobrium of a "forced decision" or "lone vote," had had a change of heart since late April. It reneged on the promise to vote by "May 10 to 15," because Chairman Nishio could not muster the rank and file. The JSP chairman Asanuma, in contrast, demanded a dissolution to put the treaty issue to the voters.[65] Kishi's choice was either a dissolution or a "forced decision." Dissolution at this stage was tantamount to admitting to government's mismanagement of the treaty ratification process. It would give ammunition to Kishi's intra-LDP opponents. Eisenhower's visit with a caretaker government would be meaningless. *Asahi* acknowledged the predicament with this headline: "THE CONSERVATIVE PARTY IN CRISIS IF TREATY ABORTED."[66] However, the JSP had repeatedly declared that it would physically obstruct any vote—on extending the session, on forcing the treaty out of the Ad Hoc Committee, or on the treaty itself. The DSP was in agreement. On the same page, *Asahi*'s editorial demanded an extension, more debate, and, if that did not resolve the issue, abandonment of treaty revision![67]

"In the nature of the case," Kishi felt, "no amount of discussion would solve it."[68] On May 17 Kishi, at a plenary meeting of all Diet members, secured the consent of the party—including even Ikeda, Ishii, and Ohno—for votes to extend the session and on the treaty. The LDP stood by for the right moment. On Thursday morning, May 19, the LDP formally proposed a 50-day extension, to be voted on in the plenary session to begin at 5:00 P.M. The JSP Dietmen and secretaries cordoned off the speaker's room to prevent him from reaching the podium. At 10:25 P.M. the LDP chairman of the Ad Hoc Committee reconvened the meeting. In a surprise move, he sought to close the debate. With the Socialists stomping out in protest, he managed to get an affirmative vote on the treaty.

At 10:35 P.M. the last bell for the plenary session sounded and the LDP members entered the chamber. Speaker Kiyose was still locked up in his office, and his repeated pleas for civility, broadcast over the public address system, had been falling on deaf ears for over five hours. Some LDP Dietmen became irate over his efforts to appease his captors. But Kiyose proved his mettle and repaid Kishi's trust in him. He finally ordered 500 policemen to the Diet to break up the barricade at 11:00 P.M. With only the LDP members present, he took a vote on extension. But Kishi had secretly decided to put the treaty to a vote as well, because there was little sense in repeating a major fracas.[69] At six minutes past midnight, Kiyose opened a new session to vote on the report of the Ad Hoc Committee. Kono, Ishibashi, Miki, Matsumura, and their followers voted only for the extension, claiming that they knew nothing of the treaty vote. Ikeda, who had favored "careful deliberation" but declined to "wave a flag," voted for both measures.[70] So did Ishii and Ohno. The treaty passed, and its automatic passage through the upper house was assured in one month.

Everyone was conscious of the precedent of the police bill affair, and it was almost a forgone conclusion that the focus would switch to Kishi and "parliamentary democracy." No conservative could afford to oppose the treaty. But Kishi and his "dictatorship" were a fair game. The whole nation seemed to unite in condemning him. The Communists alone cried out in anguish that the United States was the main enemy, and that "Kishi" was draining off the anti-American animus in public opinion.

Kishi and parliamentary democracy became the issue because of the simple, brutal fact that all the obstructionist tactics of the JSP were ignored in the media. According to the research of the Japan Press Association, of the 49 editorials of its members between May 21 and 23, only 15 blamed both sides. Thirty-three condemned Kishi and demanded his resignation and Diet dissolution. One rested its hopes on deliberations in the upper chamber.[71] Of the 15 "evenhanded" editorials, most comments critical of the opposition were perfunctory; they demonstrated a newspaper's "fairness." But it was obtuse to be evenhanded in this instance. Add the 33 that denounced only Kishi, and we have a mechanism for extraparliamentary mobilization on critical issues.

On those questions that aroused the JSP and the media, a majority vote became inoperative. A government that refused to take a "low posture" and "forced a decision" ran the risk of becoming mortally wounded because the LDP majority, though overwhelming on paper, would crack along the Yoshida-revisionist cleavage and in addition along the factional lines. Formally in existence since 1956, the factions proved their lethal power in 1960. On critical "peace" issues, therefore, Kishi's successors would begin to opt for a decision by unanimity that encompassed the ideological opposition. In this way, the JSP's legislative influence, confined initially to procedural matters, began to extend to the substance of a bill. This was the beginning of decision-making by "consensus": it was alien to Japanese politics until then, and it certainly was not Japan's cultural heritage, as standard history alleges.[72] The final arbiters in deciding whether a vote should be unanimous or not were the JSP and the giant commercial newspapers such as *Asahi* and *Mainichi*. Although incompetent, disorganized, and unsure of itself, the JSP played an indispensable role in establishing the "consensus" decision-making rule within the 1955 system, thereby changing the character of the system from confrontational to issueless (van Wolferen).[73]

Foreign policy issues were particularly vulnerable to extraparliamentary pressure because Japanese politics embodied the Cold War division. Yet, though foreign intervention was just as intense as it had been in 1955–56, it worked to a different end this time. Kishi, who sought to avoid Hatoyama's fate by working closely with Dulles, isolated himself instead. His denunciation of the JSP and its foreign friends was met with the reply that he too worked for foreign friends. Standing between Kishi and the JSP, Yoshida alone was independent. Everyone else—including the JSP, the LDP revisionists, Moscow, Peking, and Washington—were ministering to his end. Given the 1955 system, Yoshida's course alone insured Japan's "independence."

Kishi took the May 19 vote to insure that the treaty would be ratified in time for Ike's visit on June 19. Now Eisenhower was added to the issue. Immediately the JSP and DSP demanded a postponement of the visit. The JSP insisted that the vote extending the session was invalid and demanded Kishi's resignation, a new election, calling for a switch in tactics to extraparliamentary action. Between May 20, the day after the "forced decision," and July 18, the JSP boycotted all Dietary proceedings. Nishio, the chairman of the DSP, kept trying to mediate between the ruling party and the JSP while trying to keep his own party in the Diet. He maintained—against internal opposition—that the DSP would recognize the extension if the LDP agreed to scuttle the treaty, force Kishi to resign, and dissolve the Diet. Kishi knew he was doomed, but he pressed on. He had the upper house vote for an extension of its session, and he tried to have it vote on the treaty instead of relying on automatic validation of the lower house vote.

With Kishi acting as the lightning rod, the treaty's passage was assured. Much of the anti-American animus generated by the treaty controversy was dumped on Kishi, and that seemed to relieve the anti-American tension.[74] The psychological mechanism of issuetransformation was described by Kaiko Takeshi, a popular novelist:

> I'll tell you how I felt as a novelist when I saw the morning paper on May 20. The moment I saw the picture of scuffles. . . . Hitherto I had a gloomy feeling, lectur-

ing and demonstrating here, there, and everywhere. And I had this feeling that the people on the street do not understand the treaty question. . . . But that [forced vote] was a splendid clean hit. Now we have a really truly simple powerful goal. . . . Kishi Nobusuke is unparalleled in history for being so full of the spirit of self-sacrifice.[75]

The new issue was put this way by Takeuchi Yoshimi, a leading China specialist:

I have been opposed to the security treaty, and I have been campaigning against it. But I no longer wish to argue with those who support it. I have no time for it. Let us rebuild democracy first. There are those who say, our goal is to smash the new security treaty and *rebuilding democracy is the means.* But I disagree. . . .[76]

The treaty became irrelevant to the fight against Kishi. The shots were called by the press with banner headlines from May 20 on, and the intellectual community swung behind it overnight.

The nature of the intellectual masses that mobilized themselves against Kishi after May 20 is difficult to define. Their self-appointed pied piper was Maruyama Masao, Tokyo University political scientist, though he was objectively an instrument of the newspapers. Collectively the intellectuals viewed everything since the "reverse course" as a fall from Eden. Maruyama was still dreaming E. Herbert Norman's *kozaha* dream of having a French revolution in Japan. He felt that "parliamentarism" as it was practiced by established political parties, of both Right and Left, was a "sham program." It was terribly inauthentic; it was an "imposition"—in the sense, I infer, that any political system holds men "in chains," as Rousseau put it. Maruyama was extremely exhilarated to see the riots, which were reversing all the "reversals" inflicted on early occupation reforms. The "narcissism" of loving the "confusion qua confusion" was, he thought, the motive power to recreate the storming of the "Bastille."[77]

Only the LDP, the Communists, and perhaps the newspaper editors knew what was really happening. In contrast, the JSP, the DSP, students, professors, and demonstrators jumped at the new issue as if by reflex. It was evident that the Socialists acted without meditating the consequences of the issuetransformation. Until Kishi became the issue, the JSP stood for a foreign-policy program. It had some leverage over extraparliamentary mass movements with which to influence decisions in the Diet. But when the JSP acceded to issue change, it lost that leverage. Massive demonstrations continued, but basically politics shifted away from the street to the Diet, because parliamentary democracy was now the issue. Kishi's vote was perfectly legal, and the outcry for "democracy" could only uphold that vote—there was no way a street mob could undo it. With democracy restored by the mob, the JSP was thrust back to its minority status in the Diet. Unanimity was no longer binding. Unseating Kishi was a job for the LDP factions. The Socialists were at best a froth on the LDP's power game.

On June 10 James C. Hagerty, President Eisenhower's press secretary, arrived in Tokyo to make final preparations for the state visit. At Haneda airport the car ferrying him and Ambassador MacArthur was trapped by massed demonstrators under JCP control. The Americans escaped less than an hour later, unharmed, when police arrived. The media condemned the harassment. Undeterred, the Communists wanted to press ahead against Eisenhower. But on June 16, just before his visit, the National Congress decided to remain antigovernment but not anti-Eisenhower.[78] Just as gravity was shifting back to the Diet, the JSP found itself on the outside, bound by its vow of a Diet boycott. It toyed with the idea of mass resignations from Diet seats as a way of forcing the dissolution of the Diet, but failed to go through with it. Then it dawned on the Socialists that this was not the time to disappear from the Diet.

The LDP's factional maneuvers continued until Ikeda was selected, and they need not detain us any longer. But there was one incipient movement that pointed up one objective issue before Japan. The antimainstreamers' boycott of the treaty vote and other shameful conducts were met by a groundswell of public demand for a second conservative party.[79] Kono responded with an attempt to merge factions of the LDP and the Socialists to form the opposition in a two-party system. That was the objective need of the political system, as demonstrated by the entire upheaval. But it was too late. The JSP was too entrenched and too incompetent.

Frustration caused by the JSP's leadership, long on rhetoric and short on action, was felt within the Diet and without. Zengakuren students, mostly freshmen and sophomores since the upperclassmen had been decimated by police arrests in the month-long upheaval, felt betrayed by the turn of events after the issue change on May 19. They were to have one last jacquerie in the name of revolution on June 15, leaving one student dead. The violence shook the government, which came to the decision that Eisenhower's safety could no longer be guaranteed. The Japanese police apparatus did prove to be defective, as Kishi knew. He then discussed with his ministers the idea of calling in the Self-Defense Forces, but abandoned it because a shooting on the streets might lead to a real revolution.[80] On the following day, Kishi announced the cancellation of the state visit.

On June 17 seven major newspapers issued a highly unusual joint statement deploring violence and pleading the case for "parliamentarism." It was a self-serving document that obscured the responsibility of the media for the whole upheaval and cast doubt on their integrity.

> The bloodshed in and out of the Diet on the night of June 15 was a grievous incident that plunged parliamentarism into crisis, *quite apart from the reasons for its origin.* Democracy ought to be contended for in speech alone. *No matter what the cause,* violence . . . is absolutely impermissible.[81]

The newspapers' call *"to abandon the point hitherto at issue"* struck the radicals as evenhanded injustice this time. Nakano Yoshimi protested that it was those very newspapers that had agitated against the May 19 vote by saying, "Everything is Prime Minister Kishi's responsibility," or "We can never accept [the vote]."[82]

Amid the din of street battles that engulfed Nagatacho on the night of June 19, Kishi was alone with his brother in the prime minister's official residence. Police advised him that his safety could not be guaranteed there, but he insisted on staying. Having abandoned the treaty vote in the upper house, he was waiting for midnight, when the lower house vote would automatically complete the ratification. At midnight Kishi and Sato toasted each other. Then the morning after, following the exchange of the instrument of ratification between the foreign minister and Ambassador MacArthur, Kishi announced his resignation.[83]

Because Kishi had been the deus ex machina that transformed the issue, his resignation restored Japan to calm, as if nothing had happened. Incredulous, people began asking, What was *anpo* all about?[84] The question arose because no one came forth to take credit for the treaty. Kishi wanted to but could not.[85] The United States and Secretary Dulles could not. And the JSP certainly could not. Characteristically, the real winner discreetly distanced himself from the United States.

Prime minister Ikeda's first "state of the union" speech was devoted to the goals of healing wounds at home and restoring Japan's credibility abroad. He declared he would practice the politics of "tolerance and patience," or what came to be more popularly called "politics of low posture." The centerpiece of his policy was the plan to double average income in 10 years. The rate of GNP growth in 1959 was 14 percent, well above what he needed to achieve his goal. Ikeda dissolved the Diet in October for a lower house election, and the LDP won as expected.

In early December the new Diet voted to choose the prime minister. Kishi and Sato, holding the largest bloc of votes, supported Ikeda's candidacy for the prime ministership, as they had previously agreed to. The Eisenhower administration, too, was supporting Ikeda in exchange for his treaty vote.[86] Kishi refused to support Kono, Miki, Matsumura, or their choice, all professional politicians who had stabbed him in the back. The vote split the LDP neatly along the bureaucrat-professional line, 302 to 194, in Ikeda's favor. The days of bureaucratic dominance in Japanese politics was on hand. At the time there were 135 bureaucrat-turned-politician in the Diet, most of them in the LDP.[87]

A new orthodoxy in foreign and domestic policy was being erected by Ikeda and his bureaucratic brain trust. Having written the treaty themselves this time, there was no chance for the Japanese to disclaim responsibility for it. Still, politicians of the Yoshida School emphasized the economic benefits that was said to accrue to Japan from the treaty (the *anpo* utility thesis or *anpo koyoron*). Japan continued to act as if it were semi-neutral on political and strategic matters. In fact it was only after the conservative defenders of the constitution wrested power that Japan's pacifist self-abnegation was reinforced. The three principles of nuclear disarmament (whereby the Diet resolved not to introduce, manufacture, or possess nuclear weapons), a ban on the export of weapons, 1 percent of GNP as a defense budget ceiling, and the like were added after 1960. The new Venice was born. It took 10 years for Japan to win the status that Yoshida and MacArthur staked out for it back in 1950.

The crisis-and-compensation tactic, with which the conservatives would compromise their principles and buy off the opposition (with "income doubling," as in this case), became the LDP's stock in trade at this point.[88] Shortly thereafter, the tactic coalesced with the diplomacy of pacifist self-abnegation, to produce the crisis-and-compensation diplomacy. It would tempt foreign governments to criticize Japan with the expectation of getting compensated.[89]

The American people were shocked by the upheaval in Japan, especially because they could not make head or tail of the dust and din over Tokyo. TV reporting on the Hagerty siege—focusing on the deluge of red flags and hostility—underscored the need for a reorientation of America's Japan policy. In the fall of 1960 a series of reports and testimonies were offered to the Senate as it searched for a new policy. It is difficult to say that the Senate was getting the truth from these documents. They agreed on two points: that the trouble in Japan was primarily a domestic matter caused by the immaturity of its democratic institutions; and that the remedy was economic stability. These points were present in America's diagnosis of any problem anywhere, but perhaps that did not matter. There was really only one direction in which the United States could move: detachment and benign neglect. The treaty of 1960—mutual and not mutual—had already pointed the way by enshrining the MacArthur legacy and the constitution.

President Kennedy's appointment of Edwin O. Reischauer, father of the modernization paradigm, as ambassador to Japan in 1961 could not have been more appropriate or better timed. A Douglas MacArthur of culture, as it were, Reischauer ushered in the era of "partnership" across the Pacific. "Partnership" was the synonym of the mutual but not mutual treaty.

## NOTES

1. Shakai-shugi Kyokai, ed., *Nitchu "kyodo seimei" to Shakaito* [Japan-China "joint statement" and the JSP] (Tokyo: Shakai-shugi Kyokai, 1975), p. 40.

2. See Yoshihisa Hara, *Sengo Nihon to kokusai seiji: anpo kaitei no seiji rikigaku* [Postwar Japan and international politics: political dynamism of anpo revision] (Tokyo: Chuo Koronsha, 1988), pp. 166–78.

3. Douglas MacArthur II and Yoshihisa Komori, "Rokuju-nen anpo kaitei no shinso," *Chuo Koron* (November 1981), p. 184. At what point did Eisenhower and Dulles make the specific decision to consider drafting of an entirely new treaty? Hara places that decision at early June, 1958. Hara, pp. 176–77.

4. Aiichiro Fujiyama, *Seiji waga michi* [Politics my way] (Tokyo: Asahi Shimbunsha, 1976), p. 61–62, says the date was August 1. Fumihiko Togo, *Nichi-Bei gaiko sanjunen: anpo-Okinawa to sonogo* [Thirty years of Japan-U.S. relations: anpo-Okinawa and after] (Tokyo: Sekaino Ugokisha, 1982), p. 63, puts the date at August 25. I take the latter. See also Hara, p. 179.

5. *Asahi Shimbun,* September 13, 1958, p. 3. Kishi met "several tens of times" with Ambassador MacArthur, thrashing out an early draft, while Fujiyama and his staff met the ambassador separately in the Imperial Hotel some 15 times before the meeting was disrupted in mid-December by trouble in the Diet. Ikuzo Tajiri, *Showa no yokai Kishi Nobusuke* [Kishi Nobusuke: the spectre of Showa] (Tokyo: Gakuyo Shobo, 1979), p. 178; Fujiyama, *Seiji waga michi,* p. 77.

6. Townsend Hoopes, *The Devil and John Foster Dulles* (Boston: Little Brown, 1973), p. 445.

7. Ibid., pp. 442–49.

8. "NSC Staff Study of U.S. Policy Toward Communist China, (NSC 166/1)," *Foreign Relations of the United States* (Washington, DC: GPO, 1976), 1952–54, XIV, 282–306; John L. Gaddis, *Strategies of Containment: A Critical Appraisal of Postwar American National Security Policy* (New York: Oxford Univ. Press, 1982), p. 143.

9. Takeo Shinmyo, "Anpo jyoyaku no kuroi kage" [The dark shadow of the security treaty], *Bungei Shunju* (January 1959), p. 106.

10. *FRUS,* 1950, VI, 1243. He says the war can be used to awaken the Japanese from their "postwar stupor" to the need for defense.

11. George R. Packard III, *Protest in Tokyo: The Security Treaty Crisis of 1960* (Princeton, N.J.: Princeton Univ. Press, 1966), mentions the international crisis in passing (pp. 62–63) but does not relate it to the decisions by Kishi or Dulles. Hence he blames the fiasco on Kishi's domestic "handling" of revision. Packard, p. 152.

12. Shinmyo, *Chuo Koron* (January 1959), p. 106; *New York Times,* August 26, p. 1; Fujiyama, *Seiji waga michi,* p. 72.

13. Of the two explanations for the JSP's change of policy—political and sociological, referred to in the previous chapter—the former was decisive.

14. Japan Socialist Party, *Nihon Shakaito no sanjunen* [Thirty years of the JSP] (Tokyo: JSP, 1974), II, 213.

15. To view Japan's domestic politics in isolation necessarily results in a bias against Kishi. See how Kosaka resembles the Socialists on this point, in Masataka Kosaka, *Saiso Yoshida Shigeru* [Prime minister Yoshida Shigeru] (Tokyo: Chuo Koronsha, 1968), pp. 124–28.

16. Hara, pp. 244–57. In my judgment, the pivot in this turnaround was the Quemoy-Matsu incident. But Hara seems to think that the turnaround was independent of the incident.

17. MacArthur and Komori, "Rokuju-nen anpo kaitei no shinso," *Chuo Koron* (November 1981), p. 186; Hara, p. 283.

18. See Chapter 9, note 1.

19. *Asahi Shimbun,* December 28, 1958, p. 1. This is the number that supported Ikeda's subsequent resignation from the cabinet.

20. Ibid., November 20, 1958, p. 1. The Japanese government denounced it as "intervention."

21. Ibid., December 4, 1958, p. 1.

22. "Seifu no anpo jyoyaku kaitei koso ni hantai suru" [In opposition to the government's idea of security-treaty revision], *Chuo Koron* (June 1959), p. 44.

23. Ibid., p. 48.

24. Nishio of the rightwing felt it was utterly irresponsible to oppose both the existing treaty and its revision. He later walked out on the JSP.

25. Tadao Okada, *Seiji no uchimaku* [Inside story of politics] (Tokyo: Yuki Shobo, 1959), pp. 179–81.

26. Hara, p. 209; Okada, pp. 171–79.

27. "Kono Ichiro shi: sono genjitsu kankaku" [Mr. Kono Ichiro: his sense of realism], *Chuo Koron* (February 1959), pp. 70–71. This was the mindset that gave rise to the LDP's factionalism in 1956 and after 1958.

28. Okada, pp. 20, 29; *Nihon naikaku shiroku,* V, 431.

29. *Asahi Shimbun,* January 24, 1959, p. 1.

30. Fujiyama, *Seiji waga michi* p. 80.

31. Ibid., pp. 80, 95.

32. Informal JSP-JCP cooperation had commenced during the campaign against the small-district bill back in 1956. *Nihon Shakaito no sanjunen,* II, 120; Packard, p. 93.

33. Seizaburo Shinobu, *Anpo toso shi* [History of the anpo struggle] (Tokyo: Sekai Shoin, 1961), p. 47; *Nihon Shakaito no sanjunen,* II, 239–47.

34. Koken Koyama, *Sengo Nihon Kyosanto shi,* pp. 205–12.

35. Packard, p. 93.

36. *Nihon Shakaito no sanjunen,* p. 247. Packard offers the most comprehensive account of the radical movement, pp. 101–24.

37. Packard, p. 117.

38. See Jiro Fukushima, "Seiji teki jiba no henka ni tsuite" [On the shift in the political magnetic field], *Chuo Koron* (January 1959), pp. 56–64; Yarumasa Oshima, "Chukan teki kaigi chitai no rinri" [On the ethics of the centrist skeptic zone], *Chuo Koron* (January 1959), pp. 142–52.

39. Ichiro Ohinata, *Kishi seiken 1241 nichi* [The 1241 days of Kishi government] (Tokyo: Gyosei Mondai Kenkyujo, 1985), p. 192.

40. Kiichi Shioguchi, *Bunsho Ikeda Hayato* [Stories about Ikeda Hayato] (Tokyo: Asahi Shimbunsha, 1975), pp. 188–92.

41. *Kishi Nobusuke no kaiso,* p. 199.

42. Hara, p. 267, citing Miki Takeo in an interview.

43. Hajime Terazawa, "Jiyuuminshuto no gaiko kankaku" [The LDP's diplomatic sense], *Chuo Koron* (August 1959), pp. 177–80.

44. Kishi and Gaimusho planned to initial the draft by January 1959; April 1959; and June 1959, immediately after the election.

45. Shinobu, *Anpo toso shi,* p. 121.

46. Fujiyama, *Seiji waga michi,* p. 87.

47. Hara, p. 313.

48. Fujiyama, *Seiji waga michi,* pp. 81–84; Packard, pp. 369–73, for Kishi-Herter letters; *Nihon naikaku shiroku,* V, 438.

49. Martin E. Weinstein, *Japan's Postwar Defense Policy, 1947–1968* (New York: Columbia Univ. Press, 1971), notes this fact (p. 87) without a mention of American concessions. See a file of documents relating to the U.S. embassy actions, made available to this author by Richard Snyder, Ambassador MacArthur's aide.

50. Cited in Shinobu, *Anpo toso shi,* p. 30.

51. Ohinata, pp. 227–31.

52. Packard noted this also, p. 215.

53. (1) That the "prior consultation" between the two governments over the deployment of U.S. forces be replaced by "prior agreement," (2) that the purpose of U.S. forces in Japan (Article VI) be limited to the maintenance of Japanese security only, (3) that all clauses that cast doubt on the constitutionality of the treaty be removed, and (4) that the 10-year term of the treaty be reduced. *Asahi Shimbun,* January 14, 1960, p. 1.

54. Here is another disagreement I have with Hara, who virtually ignores the media.

55. *Asahi Shimbun,* January 28, 1960, p. 1.

56. The two most controversial points had to do with the *makikomareru* thesis. One was the definition of "treaty area" and "Far East." The other was whether Japan possessed a veto over U.S. military operations staged from the bases in Japan. A third, a procedural one, concerned the question of whether the Diet had the authority to amend the treaty that had already been signed. The government had to say that the treaty was to be accepted or rejected in toto. See Hara, pp. 338–59

57. See Hara's statement to this effect, p. 393.

58. See Packard, pp. 128–31, for a good summary of its platform.

59. *Asahi Shimbun,* March 24, 1960, p. 7. Ikeda demanded a new opening toward Peking in January 1960. Ibid., January 10, 1960, p. 1.

60. Ibid., March 21, 1960, p. 2.

61. Ibid., March 20, 1960, p. 1.

62. Hara, p. 363.

63. *Asahi Shimbun,* April 22, 1960, p. 1; ibid., April 23, 1960, p. 1; ibid., April 24, 1960, p. 1; ibid., April 25, 1960, p. 1.

64. Packard, pp. 229–30.

65. *Asahi Shimbun,* May 19, 1960, p. 5.

66. Ibid., May 17, 1960, p. 2.

67. Ibid., editorial, May 17, 1960, p. 2.

68. Ibid., May 13, 1960, p. 2.

69. Hara, p. 400.

70. Shinobu, *Anpo toso shi,* p. 151.

71. *Asahi Shimbun,* May 26, 1960, p. 10.

72. Yasusuke Murakami, Shunpei Kumon, Seizaburo Sato, *Bunmei to shiteno ie shakai* [The *ie* society as a civilization] (Tokyo: Chuo Koronsha, 1985).

73. Hara says, "It is difficult to find instances in which the JSP had impacted directly and continuously on the process of treaty revision." Hara, p. 245. With this I disagree. Neither the origin nor the conduct of the LDP's factionalism can be explained except in the context of the Socialist opposition and the "peace" issue.

74. Suekichi Aono, cited in Shinobu, *Anpo toso shi,* p. 271.

75. "Giji puroguramu kara no dakkyaku" [Transcending phony programs], *Chuo Koron* (July 1960), p. 32.

76. Cited in Shinobu, *Anpo toso shi,* p. 289. (Emphasis added.)

77. Maruyama et al., *Chuo Koron* (July 1960), pp. 35–36.

78. Packard, p. 294.

79. *Sankei Shimbun,* May 21, 1960, p. 2; *Asahi Shimbun,* June 3, 1960, p. 2.

80. Hara, p. 425–28.

81. *Asahi Shimbun,* June 17, 1960, p. 1. (Emphasis added).

82. Shinobu, *Anpo tososhi,* pp. 421–22.

83. There followed an extensive and soul-searching postmortem by Japanese scholars and analysts. They must be read by any serious student of Japanese politics, though we dispense with their writings here. Some outstanding examples are Jun Eto, "Sengo chishiki-jin no hasan" [The bankruptcy of postwar intellectuals], *Bungei Shunju* (November 1960), pp. 98–106; Jun Eto, "Koe naki mono mo tachi-agaru" [Even the voiceless rise up], *Chuo Koron* (July 1960), p. 53; Yoshikazu Sakamoto, "Kakushin nashonarizumu shiron" [A trial thesis on radical-liberal nationalism], *Chuo Koron* (October 1960), pp. 42–53.

84. Shintaro Ryu, editorialist of *Asahi,* "Anpo kaitei o do shitara yoika" [How to handle the *anpo* revision], *Bungei Shunju* (June 1960), pp. 64–72.

85. Taro Akasaka, "Migi mo hidari mo nairan" [Revolts on the right and left], *Bungei Shunju* (November 1960), p. 114.

86. Hara, pp. 377–78.

87. Interior 53, Finance 21, Agriculture 19, Foreign Ministry 11, Post and Telegraph 9, MITI 8, and others 2. Chiyoda roshi, "Inochi mijikashi Kishi naikaku" [The short-lived Kishi cabinet], *Bengei Shunju*(December 1959), p. 94.

88. Kent E. Calder, *Crisis and Compensation: Public Policy and Political Stability in Japan, 1949–1986* (Princeton, NJ: Princeton Univ. Press, 1988).

89. In these exchanges, Japan makes up with money for the lack of adequate military defense. The so-called defense-trade linkage that became so controversial in the FSX (Japan's jet fighter, fighter support experimental) dispute of 1989 was in fact initiated by Japan itself.

# Chapter 9

# Conclusion

This book offers for the first time an honest and politically uninhibited account of the origin of Japan's postwar regime. Let me summarize some of the more important findings by way of conclusion.

The United States and Japan were intimately involved with each other in the founding of Japan's postwar regime. The Japan Problem, so-called, has its origin in that regime, which may be best defined in terms of the tension between the constitution and the security treaty. Japan's foreign policy and domestic political institutions (such as the LDP's one-party dominance) can only be explained in this way.

The founding of the postwar regime began with Japan's surrender and the imposition of the constitution, went on to the incomplete reversal of the early occupation reforms in the course of negotiation over the peace and security treaties, and was not finalized until 1960. Yoshida Shigeru, Douglas Mac-Arthur, and Pentagon imperialism must bear a large part of responsibility for the result. It took 15 years, a very long time, before the Japanese accepted the regime, because men like Hatoyama, Kishi, and Dulles refused to accept inequality.

Japan is in debt to Douglas MacArthur for his magnanimity immediately after the surrender. It is unfortunate that he should have been consumed by a strange passion thereafter, and that his racially tinged legacy should have become the cornerstone of the U.S.-Japan security tie.

During the negotiation over the peace and security treaties, six parties, three Japanese and three American, vied with each other. The most important demand of the United States, represented by the Defense Department, was to secure continued occupation or de facto occupation of Japan. John Foster Dulles and the State Department took an ambivalent position: without overriding the Pentagon's demand for military bases, they insisted on a peace treaty granting Japan formal equality; the Japanese revisionists endorsed Dulles and State insofar as they stood for equality. MacArthur and Yoshida bowed to the dictate of de facto occupation, felt formal equality was a chimera, and urged Japan to do its own thing under the American rule. If Yoshida's real motive was to keep Japan out of the Korean War, the revisionists might have forgiven him. But the point remains moot. The Japanese Socialists called for genuine neutrality as the closest approximation to autonomy.

I find Dulles's argument that Japan should take active part in its own defense above reproach. Had he been able to work in harmony with Hatoyama, Japan could have developed into a different country both in its security and nonsecurity aspects. The critical turning point was the peace negotiation with Moscow. The United States made a fatal error in first endorsing and later vetoing that negotiation. After the downfall of Hatoyama, the constitution could not be changed.

For all their good intentions, Kishi and Dulles had to seek "mutuality" within the constitutional framework. In that sense, they were doomed to failure. But they were also doomed to failure if they left unattended the legitimate discontent of the Japanese against the original security treaty.

Kishi and Dulles also made tactical errors in submitting the police duties bill and in plunging the revision process into the Quemoy crisis. Their errors served the symbolic purpose of underscoring Yoshida's point that no revision that was not preceded by constitutional revision could change the basic inequality in the U.S.-Japan relations.

Kishi's predicament was tragic. The same cannot be said of John Foster Dulles inasmuch as he wavered over Hatoyama's peace treaty, thereby forfeiting the chances for constitutional revision.

But there were extenuating circumstances for Dulles: the use and abuse of purge by MacArthur and Yoshida made certain that Hatoyama and the revisionists resented the United States while the Americans grew suspicious of the "militarists." The abuse stretched over nearly six years and grew more intense as the end of the occupation came into sight. Their purpose was to insure the perpetuation of the constitution and to determine Japan's foreign policy. They also ended up determining U.S. foreign policy toward Japan.

The contention between professional politicians and bureaucratic politicians or between the Diet and the central ministry bureaucracies has been one of the central themes of Japan's postwar politics. The contention ranged over the entire spectrum of Japan's foreign and domestic policy, leaving its imprint everywhere. This contention also has had its origin in the use and abuse of the purge program.

The settlement of 1960 left both Japan and the United States dissatisfied. Having been denied formal equality, Japan switched to the developmental track while standing semidetached from the United States. The United States was not getting adequate burden sharing by Japan, a fact that may account for America's dissatisfaction with Japan today.

So far the establishments in both America and Japan have endorsed Yoshida overwhelmingly—without knowing what he really was. The ultimate source of his conduct was his intense nationalistic passion. The constitution was a mere tool and a temporary stopgap for him. Just before his death, Yoshida admitted that his defense of the constitution was overdone and that Japan was veering off in an unhealthy direction in the hands of his followers. He was after all a selective revisionist and was in favor of constitutional revision after an interval.[1]

Since 1960, Japan has been accused of indulging in a free ride and of exploiting American goodwill. But in reality, it was with great reluctance that the Japanese chose to forego mutuality and equality in favor of economic development. The psychological springboard of Japan's economic "miracle" is not a desire for a parasitic life but, on the contrary, a wish among the elites to escape their inferior political status, a wish that turned into a kind of social contract after the upheaval of 1960. Max Weber explains such a predicament in this way:

> National or religious minorities which are in a position of subordination to a group of rulers are likely, through their voluntary or involuntary exclusion from positions of political influence, to be driven with peculiar force into economic activity. Their ablest members seek to satisfy the desire for recognition of their abilities in this field, since there is no opportunity in the service of the State.[2]

It is a misreading of history to suppose (as standard history does) that postwar Japan become a democracy because of the no-war constitution or that it will revive militarism if the constitution is revised. Initially, Japan accepted the constitution strictly for the instrumental purpose of saving the emperor. Then Yoshida retained it for foreign policy purposes. That is to say, Japan restored democracy and kept it for reasons that were independent of the constitution. The constitution's greatest impact was felt in the politician-bureaucrat struggle and foreign policy.

Arguably Japan is a "stateless nation."[3] If so, the United States and Yoshida must share the blame. Japan cannot be a normal state as long as the Socialists, the constitution, and the security treaty remain. However, now that the Cold War is over, the constitution and the security treaty will become an issue every time a military crisis affecting Japan's interests arises. Then Japan will be forced to choose between paying for American mercenaries or self-help.[4]

Had Japan entered into regional collective security with South Korea, as

Dulles proposed, Japan's relationship with it would have been vastly different. As it is, Japan has virtually no security arrangement with South Korea.

There really ought to be no major conflict of interest between the United States and Japan. They are both democratic and capitalist nations, and they can mutually benefit from friendly competition and thriving trade. But the U.S.-Japan relations are beset by major problems today. I believe these problems stem primarily from the fact that the existing security alliance has made Japan excessively dependent on the United States. Dependence began in the security tie. Then Japan was forcibly cut off from its natural markets and was integrated into the North American market. In the decade of 1980s, the United States became critically dependent on Japan for fiscal resources as a result of its last major arms expansion. That in turn created the huge trade imbalance.

One proposed solution, called Amerippon, seeks to further increase the mutual dependence that now exists: the United States will exchange military protection for Japan's fiscal contribution, not to say tax payments.[5] But this idea is inherently undemocratic and will exacerbate the existing problems, which come from excessive integration. For instance, can America really afford to see Detroit concede the commanding position to Japanese auto makers, as is likely to happen in less than 10 years? The only viable solution is devolution of military responsibility, reduction of U.S. military budgets, greater military autonomy for Japan, and greater mutuality in defense and trade—but not in political or commercial separation.

It is a great pity that the United States and Japan have missed the chance to build a relationship based on greater equality, mutual help, and firm trust in all the Cold War years when they faced a common enemy and that, through a false reading of history, they have learned to fear men like Hatoyama Ichiro and Kishi Nobusuke as militarists and John Foster Dulles as an imperialist, instead of paying tribute to them.

## NOTES

1. In a book published a year before his death in 1964 at the age of 89, Yoshida said of his earlier objection to rearmament, "But that was when I was serving in the cabinet. In view of subsequent developments, I have come to have many doubts over the reality of Japan's defense." He went on to say that during his latest travels through Europe, he had had a chance to observe the leaders of the free world in their efforts to "contribute to the peace and prosperity of the world as their own responsibility." He was "moved" by the sight and "came to feel that Japan, too, ought to make [a similar] contribution. . . ." Furthermore, in an obvious reference to the Ikeda government's way of using the constitution, he said, "As for the constitution's *tatemae* and the government's policy, I am not one to evade my own share of responsibility. As an official in

charge of the constitutional debate and the subsequent administration of the government, I am painfully aware of my responsibility for it." Yoshida Shigeru, *Sekai to Nihon* [The world and Japan] (Tokyo: Bancho Shobo, 1963), pp. 202, 206.

There are reasons to believe that Yoshida's support for Kishi after the Quemoy crisis was rendered not merely out of an ulterior motive to wrest power from the revisionists, but from a genuine fear of the monster he had created out of the pacifist Left. Shunichi Kase, *Yoshida Shigeru no yuigon* [Treatment of Yoshida Shigeru] (Tokyo: Yomiuri Shimbunsha, 1967), pp. 124–29.

2. *The Protestant Ethic and the Spirit of Capitalism* (New York: Unwin, 1958), p. 39.

3. The revisionists in Japan have always maintained this point. For a latest example, see Ikutaro Shimizu, *Nihon yo kokka tare* [Japan, be a state!] (Tokyo: Bungei Shunjusha, 1980).

4. Van Wolferen's rhapsodic characterization of the Japanese System is bungled and inadequate. The System is the ideology of Japan as the merchant nation, an ideology that mythologizes Yoshida's policy line. Its empirical referents are those who advocate it. It appears as "culture," "tradition," "consensus," and the like but steadfastly refuses to appear in the guise of nationalism (e.g., Prime Minister Ohira's use of "culture"). It is broader in compass than the state, coming closer to the concept of community. Such a community was formed in the wake of the 1960 upheaval, when the Japanese society entered into a contract with itself to pursue economic development.

5. Zbigniew Brzezinski, "America's New Geostrategy," *Foreign Affairs* (spring 1987), pp. 680–99.

# Appendix I

# Genealogy of the Conservative Political Parties

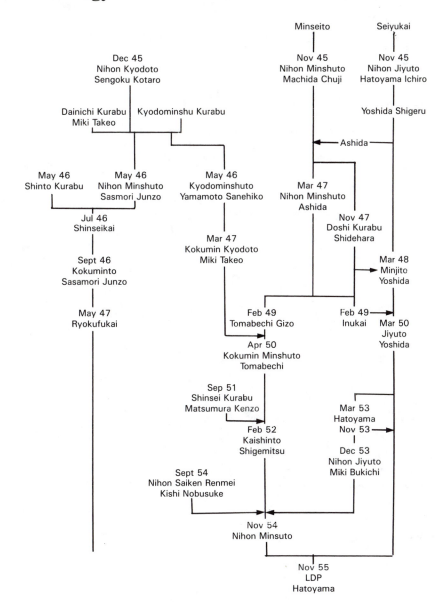

# Appendix II

# Security Treaty between the United States and Japan, September 8, 1951

Japan has this day signed a Treaty of Peace with the Allied Powers. On the coming into force of that Treaty, Japan will not have the effective means to exercise its inherent right of self-defense because it has been disarmed. There is danger to Japan in this situation because irresponsible militarism has not yet been driven from the world. Therefore, Japan desires a Security Treaty with the United States of America to come into force simultaneously with the Treaty of Peace between the United States of America and Japan. The Treaty of Peace recognizes that Japan as a sovereign nation has the right to enter into collective security arrangements, and further, the Charter of the United Nations recognizes that all nations possess an inherent right of individual and collective self-defense.

In exercise of these rights, Japan desires, as a provisional arrangement for its defense, that the United States of America should maintain armed forces of its own in and about Japan so as to deter armed attack upon Japan.

The United States of America, in the interest of peace and security, is presently willing to maintain certain of its armed forces in and about Japan, in the expectation, however, that Japan will itself increasingly assume responsibility for its own defense against direct and indirect aggression, always avoiding any armament which could be an offensive threat or serve other than to promote peace and security in accordance with the purposes and principles of the United Nations Charter.

Accordingly, the two countries have agreed as follows:

*Article I.* Japan grants, and the United States of America accepts the right, upon the coming into force of the Treaty of Peace and of this Treaty, to dispose United States land, air, and sea forces in and about Japan. Such forces may be utilized to contribute to the maintenance of the international peace and security in the Far East and to the security of Japan against armed attack from without, including assistance given at the express request of the Japanese Government to put down large-scale internal riots and disturbances in Japan, caused through instigation or intervention by an outside Power or Powers.

*Article II.* During the exercise of the right referred to in Article I, Japan will not grant, without the prior consent of the United States of America, any bases or any rights, power, or authority whatsoever, in or relating to bases or the right of garrison or of maneuver, or transit of ground, air, or naval forces to any third Power.

*Article III.* The conditions which shall govern the disposition of armed forces of the United States of America in and about Japan shall be determined by administrative agreements between the two Governments.

*Article IV.* This Treaty shall expire whenever in the opinion of the Governments of the United States of America and of Japan there shall have come into force such United Nations arrangements or such alternative individual or collective security dispositions as will satisfactorily provide for the maintenance by the United Nations or otherwise of international peace and security in the Japan Area.

*Area V.* This Treaty shall be ratified by the United States of America and Japan and will come into force when instruments of ratification thereof have been exchanged by them at Washington.

IN WITNESS WHEREOF the undersigned plenipotentiaries have signed this Treaty.

DONE in duplicate at the city of San Francisco, in the English and Japanese languages, this eighth day of September, 1951.

# Appendix III

# Treaty of Mutual Cooperation and Security between the United States and Japan, Signed at Washington, D.C., January 19, 1960

The United States of America and Japan,

Desiring to strengthen the bonds of peace and friendship traditionally existing between them, and to uphold the principle of democracy, individual liberty, and the rule of law,

Desiring further to encourage closer economic cooperation between them and to promote conditions of economic stability and well-being in their countries,

Reaffirming their faith in the purposes and principles of the Charter of the United Nations, and their desire to live in peace with all peoples and all governments,

Recognizing that they have the inherent right of individual or collective self-defense as affirmed in the Charter of the United Nations,

Considering that they have a common concern in the maintenance of international peace and security in the Far East,

Having resolved to conclude a treaty of mutual cooperation and security,

Therefore agree as follows:

*Article I.* The Parties undertake, as set forth in the Charter of the United Nations, to settle any international disputes in which they may be involved by peaceful means in such a manner that international peace and security and justice are not endangered and to refrain in their international relations from the threat or use of force against the territorial integrity or political independence of any state, or in any other manner inconsistent with the purposes of the United Nations.

The Parties will endeavor in concert with other peace-loving countries to strengthen the United Nations so that its mission of maintaining international peace and security may be discharged more effectively.

*Article II.* The Parties will contribute toward the further development of peaceful and friendly international relations by strengthening their free institutions, by bringing about a better understanding of the principles upon which these institutions are founded, and by promoting conditions of stability and well-being. They will seek to eliminate conflict in their international economic policies and will encourage economic collaboration between them.

*Article III.* The Parties, individually and in cooperation with each other, by means of continuous and effective self-help and mutual aid will maintain and develop, subject to their constitutional provisions, their capacities to resist armed attack.

*Article IV.* The Parties will consult together from time to time regarding the implementation of this Treaty, and, at the request of either Party, whenever the security of Japan or international peace and security in the Far East is threatened.

*Article V.* Each Party recognizes that an armed attack against either Party in the territories under the administration of Japan would be dangerous to its own peace and safety and declares that it would act to meet the common danger in accordance with its constitutional provisions and processes.

Any such armed attack and all measures taken as a result thereof shall be immediately reported to the Security Council of the United Nations in accordance with the provisions of Article 51 of the Charter. Such measures shall be terminated when the Security Council has taken the measures necessary to restore and maintain international peace and security.

*Article VI.* For the purpose of contributing to the security of Japan and the maintenance of international peace and security in the Far East, the United States of America is granted the use by its land, air, and naval forces of facilities and areas in Japan.

The use of these facilities and areas as well as the status of the United States armed forces in Japan shall be governed by a separate agreement, replacing the administrative Agreement under Article III of the Security Treaty between the United States of America and Japan, signed at Tokyo on February 28, 1952, as amended, and by such other arrangements as may be agreed upon.

*Article VII.* This Treaty does not affect and shall not be interpreted as affecting in any way the rights and obligations of the Parties under the Charter of the United Nations or the responsibility of the United Nations for the maintenance of international peace and security.

*Article VIII.* This Treaty shall be ratified by the United States of America and Japan in accordance with their respective constitutional processes and will enter into force on the date on which the instruments of ratification thereof have been exchanged by them in Tokyo.

*Article IX.* The Security Treaty between the United States of America and Japan signed at the city of San Francisco on September 8, 1951, shall expire upon the entering into force of this Treaty.

Article X. This Treaty shall remain in force until in the opinion of the Governments of the United States of America and Japan there shall have come into force such United Nations arrangements as will satisfactorily provide for the maintenance of international peace and security in the Japan area.

However, after the Treaty has been in force for ten years, either Party may give notice to the other Party of its intention to terminate the Treaty, in which case the Treaty shall terminate one year after such notice has been given.

IN WITNESS WHEREOF the undersigned Plenipotentiaries have signed this Treaty.

DONE in duplicate at Washington in the English and Japanese languages, both equally authentic, this 19th day of January, 1960.

# Index